HEALTH
COMMUNICATION
RESEARCH

HEALTH COMMUNICATION RESEARCH

A Guide to Developments and Directions

EDITED BY

Lorraine D. Jackson
and Bernard K. Duffy

GREENWOOD PRESS

Westport, Connecticut · London

Library of Congress Cataloging-in-Publication Data

Health communication research : a guide to developments and directions
/ edited by Lorraine D. Jackson and Bernard K. Duffy.
    p.   cm.
   Includes bibliographical references and indexes.
   ISBN 0–313–29925–0 (alk. paper)
   1. Communication in medicine—Research.   I. Duffy, Bernard K.
II. Jackson, Lorraine D., 1968– .
   R118.H435   1998
   610.69'6—dc21   98–14240

British Library Cataloguing in Publication Data is available.

Library of Congress Catalog Card Number: 98–14240
ISBN: 0–313–29925–0

First published in 1998

Greenwood Press, 88 Post Road West, Westport, CT 06881
An imprint of Greenwood Publishing Group, Inc.

Printed in the United States of America

The paper used in this book complies with the
Permanent Paper Standard issued by the National
Information Standards Organization (Z39.48–1984).

10 9 8 7 6 5 4 3 2 1

For my family and friends, and the health care professionals
who care for them.
L. D. J.

For Susan and Elizabeth.
B. K. D.

Contents

Preface

This book surveys the field of health communication at a time when the system of medical care is undergoing rapid and accelerating change. In the past, most major changes in medicine were the product of new scientific discoveries, medical equipment, and techniques. Today, some significant changes are occurring because of the research of social scientists and humanists, applied not only to medical practice and the health care industry, but also to larger issues of public health. As with every major social institution, the medical institution is the object of wide-ranging scholarly inquiry. Virtually every branch of the academy, from sociology, political science, and history to education, economics, and business management, has addressed some aspect of medicine. Within the last two decades students of communication have also begun framing a view of how they can assist in understanding and improving medical care. Communication specialists are attempting to establish and legitimate themselves and their academic specialty within the health care arena. This is an era of increasing professionalization for health communication researchers and educators.

Few in the medical community, however, fail to recognize that more successful communication might contribute to the understanding and improvement of medical care. Improved communication increases the efficiency of the health care system, the satisfaction with health care, and the health of the general public. Although every health care constituency acknowledges the importance of communication in health care, health care educators and health communication researchers are still developing a sophisticated understanding of how communication operates in health care settings and how it can be improved.

What is the compass of health communication? Although this is a question to which the book provides the fullest answer, in essence, the study of health communication focuses on the interaction of people involved in the health care process and the elucidation and dissemination of health-related information. Health communication research examines the role of communication in medical education, health professional/client relationships, creating and maintaining cultures, promoting adherence with courses of treatment, ethical issues, the flow of information within and between health organizations, the design and effectiveness of health information for various audiences (including media strategies to promote public health), as well as the planning and evaluation of health care policy. By its nature the area is interdisciplinary and is relevant to scholars and practitioners in communication, psychology, sociology, medicine, nursing, physical therapy, dentistry, pharmacy, public health, and the allied health professions.

Although a system of governmental health insurance, proposed by the Clinton administration, was incrementally diluted to the point of essential defeat in 1994, the debate it engendered underscored problems and opportunities that continue to be addressed in both the private and public sectors. The public was made aware that health care had reached a point of impasse. The Clinton administration repeatedly linked the failure to control health care costs in Medicare and other public programs to the impossibility of balancing the budget. Furthermore, proponents of governmentally sponsored health care dramatized such concerns as the low standard of care received by many children throughout the nation. No matter what the fate of national health insurance, increased government intervention in health care, cost control, and managed care were clearly on the horizon. At the same time, consumerism in health care had been coming of age. While the role of physicians has been affected by the oversight of health maintenance organizations (HMOs) and insurance officials, it has also been realigned by the demand of patients for greater information and participation in health care decisions. Physicians, particularly those trained recently in U.S. medical schools, have become more sensitive to patient backgrounds, to their emotional needs, and to the nonmedical consequences of their treatment. Specialists in interpersonal communication have attempted to assist medical school officials in developing appropriate courses in improving patient-physician communication. Greater social sensitivity to cultural and gender issues in communication has also influenced the delivery of health care. Even outside of medical schools there has been a spate of new programs which encourage physicians to consider ways to adapt to a diverse group of patients. Interestingly, such training programs have been spurred by Medicaid HMOs with their emphasis on reducing costs (*Wall Street Journal* 4 September 1997, p. B1).

The government's role in protecting and improving public health has been solidified by epidemics such as HIV/AIDS, and by anti-drug and alcohol campaigns, as well as by legal efforts to hold tobacco manufacturers responsible for the public cost of treating tobacco related illness. The role of the surgeon general, for example, has shifted from that of a public administrator, offering mild blandishments and measured admonitions, to that of a vigilant guardian of public health, spearheading public health campaigns against such health concerns as teen drug consumption during pregnancy, alcoholism, or unsafe sex. Not only has the role of the surgeon general been enhanced, it has also been politicized to an extent unimagined by earlier generations of Americans. Health care has become as politically charged an issue in the present decade as Reaganomics was during the last. And, with an aging population, the likelihood is that high-visibility public debates concerning the politics and administration of health care and the wave of increased governmental activism in health care are unlikely to recede. For example, the Clinton/Gore administration has recently inaugurated a national campaign to promote organ donations. The increasing use of public relations and communication media technology to wage campaigns concerning health care issues and to influence perceptions of health risks and alter health behaviors has inspired considerable theorizing about which communication campaign strategies are most effective.

The time, in other words, is ripe for the field of communication to consolidate with the field of medicine. The compass of research and research applications has been so broad that it seemed necessary to survey and evaluate it in a book such as this. As is common in a nascent academic specialty, academics are publishing their research in scholarly journals, but precisely because of its rapid development, the field has suffered from a degree of fragmentation. Health communication is a newly formed universe of ideas, and the swirling particles have not yet been formed into discrete bodies. While the specialty of health communication is still coalescing, there is a particular need for this research to be summarized systematically, evaluated critically, and presented clearly in one source, as is done in the present book. Even when this universe of discourse is more mature, there will necessarily continue to be intersections in the orbits of such subfields as interpersonal communication and communication in the field of public health. Health communication will continue to develop dynamically in response to new exigencies and opportunities.

THE CHAPTERS

Chapter 1 overviews the development of the field over the last 25 years. Gary Kreps, Ellen Bonaguro, and Jim Query describe the scope of communication inquiry, including various channels, levels, and contexts. They contend that the tools of social science shaped this multidisciplinary field and that the resulting scholarship generated a need for new journals, books, professional divisions, conferences, and, recently, web pages.

At the core of the medical system lies the training and education of physicians. In Chapter 2, Gregory Makoul notes that informal instruction in ''bedside manner'' is giving way to formalized instruction and evaluation of communication skills in medical education. As an example, Makoul describes the Communication Skills Unit at Northwestern Medical School. Communication with patients, family members, other health professionals, and use of telemedicine and distance learning present both opportunities and challenges to communication scholars.

In Chapter 3, Teresa Thompson examines the defining transaction wherein medical care occurs: the conversation between patient and physician. Using her earlier reviews as a base, she focuses on research published since the early 1990s, noting changes, trends, improvements, and areas in need of development.

Chapter 4 focuses on the social and cultural factors related to doctor-patient interaction. Rebecca Cline and Nelya McKenzie argue that differences in education, specialized language use, social characteristics, and power make most doctor-patient interactions similar to intercultural exchanges. Such differences may often lead to communication that is disconfirming, distant, and dissatisfactory. Gender, age, ethnicity/race, socioeconomic status, and education are reviewed as influences on patterns of interaction.

Another serious challenge to medical treatment is the problem of patient adherence. M. Robin DiMatteo and Heidi Lepper note that on average, four out of every ten patients misunderstand, forget, or ignore medical instructions. This can be costly in terms of human suffering to patients and inefficient for the medical system as a whole. Therefore, Chapter 5 examines the connection between communication and adherence and outlines a research agenda, as well as clinical applications of provider-patient negotiation.

Chapter 6 examines the role of communication in ethical medical decision making. Physicians and medical educators realize that they must do more than diagnose and treat illness; they must also attend to the emotional, philosophical, and social needs of patients. There is also now a greater emphasis on determining treatment through a consultative rather than a prescriptive process. Questions of appropriate disclosure, informed consent, and confidentiality have altered the nature of communication in medical ethics.

In Chapter 7 Robert O'Connor, Shriti Hallberg, and Richard Myles discuss the revolutionary transformation in health care organization and administration. Health care providers must offer more and better information not only to patients but also to insurers. The trend toward managed care and cost control has necessitated that decisions concerning health care often be shared by all those who hold a stake in the quality of care and its cost. Communication within organizations and between organizations are both discussed.

Chapter 8, written by Mary Jo Deering, focuses on health communication and health policy, exploring the importance of reducing the need for medical care through governmentally sponsored prevention programs. Deering discusses individual choices concerning lifestyle and care seeking, and shows how those choices affect long-term health. She also considers the availability of consumer health information and how the government can improve availability through the Agency for Health Care Policy and Research in the Department of Health and Human Services.

In Chapter 9 Maria Knight Lapinski and Kim Witte continue the discussion of health and the media, focusing on health education campaigns. They explore research concerning campaign strategy and emphasize the importance of developing and applying theories of attitude and behavior change to improve the effectiveness of health campaigns. They discuss concepts related to campaigns such as diffusion and social marketing, community empowerment, fear appeals, the health belief model, and the extended parallel process model, which seeks to explain reactions to health threats.

Nancy Signorielli assesses the influence of the media on perceptions of health in Chapter 10. She particularly addresses popular media images and representations of health and illness, medical professionals, contraception and sexually transmitted diseases, alcohol and drugs, as well as food and nutrition. The chapter also deals with the intentional embedding of health messages in television programs and with advertising campaigns employed by industry, such as the manufacturers of spirits, that affect the public health.

The book lacks a chapter on alternative medicine, for example, folk medicine, Chinese medicine, so-called holistic medicine, faith healing, as well as variants on traditional medicine such as hospice care and midwifery. Interestingly, in many of these forms of medicine, communication appears to be a more important variable in the success or failure of the treatment than in traditional Western medicine. In a certain sense, holistic and other alternative methods of treating illness seem to be a reaction against the perceived sterility and lack of personalization in Western medicine with its focus on compartmentalization and specialization. Alternative medicine represents a pole in the dialectic concerning the degree to which the patient and physician should be subjectively involved in treatment.

THE ORGANIZATION OF THE CHAPTERS

Chapter authors were asked to follow a format, though they were allowed considerable latitude. Each chapter opens with a synopsis, followed by an explication of research done in the subfield on which the chapter focuses. A central purpose of each chapter is to mark the current boundaries of the subfield, noting the directions current research has taken, and secondarily to suggest the subfield's extensions and new areas of inquiry.

Most of the contributors to the book are very well known in the field, and were chosen based on their previous published research and, in several cases, on their direct practical experience in the medical area addressed. Although we determined the format for the book, it is the contributors finally who are most directly responsible for the substance and character of the book. Without their work this volume would not exist.

This book simultaneously addresses several audiences. First, though not foremost, it is intended for health communication researchers and their students. Second, this reference book is also designed to be useful to health professionals and medical educators. As editors we have taken care that the prose should not be ''harsh and crabbed,'' as rhetorician Richard Weaver described the character of some social scientific writing, and that authors of individual chapters do more than explicate studies but provide explanation and context. Therefore, the book is written for a professional and academic audience, and not solely an audience of health communication researchers.

We would like to thank the dedicated scholars who contributed chapters to the book and the scholars whose work they cite. We also appreciate the assistance of our editors at Greenwood Press, Cynthia Harris and Nita Romer, for their support and useful suggestions, and our production editor, John Donohue, who guided the book to its completion. A summer grant from the California State University, and smaller research grants from Cal Poly, the encouragement of health professionals, educators, and our counterparts at other institutions were important in the completion of this project. We especially appreciate the work of one of our students, Jacqualine Bainbridge, who spent many hours preparing the author index. We also thank Rocio Alvear for offering technical assistance with the list of works cited and our families and friends for their patience and kindness when our work caused them inconvenience.

HEALTH
COMMUNICATION
RESEARCH

1

The History and Development of the Field of Health Communication

Gary L. Kreps, Ellen W. Bonaguro,
and Jim L. Query, Jr.

SYNOPSIS

This chapter provides an historical background for the growing discipline of health communication and discusses the important role of communication in providing health care and health information. Health communication is defined across various levels of communication, including intrapersonal, interpersonal, group, organizational, and societal. Research in this area examines provider/client relationships and mass-mediated campaigns, as well as health communication in homes, schools, clinics, and hospitals. Two major interdependent branches of health communication inquiry, the provision of health care and the promotion of public health, are discussed.

The study of health communication is simultaneously social scientific, humanistic, and professional in orientation. Health communication inquiry builds upon the scholarship of the social sciences (i.e., communication studies, sociology, psychology, linguistics, and anthropology), draws upon theories from the humanities (i.e., rhetoric, philosophy, art, ethics, theater, and literature), and applies principles from many professional fields (i.e., the allied health care professions, education, management, law, marketing, and theology). In many respects, health communication is a convergent discipline that connects and builds upon many ideas of inquiry.

The field of health communication emerged in the professional associations of the communication discipline when the International Communication Association (ICA) established the Therapeutic Communication Interest Group in 1972, later becoming the Health Communication Division. In 1985, the Speech Communication Association (SCA, now NCA) formed the Commission for Health Communication, which also became the Health

Communication Division. The professional associations published defining work on health communication in major scholarly publications and began to hold important conferences on health communication that allowed a growing number of professionals interested in this topic to interact, collaborate, and develop health communication research and educational projects.

In the 1980s the first books about health communication written by communication scholars began to appear in print, including *Health Communication: Theory and Practice* (Kreps & Thornton, 1984), *The Physician's Guide to Better Communication* (Sharf, 1984), and *Health Communication: A Handbook for Professionals* (Northouse & Northouse, 1985). The first dedicated refereed scholarly journal in this area, *Health Communication*, began publication in 1989, followed by publication of *The Journal of Health Communication* in 1996.

Several colleges began to offer undergraduate and graduate health communication courses and majors. Medical schools also introduced health communication courses. Information regarding the many different academic programs available in health communication have been jointly compiled and are made available by the ICA and the National Communication Association (NCA) health communication divisions. Additional information about health communication education can be accessed through numerous health communication web sites (listed in this chapter).

As academic interest in the field of health communication has grown, researchers have increasingly attracted significant federal and private research funding. Numerous state and federal agencies have institutionalized health communication as major parts of important research centers sponsored by organizations such as the Centers for Disease Control, the National Cancer Institute, and the Federal Agency for Health Care Policy and Research. There is growing demand for scholars and educators with expertise in health communication in universities and research centers. The field of health communication is moving toward a sophisticated multidimensional agenda for applied research that we believe will help improve the quality of health care delivery and public health promotion.

THE STUDY OF HEALTH COMMUNICATION

Health communication has developed over the last 25 years as a vibrant and important field of study concerned with the powerful roles performed by human and mediated communication in health care delivery and health promotion. Health communication inquiry has emerged as an exciting applied behavioral science research area. It is an applied area of research not only because it examines the pragmatic influences of human communication on the provision of health care and the promotion of public health, but also because the work in this area is often used to enhance the quality of health care delivery and health promotion. To this end, health communication inquiry is usually problem-based, focusing on identifying, examining, and solving health care and health promotion problems.

COMMUNICATION AND HEALTH INFORMATION

Within the health communication field, communication is conceptualized as the central social process in the provision of health care delivery and the promotion of public health. Communication is pervasive in creating, gathering, and sharing "health information." Health information is the most important resource in health care and health promotion because it is essential in guiding strategic health behaviors, treatments, and decisions (Kreps, 1988).

Health information is the knowledge gleaned from patient interviews and laboratory tests that is used to diagnose health problems. It represents the precedents developed from clinical research and practice used to determine the best available treatment strategies for a specific health threat. The data gathered in check-ups used to assess the efficacy of health care treatments are essential to evaluating bioethical issues and weighing consequences in making complex health care decisions. Health information also provides warning signs needed to detect imminent health risks and direct health behaviors designed to avoid these risks. Health care providers and consumers use their communication abilities to generate, uncover, and exchange relevant health information for making important treatment decisions, for adjusting to changing health conditions, and for coordinating health-preserving activities. The process of communication also enables health promotion specialists to develop persuasive messages that will disseminate relevant health information over salient channels to target audiences, thereby influencing their health knowledge, attitudes, and behaviors.

While communication is a powerful process in health care, the dynamics of communication in health contexts are also very complex, the communication channels used numerous, and the influences of communication on health outcomes powerful. Health communication inquiry has developed to demystify the complexity of the multifaceted roles performed by communication in health care and health promotion. Such inquiry is conducted to increase knowledge about the influences of communication on health outcomes and to direct the knowledge gained toward helping participants in the modern health care system use communication strategically to accomplish their health goals.

THE COMPLEXITY OF HEALTH COMMUNICATION INQUIRY

Health communication is an extremely broad research area, examining many different levels and channels of communication in a wide range of social contexts. The primary levels for health communication analysis include intrapersonal, interpersonal, group, organizational, and societal communication. Intrapersonal health communication inquiry examines the internal mental and psychological processes that influence health care, such as the health beliefs, attitudes, and values that predispose health care behaviors and decisions. Interpersonal health communication inquiry examines the relational influences on health outcomes, focusing on the provider/consumer relationship, dyadic provision of health education and therapeutic interaction, and the exchange of relevant information in health care interviews. Group health communication inquiry examines the role communication performs in the interdependent coordination of group members in health care teams, support groups, ethics committees, and families, as these group members share relevant health information for making important health care decisions. Organizational health communication inquiry examines the use of communication to coordinate interdependent groups, mobilize different specialists, and share relevant health information within complex health care delivery systems in order to enable effective multidisciplinary provision of health care and prevention of relevant health risks. Societal health communication examines the generation, dissemination, and utilization of relevant health information communicated through diverse media to a broad range of professional and lay audiences to promote health education, health promotion, and enlightened health care practice.

Health communication inquiry involves examination of a broad range of communication channels. Face-to-face communication between providers and consumers, members of health care teams, and support group members are the focus of many health communication studies. A broad range of communication media, personal (telephone, mail, fax, e-mail), and mass (radio, television, film, billboards) communication are also the focus of health communication inquiry.

The settings for health communication inquiry are also quite diverse. They include all of the settings where health information is generated and exchanged, such as homes, offices, schools, clinics, and hospitals. Health communication research has examined such diverse issues as the role of interpersonal communication in developing cooperative health care provider/consumer relationships, the role of comforting communication in providing social support to those who are troubled, the effects of various media and presentation strategies on the dissemination of health information to those who need such information, the use of communication to coordinate the activities of interdependent health care providers, and the use of communication for administering complex health care delivery systems.

TWO COMPETING PERSPECTIVES IN HEALTH COMMUNICATION INQUIRY

There are two major interdependent branches of inquiry in the field of health communication. The first is the health care delivery branch, whose focus is self-explanatory. The second is the health promotion branch, which studies the persuasive use of communication messages and media to promote public health.

These two branches parallel a division found within the larger discipline of communication between an academic interest in human and in so-called mediated communication, that is, communication through electronic media. The health care delivery branch of the field has attracted communication scholars who have primary interests in the ways interpersonal and group communication influence health care delivery, focusing on issues such as the provider/consumer relationship, therapeutic communication, health care teams, health care decision making, and the provision of social support. The health promotion branch has attracted many mass communication scholars concerned with the development, implementation, and evaluation of persuasive health communication campaigns designed to prevent major health risks and promote public health. For example, health communication scholars have developed campaigns for preventing public risks for contracting diseases such as HIV/AIDS, heart disease, and cancer. Many health promotion scholars are also concerned with evaluating the use of mediated channels of communication to disseminate relevant health information and with examining the ways health and health care are portrayed by the popular media.

Unfortunately, many of the scholars representing the two branches of the field of health communication (health care delivery and health promotion) have perceived themselves as directly competing with each other for institutional resources, numbers of conference programs, journal space, and research grants. Yet, in recent years this competition has begun to diminish, first as more health communication scholars have started working in both of these areas, second as health care delivery systems have begun utilizing an increasingly broader range of human and mediated channels of communication (in areas such as telemedicine, health care marketing, and health education), and third as health promotion specialists have enlisted more interpersonal (support groups, personal appeals, family involvement programs) and macrosocial (neighborhood, workplace, and government interventions) health promotion strategies. Over time, these two branches of the health communication field should continue to grow closer together and eventually merge. The fusion of these two areas will be most advantageous because health care delivery and health promotion are closely related activities. Health promotion must be recognized as a primary professional activity of health care practice, with doctors, nurses, and other providers devoting increasing energy to health education, and health promotion efforts must be coordinated with the many related activities and programs of the health care delivery system (Kreps, 1990a, 1996a).

DEVELOPMENT OF THE FIELD: SOCIAL SCIENTIFIC INFLUENCES

There were many starting points in the development of the field of health communication. One influential starting point was rooted in the communication discipline's emulation of other social sciences, such as psychology and sociology, which were actively studying the health care system. The communication discipline has a long-standing history of adopting theories and methods from these two social science disciplines, and the move toward adopting the health care context as a topic of study was a natural disciplinary trend. Moreover, scholars in these social sciences were themselves beginning to examine communication variables in health care (Bandura, 1969; Feldman, 1966; Kosa, Antonovsky, & Zola, 1969; McGuire, 1969; Tichenor, Donohue, & Olien, 1970; Zola, 1966), which encouraged communication scholars to follow suit.

The field of psychology generated a large body of literature that prepared the ground for the development of health communication inquiry. The humanistic psychology movement of the 1950s and 1960s, for example, pioneered by scholars such as Carl Rogers (1951, 1957, 1961, 1962, 1967), Jurgen Ruesch (1957, 1959, 1961, 1963), and Gregory Bateson (Ruesch & Bateson, 1951), stressed the importance of therapeutic communication in promoting psychological health and was most influential in the development of the health care delivery perspective to health communication inquiry. This exciting body of psychological literature captured the imagination of many communication researchers. In fact, the *Journal of Communication* devoted an entire issue in 1963 to the topic of "Communication and Mental Health."

The Pragmatics of Human Communication by Watzlawick, Beavin, and Jackson, published in 1967, builds on the literature of humanistic psychology, inextricably tying together humanistic psychology and human communication. This powerful book encourages the growth of scholarship in the fields of interpersonal communication and health communication. Written from an interactional family therapy perspective, it examined the ways communication defines and influences interpersonal relations, clearly illustrating how the quality of relational communication can lead to therapeutic or pathological outcomes. The work, along with other literature in humanistic psychology, provided an influential springboard to the development of current interest in the field of health communication in provider/consumer relations, therapeutic communication, and the provision of social support.

The psychological literature about persuasion and social influence (Bandura, 1969, 1971; Festinger, 1957; Fishbein & Ajzen, 1975; Hovland, Janis, & Kelley, 1953; Katz & Lazarsfeld, 1955; Rokeach, 1973) also provided a broad theoretic foundation for the field of health communication, influencing the development of the health promotion approach to health communication inquiry. The persuasion literature, in combination with the complementary sociologically based diffusion of innovations literature that focused on the exportation and acceptance of technological innovation (Rogers, 1973; Rogers & Shoemaker, 1971), social scientific theories about mass media influence (Klapper, 1960; McCombs & Shaw, 1972–1973; Tichenor, Donohue, & Olien, 1970; Schramm, 1973) and emerging literature about social marketing (Kotler, 1972; Kotler & Zaltman, 1971) encouraged communication scholars to study the role of communication in health promotion and develop persuasive communication campaigns to promote public health. A notable example of an early health communication campaign based on a combination of social scientific theories is the Stanford Heart Disease Prevention Program. This landmark study illustrated the role of communication in health promotion with a longitudinal field experimental evaluation of a multi-city health promotion intervention program. Initiated in the early 1970s as a collaboration between cardiologist Jack Farquhar and communication scholar Nathan Maccoby, this study clearly demonstrated the powerful influences of communication campaigns on public health promotion.

The medical sociology literature (Freeman, 1963; Jaco, 1972; Mechanic, 1968) was also influential in developing the field of health communication. Medical sociologists have long been interested in the doctor–patient relationship and the social structure of health care delivery systems. Zola (1966) for example, in a now famous study, examined the ways that culture influences patients' presentations of health problems to health care providers, illustrating the need for practitioners to understand the backgrounds and orientations of their client and develop situationally specific strategies for communicating with individual patients. Kleinman's (1980) moving book, *Patients and Healers in the Context of Culture*, further reinforced this lesson about cultural influences on doctor-patient interactions and has encouraged current work on culture and health communication (see for example, Kreps & Kunimoto, 1994).

Important literature from the field of medicine has also increased interest in health communication. Korsch and Negrete's (1972) influential article "Doctor–Patient Communication," published in the prestigious international journal, *Scientific American*, made communication in health care delivery an important academic and public issue that communication scholars raced to address. Several important books about doctor–patient communication, such as Bird's (1955) *Talking with Patients*, Blum's (1972) *Reading Between the Lines: Doctor–Patient Communication*, Bowers's (1960) *Interpersonal Relations in the Hospital*, Browne and Freeling's (1967) *The Doctor–Patient Relationship*, Ley and Spelman's (1967) *Communicating with Patients*, Starr's (1982) *The Social Transformation of American Medicine*, Verwoerdt's (1966) *Communication with the Fatally Ill*, and Vorhaus's (1957) *The Changing Doctor–Patient Relationship*, also set the stage for development of the field of health communication.

INSTITUTIONALIZATION OF THE FIELD OF HEALTH COMMUNICATION

A field of study is largely defined by the body of literature it generates, and the field of health communication has a rich and varied literature. The first books concerning health communication written by communication scholars began appearing in the 1980s with Kreps and Thornton's (1984) introductory survey text written for an interdisciplinary audience of health care providers and consumers, *Health Communication: Theory and Practice*, Sharf's (1984) succinct text for medical students and practicing physicians, *The Physician's Guide to Better Communication*, and Northouse and Northouse's (1985) survey text geared toward nursing students and other health care professionals, *Health Communica-*

tion: A Handbook for Professionals. These first three texts were followed in rapid succession by important health communication books, edited volumes, and a burgeoning literature of journal articles in journals such as *Communication Yearbook* and *Health Communication*, solidifying and enriching the field of health communication.

As literature concerning the role of communication in health care and health promotion began to increase, communication scholars studying the role of communication in health felt a growing need for academic legitimization. In response to this need, communication scholars interested in health care and health promotion banded together in 1972 to form the Therapeutic Communication interest group of the International Communication Association (ICA). The formation of this professional group is one of the most influential events in the genesis of the modern field of health communication because it provided an academic home for an eclectic group of scholars, communicated to the rest of the communication discipline that health was a legitimate topic for communication research, and encouraged scholars in the discipline to consider health-related applications of their work.

The annual ICA conventions were very important sites for an emerging group of health communication scholars to meet, present their research, and generate new ideas and new directions for this new field of study. At the 1975 ICA convention, held in Chicago, another important milestone in the development of this field was reached. At this conference the members of the Therapeutic Communication Division voted to give this group the broader title of ''Health Communication,'' in recognition of the many ways that communication influences health and health care. This was an important change because the new name represented a much larger group of communication scholars than the title ''Therapeutic Communication'' did. The *therapeutic communication* title was most attractive to interpersonally oriented communication scholars, while the name *health communication* appealed broadly to scholars interested in persuasion, mass communication, communication campaigns, and the organization of health care services, as well as those interested in interpersonal communication.

The ICA Health Communication Division not only provided academic legitimization for a growing body of college faculty and graduate students, but the conference programs encouraged other communication scholars to conduct health communication research and submit it for presentation at ICA conferences. The ICA Health Communication Division began publishing the *ICA Newsletter* in 1973, communicating relevant information about health communication research, education, and outreach opportunities to a growing body of scholars. In 1977 the ICA began publishing an annual series, the influential *Communication Yearbook*, which included important chapters about the emerging field of health communication.

In the first four volumes of the *Communication Yearbook* series, each of the divisional interest groups (including the Health Communication Division) was allotted sections of the book to present research overviews and exemplary studies. In each of the first four volumes, Health Communication Division officers wrote important definitional overview chapters about the nature, purposes, and scope of health communication inquiry (see Cassata, 1978, 1980; Costello, 1977; Costello & Pettegrew, 1979). These overview chapters along with the accompanying research reports provided an excellent showcase for the developing field of health communication. Later issues of *Communication Yearbook* moved to a revised format of showcasing major review chapters along with accompanying responses from accomplished scholars representing the different ICA Divisions. The major review chapters concerning health communication were instrumental in defining this field of inquiry, and the chapter responses helped to frame the major issues in the field for a large audience of scholars (see Kreps, 1988; Pettegrew, 1988; and Reardon, 1988 for an example of a series of important health communication chapters in *Communication Yearbook 11*).

In 1985 the number of communication scholars interested in the field of health communication had grown enough that a groundswell of interested scholars formed the Commission for Health Communication within the Speech Communication Association (SCA), the largest of the communication discipline's professional societies. Many members of the ICA Health Communication Division also became members of the SCA Commission on Health Communication, and a large body of communication scholars who had limited exposure to health communication because they did not participate in the ICA now learned more about this field of inquiry. In an uncommon example of cooperation between ICA and SCA, the two groups decided to share the publication of the *Health Communication Newsletter*, now renamed *Health Communication Issues*. Within a few years, the Commission for Health Communication had grown so rapidly that it surpassed the size of the ICA Health Communication Division and qualified to become the SCA Health Communication Division.

HEALTH COMMUNICATION CONFERENCES AND MINI-CONFERENCES

The health communication conference programs at ICA and SCA became increasingly popular within the field, and in the mid-1980s several health communication mini-conferences were founded to meet the burgeoning scholarly interest in this area. One of the first of these conferences was the Medical Communication Conference held at James Madison University in Harrisonburg, Virginia, and hosted by Anne Gabbard-Alley. This mini-conference was quickly followed by a Summer Conference on Health Communication held at Northwestern University in July 1985, hosted by Paul Arntson and Barbara Sharf. This very successful conference, which included a proceedings volume of contributed conference papers, began a popular trend of small research conferences focusing on health communication inquiry.

The Northwestern conference was followed by the first of several very effective annual Communicating with Patients conferences sponsored by the Communication Department of the University of South Florida and hosted by David Smith, Loyd Pettegrew, and others. Two important international conferences were organized in 1986, the Oxford University/ICA Conference on Health Education in Primary Care, held at Oxford University (UK) and hosted by David Pendleton and Paul Arntson, as well as the International Conference on Doctor–Patient Communication, held at the University of Western Ontario (Canada) and hosted by Moira Stewart. Since then there have been several additional international health communication conferences, expanding international interest in health communication inquiry.

In 1989 a series of ICA Mid-Year Conferences on Health Communication held at Monterey, California, and hosted by Marlene Friederichs-Fitzwater, was initiated. Under the leadership of Jim Applegate, Eileen Berlin Ray, and Lew Donohew, the University of Kentucky began a series of successful health communication conferences held in Lexington, Kentucky. In 1994 a Conference on Health Communication, Skills, Issues, and Insights was held at the State University of New York at New Paltz, and NCA recently held a Summer Conference on Health Communication in Washington, D.C. Emerson College, under the direction of Scott Ratzan, also has initiated a series of conferences on health communication. These health communication mini-conferences spurred the growth of health communication inquiry both by serving as channels for disseminating health communication research information to a very large and often diverse audience of scholars and by providing health communication scholars with attractive outlets for presenting their work.

HEALTH COMMUNICATION JOURNALS

In 1989 the first refereed social scientific quarterly journal, *Health Communication*, dedicated exclusively to health communication inquiry appeared, with Teresa Thompson as its founding editor. The publication of this journal marked the coming of age of this young field of study and encouraged scholars from around the globe to take this field of study seriously.

The first issue of *Health Communication* featured five important invited essays by noted health communication experts evaluating the current status of the field of health communication and recommending directions for future development of the field. The lead article, by Barbara Korsch (1989), reviewed current knowledge about doctor–patient communication and identified fruitful directions for future inquiry. Gary Kreps's article described the theory-building, theory-testing, discipline-building, and pragmatic health care delivery system benefits of rigorous and relevant health communication inquiry. David Smith, in his essay, examined the ways health communication research has debunked the traditional medical model of doctor control and patient compliance, and advocated a sophisticated view of communication in future communication inquiry. In his contribution, Paul Arntson argued for a focus on developing citizens' health competencies in future health communication research, thus empowering citizens to make active and enlightened health care decisions. In the final invited essay in this inaugural issue of *Health Communication*, Jon Nussbaum provided a charge to scholars to conduct important, sophisticated, and influential health communication research. This first issue of *Health Communication* marked an important point in the academic maturation of health communication inquiry, and over the years the journal has provided the field with a respected outlet for health communication research.

In 1996 a second dedicated refereed quarterly health communication journal, the *Journal of Health Communication*, appeared. It departed from the established journal *Health Communication* by taking a more international orientation and health care practice perspective to health communication. While *Health Communication* is a rigorous research journal, the new journal, the *Journal of Health Communication*, melds research and practice. The two journals complement each other and provide excellent, current health communication information. They are both important scholarly outlets for health communication scholarship, indicative of the growth and maturation of this field of study.

CURRICULAR GROWTH IN HEALTH COMMUNICATION

Along with the growth of health communication literature and professional organizations came the introduction of both undergraduate and graduate health communication courses. Some of the earliest health communication courses were housed in Departments of Speech Communication at large research universities such as the University of Minnesota (taught by Don Cassata), Pennsylvania State University (taught by Gerald M. Phillips), and the University of Southern California (taught by Gary Kreps). Several medical schools also began offering health communication courses focusing on interviewing skills for physicians at the University of Illinois (taught by Barbara Sharf), Southern Illinois University (taught by Susan Ackerman-Ross), the University of North Carolina (taught by Don Cassata), and the University of Calgary (taught by Suzanne Kurtz). These courses were precursors to the development of many more undergraduate and graduate health communication courses in colleges both nationally and internationally.

Several undergraduate and graduate health communication majors are now offered at colleges (such as the University of Maryland, Emerson College, the University of Toledo, Bowling Green State University, the University of South Florida, the University of Florida, Northwestern University, Indiana University–Purdue University at Indianapolis, Rutgers University, Ohio University, the University of Georgia, Michigan State University, Stanford University, the University of Pennsylvania, and the University of Oklahoma). The Emerson College health communication graduate program is unique. It is a collaboration between Emerson's communication program and Tufts University's School of Medicine, enrolls students from both Emerson and Tufts, and offers courses taught by faculty from both institutions. This level of innovative interdisciplinary (and for that matter, interprofessional and interinstitutional) collaboration is unique and offers students in this program an opportunity for a health communication education emphasizing the intricacies of both the communication process and the health care delivery system. A concise pamphlet describing important curricular information about the many different health educational programs currently available at colleges and universities, gathered by Kim Witte of Michigan State University and Scott Ratzan of Emerson College, is available from both NCA and ICA Health Communication Divisions.

HEALTH COMMUNICATION INFORMATION ON THE INFORMATION SUPERHIGHWAY

Recently, several innovative Internet web-pages concerning health communication have been introduced. For example, the American Communication Association (a relatively young and innovative communication professional society) sponsors one of the web-pages, which has links to many sources of information about communication and health care (http://cavern.uark.edu/comminfo/www/health.html). Stuart Ainsworth, a graduate student at the University of Georgia, has also established a health communication web-page with information about the field of study, programs of health communication study, relevant health communication literature, and links to other communication pages (http://www.arches.uga.edu/stainswo/health/). The Emerson College Department of Communication has also developed a health communication web-page that provides information about their innovative health communication graduate program, the new *Journal of Health Communication*, edited by Emerson College professor, Scott Ratzan, and about current news, conferences, and research opportunities in health communication (http://www.emerson.edu/acadepts/cs/healthcom/). Clearly, these electronic information sources provide many people with access to the field of health communication and serve important public relations, academic community building, and information dissemination functions for the health communication field.

FUTURE DIRECTIONS IN HEALTH COMMUNICATION INQUIRY

Current research on health communication clearly illustrates the powerful influences of communication on health (see, for example, Kreps & O'Hair, 1995). Health communication inquiry has become increasingly sophisticated and directed toward addressing significant social issues. With the growing sophistication of health communication has come increasing interdisciplinary and institutional credibility for health communication scholars.

Health communication scholars are more likely now than at any time in the past to attract federal research funding. Federal agencies, such as the Centers for Disease Control, the National Cancer Institute, and the National Institute for Drug Abuse, have become increasingly more familiar with the field of health communication and receptive to health communication research. The Centers for Disease Control, for example, has established an Office of Communications with a Division of Health Communication dedicated to emphasizing the development of rigorous message-based communication interventions across the CDC's many important health risk prevention initiatives. Similarly, the Federal Agency for Health Care Policy and Research has increasingly emphasized the importance of health communication research and interventions in their many publications, conferences, and outreach programs.

Health communication scholars are increasingly in demand by communication programs at universities and colleges. More faculty job advertisements than ever before list expertise in health communication as one of the preferred qualifications of applicants. Communication scholars are increasingly receiving more respect from well established social sciences, with communication scholars invited to participate in interdisciplinary research teams and to edit interdisciplinary social scientific journals, such as the *American Behavioral Scientist*. See, for example, the November 1994 issue of the *American Behavioral Scientist* devoted to "Health Communication: Challenges for the 21st Century" edited by Scott Ratzan, and the July/August 1991 issue devoted to "Communicating to Promote Health," co-edited by Gary Kreps and Charles Atkin. Similarly, a recent issue of the *Journal of Health Psychology* (Volume 1, No. 3, 1996), also edited by Kreps, entitled "Messages and Meanings: Health Communication and Health Psychology" featured current health communication research by respected communication scholars. This type of interdisciplinary respect and credibility marks the progressive maturation of the field of health communication.

There is a growing emphasis on public advocacy, consumerism, and so-called empowerment in health communication research. One effect of such research will be to revolutionize the modern health care system by equalizing power between providers and consumers. Another will be to relieve a great deal of strain on the modern health care system by encouraging disease prevention and self-care and by making consumers equal partners in the health care enterprise (see Arntson, 1989; Kreps, 1993, 1996a, 1996b). Communication research should increasingly be used to identify the information needs of consumers and suggest strategies for encouraging consumers to take control of their health and health care. Ideally, health communication research should help identify appropriate sources of relevant health information that are available to consumers, gather data from consumers about the kinds of challenges and constraints they face within the modern health care system, as well as develop and field test educational and media programs for enhancing consumers' medical literacy. Such research will help consumers negotiate their way through health care bureaucracies and develop communication skills for interacting effectively with health care providers.

Current and future health communication research will increasingly focus on the effective dissemination of relevant health information to promote public health. Modern health promotion efforts will recognize the multidimensional nature of health communication, identify communication strategies that incorporate multiple levels and channels of human communication, and implement a wide range of different prevention messages and campaign strategies targeted at relevant and specific (well-segmented) audiences (Maibach, Kreps, & Bonaguro, 1993). Modern campaigns will become increasingly dependent on integrating interpersonal, group, organizational, and mediated communication to effectively disseminate relevant health information to specific at-risk populations.

Health communication inquiry is becoming increasingly concerned with the role of culture in health and health care. We believe that the work of communication scholars will help end the prejudicial treatment of marginalized cultural groups within the modern health care system, such as those with AIDS, the poor, minorities, women, and the elderly (Kreps, 1996a). Future research will examine the health communication needs of marginalized cultural groups and identify strategies for enhancing health communication with members of these groups.

We believe the field of health communication is moving toward a sophisticated multidimensional agenda for applied health communication research that will examine the role of communication in health care at multiple communication levels, in multiple communication contexts; evaluate the use of multiple communication channels; and assess the influences of communication on multiple health outcomes. Future health communication inquiry and education will likely provide relevant information about the development of cooperative relationships between interdependent participants in the modern health care system, encourage the use of sensitive and appropriate interpersonal communication in health care, enable consumers to take charge of their own health care, enhance the dissemination of relevant health information and the use of strategic communication campaigns to promote public health, facilitate the development of pluralistic ideologies for effective multicultural relations in health care, and suggest adaptive strategies for using health communication to accomplish desired health outcomes.

WEB SITES USEFUL TO HEALTH COMMUNICATORS

American Communication Association
http://cavern.uark.edu/comminfo/www/health.html

Health Communication Division—National Communication Association
http://www.sla.purdue.edu/health comm/

Health Communication Information
University of Georgia
http://www.arches.uga.edu/stainswo/health/

Emerson College
http://www.emerson.edu/acadepts/cs/healthcom/

Medical Matrix
http://www.mediatrix.org/

National Communication Association
http://www.Natcom.org/

Physician Choice
http://www.mdchoice.com/

Six Senses
http://www.sixsenses.com/

The American Medical Association
http://ama-assn.org/

The American Diabetes Association
http://www.diabetes.org/

The American Heart Association
http://www.Americanheart.org/

The Centers for Disease Control and Prevention
http://www.cdc.gov/

The Combined Health Information Database
http://www.chid.aerie.com/

The National Alzheimer's Association
http://www.alz.org/

The National Institutes of Health Information Index
http://www.nih.gov/health/

The Pharmaceutical Information Network
http://www.pharminfo.com/

2

Communication Research in Medical Education

Gregory Makoul

SYNOPSIS

Communication is quickly becoming a hot topic in medical education. Although research on interpersonal communication is the most evident opportunity for collaboration between communication scholars and medical educators, there are a number of equally fertile grounds for research. For instance, communication researchers can do work of tremendous value by eliciting and explicating patient narratives of the illness experience as well as physician narratives about decisions made in the course of diagnosis and treatment. Furthermore, as medical education continues to move toward active learning in small-group formats and medical practice shifts to a team-based approach, scholars who study small-group communication will find ample opportunities to test their theories and methods in medical schools. Effects of the "hidden curriculum" (i.e., the culture in which the formal curriculum is situated) and the role of communication in implementing curricular reform are two natural areas for research on organizational communication. In the area of communication technology, communication scholars can work with medical educators to better understand the barriers and possibilities associated with both computer-assisted learning and tele-medicine for distance learning. To turn these opportunities into productive partnerships with medical educators, communication researchers must become familiar with past efforts, current practice, and future directions in medical education.

A multitude of important new facts and theories, of new methods and routines, so far absorb the physician's attention and arouse his interest that the personal relations have become less important, if not absolutely, at least

> relatively to the new and powerful technology of medical practice. This
> condition, for which nobody is to blame, might perhaps be modified if it
> were possible to apply to practice a science of human relations.
> —Henderson, 1935

Communication science, nascent when Henderson spoke these words to physicians at Harvard Medical School and Massachusetts General Hospital, might well have developed into the "science of human relations" he had in mind. As Delia (1987) has discussed in detail, communication emerged as a distinct field of study in the early 1940s, driven primarily by investigators with "interests in the scientific analysis of public opinion, propaganda, and the uses and effects of communication." Many of these pioneers were trained in the liberal arts or behavioral sciences and heavily influenced by the Chicago school of sociology, which espoused theory-based applied research (Delia, 1987; Schramm, 1983).

In the subsequent half-century, interpersonal communication joined mass communication as a focal point for quantitative research. As the field matured, scholars trained in communication science began developing theories and methodologies tailored to the systematic study of dyadic encounters. Rigorous qualitative empirical research conducted during this period illustrated the importance of understanding aspects of interaction, such as process and context, that were not well captured through strictly quantitative methods (Rogers & Chaffee, 1983). Acknowledging the complementary relationship between quantitative and qualitative methods added both depth and breadth to the study of interpersonal communication. Given this heritage, communication science seems well suited for elucidating the import and implications of communication between physicians and patients.

Chaffee & Berger (1987) hold that the "science of human communication rests upon the optimistic assumption that behavior can be both understood and improved through systematic study" (p. 99). With regard to physician–patient communication, few would disagree that there is a great need for understanding and much room for improvement. In fact, Henderson's (1935) concern that physicians perceive personal relations as relatively unimportant is echoed, loudly, in medical, academic, and popular circles (Harvey & Shubat, 1989; Heavey, 1988; Lancaster, 1987; Makoul, 1992; Nelson, 1989; Smith & Pettegrew, 1986; Stewart, 1995). Medical schools, residency programs, and continuing medical education courses are responding to these concerns by implementing or enhancing relevant training, with varying degrees of intensity and success. The teaching and assessment of communication skills in medical schools offers perhaps the most fertile ground for communication research, since medical school efforts are more pervasive than those at the postgraduate level.

Although communication skills will be the primary focus of this chapter, there are several other areas of important, yet largely unbroken, ground for communication research in the larger field of medical education. One goal of this chapter is to mark the boundaries of these areas and plant a few ideas within them, in the hope that communication scholars and medical educators will work together to produce viable lines of research. Accordingly, in addition to suggesting areas of research on interpersonal communication (i.e., communication skills teaching and assessment), this chapter will briefly address the growth potential of research on intrapersonal communication (i.e., patient narrative, physician narrative), small-group communication (i.e., problem-based learning, training for work in interdisciplinary teams), organizational communication (i.e., the "hidden curriculum," change in the formal curriculum), and communication technology (i.e., computer-assisted learning, telemedicine for distance learning), all in the area of medical education.

It is important to keep the relationship between theory, teaching, and research in mind when considering the examples of research opportunities outlined in this chapter (see Figure 2.1). In an ideal situation, theory-driven research would provide a basis for teaching, and teaching interventions would be evaluated via rigorous research. However, in reality, the communication-oriented teaching that goes on in medical schools and residency programs is often devoid of any theoretical foundation and rarely evaluated in a systematic manner. The need for a stronger link between research, application, and evaluation at the level of interpersonal communication is also evident at the intrapersonal, small-group, organizational, and technological levels. Since there is not much communication research literature to review within the field of medical education, this chapter will focus attention on possible lines of inquiry into the content, process, and context of medical education.

INTERPERSONAL COMMUNICATION IN MEDICAL ENCOUNTERS

The idea that communication is an essential aspect of medicine is not new (see Engel, 1978; Henderson, 1935; Peabody, 1927); it just seems that way. Despite a clear recognition of the importance of communication, there is tremendous variation in the way, and extent to which, communication skills are taught and evaluated in medical schools today (Heavey, 1988; Novack, Volk, Drossman, & Lipkin, 1993). Still, it is clear that the apprenticeship model and the conception of communication as "bedside manner" or "history taking" are giving way to more formalized instruction and a reconceptualization of communication as an essential clinical skill. Attention to communication skills in North American medical schools is likely to increase dramatically, given a resolution adopted in 1995 by the Liaison Committee on Medical Education (LCME), which reviews and accredits medical schools in the United States, and the Committee on Accreditation of Canadian Medical Schools (CACMS):

Communication skills are integral to the education and effective function of physicians. There must be specific instruction and evaluation of these skills as they relate to physician

Figure 2.1
Communication Research in Medical Education

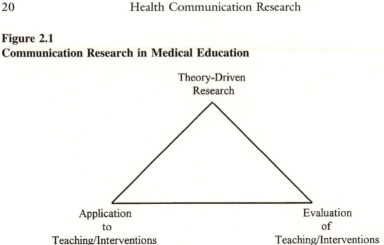

responsibilities, including communication with patients, families, colleagues and other health professionals.

This resolution suggests not simply an opportunity, but a responsibility, for communication scholars and medical educators to work together in shaping the future of communication skills teaching and assessment.

Communication Skills Teaching

An Example. The Communication Skills unit at Northwestern University Medical School is part of a comprehensive course known as Patient, Physician & Society, designed to provide and coordinate early exposure to clinical skills, as well as the social, behavioral and ethical foundations of medicine (Curry & Makoul, 1996; Makoul & Curry, 1998). The course runs two afternoons each week throughout the first and second years of the medical school curriculum. The Communication Skills unit meets one afternoon each week, beginning four weeks into the first year of medical school and continuing for 12 weeks.

To provide a vocabulary and context for thinking about and practicing communication skills, the first three weeks of the unit introduce basic concepts in interpersonal communication, explore the world of the sick, and explicate the roles and goals of physicians and patients. The next seven weeks are structured to follow the SEGUE framework (Makoul, 1995a), comprised of 25 communication tasks that focus attention on skills needed to *S*et the stage, *E*licit information, *G*ive information, *U*nderstand the patient's perspective and *E*nd the encounter (see Figure 2.2). Students meet in groups of 10 to 12 for an hour-long seminar with a clinician preceptor, during which they consider the importance of communication tasks highlighted by the SEGUE framework, and discuss skills and strategies for accomplishing them. Readings selected from communication and medical interviewing literature provide context for these discussions.

The students then practice skills for an additional hour in groups of three or four with a patient instructor, a person trained to role-play a patient and provide feedback on students' communication skills and strategies. The students see a different patient instructor each week, which allows them to interact with a diverse patient sample. In addition, while the patient instructors' biomedical "problems" remain constant throughout the unit, they change their affect (e.g., timid, frightened, angry) and psychosocial profile (e.g., living situation, work, relationships) as they interact with the different students in a group. Students receive immediate feedback from their patient instructor, as well as from their peers, and all sessions are videotaped to allow students to review their verbal and nonverbal communication behaviors.

These seminars and patient instructor sessions address components of the SEGUE framework sequentially, with each week building on the previous one (i.e., S, then SE, then SEG, etc.). After working through the SEGUE framework, students apply their growing repertoire of skills to smoking cessation counseling and other difficult situations of their choice (e.g., screening for domestic violence), again working with patient instructors. Students explore other complex skills and situations on their own outside of the classroom, and in the penultimate week, present their findings in the seminar groups. The patient instructor sessions for that week are structured a bit differently than the others: Students work one-on-one with patient instructors (i.e., rather than in groups of three or four) and view a videotape of their encounter immediately afterward, conducting a self-assessment that is reviewed by their patient instructor and faculty preceptor, as well as the Communication Skills unit director. The final week focuses on oral presentation skills and strategies for medical students, highlighting key aspects of audience analysis, organization, and delivery.

This approach differs from most extant courses for beginning students in that it: (1) makes a point of providing a conceptual context and coherent framework for learning skills; (2) addresses a broad range of communication tasks; (3) explicitly incorporates health promotion and disease prevention; (4) encourages students to explore higher-order skills and difficult situations in a learner-centered fashion. As explicated below, each of these four elements highlights important areas for communication research, particularly as medical schools continue to develop their communication training programs.

• *Conceptual Context.* Communication scholars can help medical educators provide a conceptual context for communication skills courses by conducting theory-driven research with clear application to the physician–patient encounter. Each of the three basic concepts examined in the example above is amenable to communication research. For instance, regarding roles and goals of physicians and patients (Makoul, 1992; Quill & Brody, 1996; Szasz & Hollander, 1956), how do physicians judge the extent to which patients want to be involved in decision making?

Figure 2.2
SEGUE Framework for Teaching and Assessing Communication Skills

The SEGUE Framework	Patient _____	Student _____

Set the Stage		Yes	No
1. Greet pt appropriately		| |	|
2. Establish reason(s) for visit: _____		| |	|
3. Outline agenda for visit (e.g., "anything else?", issues, sequence)		| |	|
4. Make a personal connection during visit (e.g., go beyond medical issues at hand)		| |	|
→ 5. Maintain pt's privacy (e.g., close door)		| |	|

Elicit Information	*n/a*	Yes	No
6. Elicit pt's view of health problem and/or progress	|	| |	|
7. Explore physical/physiological factors	|	| |	|
8. Explore psychosocial/emotional factors (e.g., living situation, family relations, stress)	|	| |	|
9. Discuss antecedent treatments (e.g., self-care, last visit, other medical care)	|	| |	|
10. Discuss how health problem affects pt's life (e.g., quality-of-life)	|	| |	|
11. Discuss lifestyle issues/prevention strategies (e.g., health risks)	|	| |	|
→ 12. Avoid directive/leading questions		| |	|
→ 13. Give pt opportunity/time to talk (e.g., don't interrupt)		| |	|
→ 14. Listen. Give pt undivided attention (e.g., face pt, verbal acknowledgment, nv feedback)		| |	|
→ 15. Check/clarify information (e.g., recap, ask "how much is that?")		| |	|

Give Information	*n/a*	Yes	No
16. Explain rationale for diagnostic procedures (e.g., exam, tests)	|	| |	|
17. Teach pt about his/her own body & situation (e.g., provide feedback from exam/tests, explain anatomy/diagnosis)	|	| |	|
18. Encourage pt to ask questions	|	| |	|
→ 19. Adapt to pt's level of understanding (e.g., avoid/explain jargon)		| |	|

Understand the Patient's Perspective	*n/a*	Yes	No
20. Acknowledge pt's accomplishments/progress/challenges	|	|	|
21. Acknowledge waiting time	|	|	|
→ 22. Express caring, concern, empathy	|	|	|
→ 23. Maintain a respectful tone	|	|	|

End the Encounter	Yes	No
24. Ask if there is anything else pt would like to discuss	|	|
25. Review next steps with pt	|	|

Comments:

Visit Date: / /   **Review Date:** / /   **Reviewer** _____

- *Communication Tasks.* The task approach (Pendleton, Schofield, Tate, & Havelock, 1984) outlines the objectives physicians should use their skills to achieve (e.g., check and clarify information). Inherent in this approach is the realization that different communication skills and strategies may be required to accomplish the same tasks with different people. This built-in flexibility reflects the reality of human communication (see Capella, 1987). The advent of evidence-based medicine is consistent with the notion that there should be an empirical basis for communication skills teaching. Communication scholars can conduct research to assess the value of communication tasks. For example, which communication tasks are essential? (see Makoul, 1995a); what do patients expect their physicians to do? (see Kravitz et al., 1996). Research is also needed on the outcome of accomplishing, or not accomplishing, communication tasks in the consultation (see Makoul, Arntson, & Schofield, 1995); interest in empirical studies of outcome is likely to grow in concert with the movement toward evidence-based medicine.

- *Health Promotion/Disease Prevention.* The World Health Organization (1986) defines health promotion as ''the process of enabling people to increase control over, and to improve, their health.'' Although the term is usually associated with public health campaigns or wellness programs, a health promotion perspective enriches the examination of communication in physician–patient encounters by emphasizing issues of ability, understanding, and control (Makoul et al., 1995). By focusing attention on the link between communication and control, communication researchers can help build the argument for teaching and learning to accomplish communication tasks that enhance patients' control during—and after—the medical encounter (Annandale, 1987; Greenfield, Kaplan, & Ware, 1985; Makoul, 1992). Further, there is a well-established link between many health problems (e.g., heart disease) and behavior, suggesting a great need for research on the effect and effectiveness of both screening and counseling for disease prevention.

- *Learner-Centered Learning.* Many medical schools are implementing curricular change that involves more learner-centered learning, a process by which students identify and address areas in which they need more information or practice. This suggests the need for research on the spectrum of higher-order communication skills (e.g., delivering bad news, dealing with domestic violence) that medical students identify as learning issues at different stages of their education. A better understanding of student perspectives regarding the higher-order skills would help medical educators develop stage-appropriate exposure to the curriculum and related learning resources (see Makoul, 1996). The social-learning theory concept of self-efficacy (Bandura, 1977a) provides one useful theoretical foundation for such work.

The use of patient instructors, a feature that the Communication Skills unit described above shares with courses at many other schools, is a largely untapped area of investigation, and the need for solid research in this area will increase as more institutions incorporate patient instructors into their training programs. In addition to conducting theory-driven descriptive research (e.g., to identify the content and process of feedback sessions), communication scholars can contribute to this aspect of teaching by assessing the training of patient instructors, evaluating the effectiveness of different feedback models, and determining the effect that working as a patient instructor has on an individual's interactions with his or her own physician. The same research agenda could be applied to the widespread and generally successful practice of involving patient instructors in teaching components of the physical examination (e.g., female breast and pelvic exams, male genital and rectal exams) in which effective communication is clearly essential because these exams are often anxiety provoking for both patients and physicians (Beckmann, Sharf, Baransky, & Spellacy, 1986; Lang, 1990).

Communication Skills Assessment

The increasingly vigorous calls for improving physician–patient communication coincide with increasingly rigorous attempts to assess students' clinical skills. There is a growing movement toward testing clinical skills by having medical students interact with standardized patients, people trained to role-play patients and record student behavior (see, for example, Stillman & Swanson, 1987). The term *standardized* warrants emphasis, since the standardized patients are, in effect, the test. Thus, standardized patients are trained to enact the same patient role—with the same demeanor and same information content—during each student encounter. They are also trained to use consistent criteria for evaluating each student. In contrast to patient instructors, who provide immediate feedback to students for teaching purposes, standardized patients do not leave the patient role when in the presence of a student. After a student finishes the encounter and leaves the room, the standardized patient completes a report regarding his or her assessment of that student's behavior.

An Example. At the conclusion of the two-year clinical skills sequence at Northwestern University Medical School (see Curry & Makoul, 1996), students participate in a clinical skills assessment, during which they interact with standardized patients presenting with abdominal pain. Each student has 45 minutes to talk with a standardized patient and conduct a focused physical examination, after which he or she leaves the room to complete a written challenge and update the standardized patient's chart by generating a problem list. While the medical student is working on these followup tasks, the standardized patient is filling out the SEGUE checklist to record which communication tasks were accomplished, as well as a physical examination checklist to record whether or not the student performed key aspects of the exam. All interactions are videotaped to allow for reliability checks and to provide students with an opportunity to learn by viewing their interactions.

The use of standardized patients in assessing communication skills suggests several lines of research. The two watchwords in these assessments are reliability and validity, since medical educators are using the data to make decisions about students' clinical skills. For instance, it is important to gauge how standardized patients' ability to reliably assess students' communication skills is related to the complexity of a particular case (i.e., the role itself) and the complexity of assessment tools within a case (i.e., number of tools, number of items, type of tools, type of items). From a validity perspective, research could focus on the standardized patient (e.g., to what extent is the role-play representative of a real scenario?; see Barrows, 1971) or the student (e.g., to what extent is behavior with a standardized patient representative of behavior with a real patient?; see Pieters, Touw-Otten, & DeMelker, 1994). Research could also focus on generalizability of communication measures across cases, as well as communication competence at different levels of training.

The discussion regarding assessment has, to this point, been limited to medical school settings. Assessing communication skills in residency and practice often involves analyzing videotapes of encounters with real patients. While the emphasis is no longer on the standardization of patients, it is possible to maintain standardization of assessment tools and methods. For instance, the Communication Training Program for resident physicians at the Rehabilitation Institute of Chicago involves collecting videotapes of residents with their clinic patients twice each year and using the SEGUE framework as a template for reviewing the videotaped encounters (Makoul & Sliwa, 1996). In the United Kingdom, the Royal College of General Practitioners now requires physicians applying for certification to submit several videotaped encounters, which are reviewed in a highly structured manner by both the applicant and senior physicians within the Royal College (Tate & Foulkes, 1996). In all these cases, whether they involve standardized patients or real patients, communication researchers can work with medical educators to shape evaluation and assessment exercises that afford learning opportunities, serving as both formative and summative evaluations.

INTRAPERSONAL COMMUNICATION IN MEDICINE

Illness is a subjective phenomenon (Cassell, 1976; Zinn, 1993) that, short of personal experience, can be best understood through patient narrative (see Kleinman, 1988; Mishler, 1984). Clinical interpretations and judgments can also be elucidated through the study of narrative, particularly physicians' narrative regarding decision making (see Bordage & Lemieux, 1991; Regehr & Norman, 1996). Despite the importance of understanding patients' illness experiences and physicians' decision-making processes, the research on intrapersonal communication in medicine is sparse.

Patient Narrative

Fortunately, for their sake, most medical students and residents have not personally experienced the chronic illnesses, disabilities, or hospital stays that are anything but abstractions for many patients. They have little or no idea of what it is like to be on ''the other side of the stethoscope,'' which thus sharpens the contrast between the cultures of physician and patient. Perhaps the most common feeling on that ''other side'' is a diminished sense of control (see Broyard, 1992; Cassell, 1976; Cousins, 1979; Murphy, 1990). Communication researchers can do work of tremendous value by eliciting and explicating patient narratives— stories of restitution, chaos, and quest (Frank, 1995)—and making their analyses accessible to physicians-in-training and physicians-in-practice, as well as those who teach them (Reiser, 1993).

Physician Narrative

> The practice of medicine is an interpretive activity. It is the art of adjusting scientific abstractions to the individual case. The daily life of the practicing physician is made up of observing, testing, interpreting, explaining, as well as taking action to restore the patient to health.
>
> —Hunter, 1991

Medical students and physicians must interpret information in the process of making decisions about diagnosis and treatment. Yet they seem to structure the information differently (e.g., diffused or integrated), depending on their level of experience (Bordage & Lemieux, 1991). Researchers can use narrative analysis to detect and highlight themes, crossroads, and turning points in the decision-making process, with an eye toward better understanding the factors related to appropriate clinical decisions. Both the methodology and rationale for studying physician narrative have been bolstered by advances in cognitive science (Regehr & Norman, 1996) and qualitative research (Reissman, 1993).

SMALL-GROUP COMMUNICATION IN MEDICAL EDUCATION

Given the enormous, and ever increasing, amount of medical knowledge, many people liken the process of assimilating medical information to taking a sip from a fire hose. Medical educators have responded by designing small-group-based strategies to encourage active learning and help students develop strategies for life-long learning. While the number of discussion groups and seminars is on the rise, perhaps the most pervasive small-group innovation is the problem-based learning technique.[1] Medical practice has also responded to the flood of medical information by evolving interdisciplinary, team-oriented approaches, whereby different health professionals, such as physicians, nurses, psychologists, social workers, and pharmacists, are meant to share and integrate their perspectives in the interest of patient care. Medical education can draw benefits from a focus on relevant small-group communication processes and outcomes in both areas.

Problem-Based Learning

Lectures, through which large amounts of information are intended to pass from faculty members to students, have long been a staple of medical education. Although lectures remain a valuable method of communicating basic information, the rapid advances and changes in medical knowledge make a compelling case for helping students develop skills and strategies for learning throughout their professional lives. In an effort to enhance active, life-long learning, many medical schools are reducing the amount of time devoted to lectures and increasing the use of small groups for discussion, seminars and problem-based learning.

Problem-based learning (PBL), in particular, is a technique designed to foster the "ability to identify, formulate and solve problems; to grasp and use basic concepts and principles; and to gather and assess data rigorously and critically" (Association of American Medical Colleges, 1984). It is a learner-centered activity in which students take responsibility for determining learning issues, gathering information relevant to those issues, and reporting back to their colleagues. Problems, often clinical case descriptions, are the fodder for discussion in PBL. These problems, the details of which may be revealed in stages, serve as the triggers for generating ideas regarding possible causes (e.g., the basic science pathways to the clinical manifestations), as well as collecting and integrating information. Faculty members who work with PBL groups are meant to adopt the role of facilitator rather than the role of expert.

Given the importance attached to PBL as a pathway to active, life-long learning, and the emphasis placed on relatively free-wheeling discussion, surprisingly little research has been done on the communication that occurs during PBL sessions. One of the few studies was conducted by Wilkerson, Hafler, and Liu (1991), who analyzed four PBL groups at Harvard, and identified five communication-related factors associated with differences in student-directed discussion among the groups: topic initiation, use of questions, style and pattern of tutor talk, pattern of student–tutor interaction, number of pauses and interruptions. These results illustrate the importance of understanding basic communication patterns within PBL groups, as well as how these patterns change with time.

Perhaps even more importantly, the fact that there were major differences within a small sample of groups at one institution suggests a need for "monitoring evaluations" or "implementation evaluations" (Rossi & Freeman, 1989; Shadish, Cook & Leviton, 1991) to determine the actual process and outcome of PBL (i.e., is it being implemented as specified in the program design?). Clearly, communication would be a major focus of such evaluations. Optimal group size is another neglected area of research, one of tremendous interest to medical educators who must balance the desire for small, highly integrated groups with the reality of recruiting enough faculty to facilitate them (see Ravitch, Brunner, & McGaghie, 1995).

Training for Work in Interdisciplinary Teams

We work together, but we do not learn together. This is both cause and consequence of the fragmentation that plagues health care. The walls we have erected between disciplines, between organizations, and between preventive and acute care frustrate many of our best-intentioned efforts to craft effective, safe, and waste-free processes for our patients, their families, and their communities. To improve we must forge connections.

—Berwick, 1996

There is no question that medical practice is moving toward a team-based model, one in which health care professionals with different areas of expertise will be working together toward the goal of effective and efficient patient care (see Gordon et al., 1996). At present, training for work in this collaborative environment tends to take place on-the-job rather than as part of the formal medical education process, and the product is less than optimal (Anvaripour, Jacobson, Schweiger, & Weissman, 1991). Indeed, McKegney (1989) noted that "communication patterns within the teaching hospital reinforce trainees' strivings for perfectionism and devalue the contributions of nonphysician staff." The situation is unlikely to improve unless medical educators, as well as nursing educators, pharmacy educators, and so on, develop training programs for their students. Communication scholars can build a foundation for these training programs by conducting field research on the communication patterns between team members. Systems theory (Ray & Miller, 1990), as well as theories of leadership and conflict resolution, would provide useful frameworks for these studies.

ORGANIZATIONAL COMMUNICATION IN MEDICAL SCHOOLS

Medical education can be seen as a process of socialization (Becker, 1961), and some of the strongest messages students receive about what it means to be a medical professional are inferred. In addition to stated educational objectives, students quickly learn to pay close attention to the "hidden curriculum"—the culture of the medical school in which the formal curriculum is situated. More specifically, students develop a sense of what is important by watching, talking with, and imitating role models (Bandura & Walters, 1963), as well as by applying a simple litmus test: if the material is on an examination, it is important. In many respects, medical educators' recognition of the "hidden curriculum" prompted a movement toward changing the formal curriculum. From almost any standpoint, the process of implementing change in the formal medical school curriculum is painfully slow, and it is different in every institution. Both of these topics—effects of the "hidden curriculum" and change in the formal curriculum—are rich areas for organizational communication research.

The Hidden Curriculum

Medical students learn a great deal about what it means to be a doctor by watching and talking to their role models—interns, residents, and attending physicians—just as they are adept at learning what it takes to be a successful medical student by watching their more proximal role models, the students who precede them. The formal curriculum is likely to be successful only to the extent that messages about it are consistent with what students glean from the hidden curriculum, the environment in which the formal curriculum is offered. For example, a course director might issue the following statement about the formal curriculum: "we want you to think about the big picture and try to integrate concepts—don't worry about the minutiae," but paradoxically produce exams that focus primarily on isolated facts. The message of the hidden curriculum is that students should focus on memorizing the facts rather than trying to understand the connections between concepts.

Communication scholars could conduct valuable ethnographic research to determine the extent of congruence between messages associated with formal curriculum and hidden curriculum. Indeed, the area of communication skills is a prime candidate for this type of investigation, since there may be incongruities between what students learn in their communication skills sessions and what they observe their role-models doing in clinical settings. Cognitive consistency theories (see, for example, Festinger, 1957) would be a cornerstone of such research, while faculty development to reduce mixed messages and counter-modeling would be an important outcome.

Change in the Formal Curriculum

> The major constraints to further progress in this area continue to be that faculty members are generally unable or unwilling to abandon the role of being information providers only, and cling to the lecture method because it is the most efficient way for them to provide information.
> —Association of American Medical Colleges, 1992

The move toward curriculum reform was, to a large degree, generated by medical educators' recognition of counter-messages inherent in the traditional medical curriculum (e.g., the desire for active learners was at odds with reliance on the lecture format). While the need for change has been recognized for some time now, curricular reform has not come easily. For instance, some schools attempting to shift from a departmentally organized, discipline-based curriculum to a more integrated, organ-system-based curriculum found basic science or clinical departments defending their turf, reluctant to relinquish either curricular time or "what is viewed as their right to determine independently the knowledge and skills, in their respective disciplines, that medical students should acquire" (Association of American Medical Colleges, 1992).

While organizational change often depends on clear vision and strong leadership at the top (i.e., the medical school dean), such change is unlikely to succeed unless faculty throughout the organization feel they have a voice in the process, particularly since medical education is so faculty intensive. In addition, only by soliciting honest feedback from students can medical educators get a sense of whether and how their innovations are working. Along these lines, Burg, McMichael, and Stemmler (1986) identified networks for communicating about education problems and issues, systems for obtaining consensus among the institution's constituencies, and vehicles for providing the faculty, students and administration with information—communication strategies all—as keys to managing change in medical education.

Another essential component of the change process is faculty development. For instance, faculty members who are experienced lecturers are unlikely to be immediately comfortable if asked to take a more facilitative role with a small group of students. Similarly, physicians who have taught in clinical clerkships for years may have a difficult time reflecting on their own skills and discussing their students' communication with patients unless they are equipped with strategies for doing so. Communication researchers can provide a valuable service to both faculty and students by assessing the training and support of faculty members in a new educational environment. As more and more medical schools take on the challenge of curriculum reform, organizational communication scholars can both offer and gain insight into effective models and channels for innovation (see Lemon, Yonke, Roe, & Foley, 1995).

COMMUNICATION TECHNOLOGY FOR MEDICAL EDUCATION

From database searches to self-paced tutorials to tests of diagnostic reasoning to medical imaging, the personal computer has revolutionized medical education. The Internet has accelerated that process, and some medical schools have updated their libraries and computer centers, provided high-speed network access in residence halls, and encouraged students to use Internet software. In addition, telemedicine, the delivery of health and medical services across some distance through the use of telecommunication, has facilitated distance learning, allowing physicians in remote locations to interact with colleagues and courses based in academic medical centers. While computer-assisted instruction and telemedicine capabilities are not new, they are not yet in widespread use. Communication scholars can work with medical educators to better understand the barriers and possibilities associated with both computer-assisted learning and telemedicine technology for distance learning.

Computer-Assisted Learning

Friedman (1996) has nicely summarized the promise and pitfalls of computer-assisted instruction (CAI), particularly with respect to the World Wide Web. At a conceptual level, the World Wide Web allows CAI programs to be distributed and used at any medical school, on any computer platform. At the operational level, the promise of CAI is unlikely to be realized, at least in the near future, because it is not yet fully integrated into medical curricula, students are not tested on the material they learn via CAI, the programs tend to be poorly designed and rarely updated, and not all medical schools have reasonable access or solid support for CAI (Friedman, 1996). Communication researchers can participate in the integration of CAI into the medical curriculum by evaluating the ways in which students interact with various programs.

Telemedicine and Distance Learning

Advances in communication technology have made possible high-quality transmission of digitized audio, video, and still images via telephone lines, cable television lines, or satellite links. Thus, the same technology that can be used to link remote sites with medical centers for patient care can also be used for distance learning, through which physicians at remote sites can participate in continuing medical education courses or regular seminar sessions held at the medical centers. Proponents of distance learning suggest that it will improve quality of care in rural and underserved communities by helping the physicians stay current, as well as mitigate isolation of rural practitioners by linking them to urban medical centers. However, there are many obstacles to implementing telemedicine (Makoul, 1995b) and, therefore, to realizing the promise of distance learning. Whether communication researchers examine distance learning from a regulatory, technological, or instructional perspective, this complex topic requires an integrated, communication systems approach.

THE ROLE OF COMMUNICATION SCHOLARS

Along with many exciting opportunities for research, the medical community's increasing interest in communication also reveals three major challenges that face communication scholars: (1) the ambiguity inherent in the term *health communication*, (2) the fact that a hot seat usually accompanies a hot topic, and (3) the practical reality of working in a milieu that might not be familiar with, or conducive to, communication scholarship. Each topic is addressed in turn.

Health Communication

The term *health communication* is the product of two words that already connote all things to all people. The World Health Organization definition of *health* (World Health Organization, 1947) as "a state of complete physical, mental and social well-being, not merely the absence of disease or infirmity" illustrates that concept's breadth, and there are diverse perspectives on how health can be achieved. As noted in this chapter, *communication* occurs, and is assessed, at multiple levels (e.g., intrapersonal, interpersonal, group, organizational, technological). While *health communication* is a convenient heading for association divisions, journals, and the like, overuse of the term risks conflating scholarly pursuits and deflating their import. In order to be effective, researchers must clearly articulate the value of bringing a communication perspective into the medical education arena.

Hot Topic = Hot Seat

At a very basic level, communication scholars who get involved with the health care community have either convinced someone at a medical school, pharmacy school, nursing school, school of public health, hospital, HMO, community group, public health organization, international agency, or funding foundation that communication is important to the success of a program, or have been brought in by someone who thinks a program needs a communication component. The fact that communication is now a hot topic in the medical education arena means that those who enter the arena often find themselves in a hot seat, the temperature of which depends on the particular environment.

If working in a setting where "medicine" is spoken, the credibility of communication researchers depends on the ability to speak the language and be part of a team. If arguing that precious resources—whether research funds or curricular time—should be devoted to communication, it is important to realize that there may only be one chance to prove the resources are well spent. The bottom line is medical educators are taking very seriously the promise of communication research. To build and maintain credibility, communication scholars must be sensitive to "local" criteria of quality and relevance.

Communication Scholarship and Medical Education

The most formidable challenge might be conducting research in an environment that is not necessarily conducive to communication scholarship. Consider medical schools as an example: As more schools make a real commitment to communication training and community experience, there will be more opportunities for communication scholars. However, people will likely be brought into offices or departments of medical education, most of which are committed to providing a central service to students and faculty. In other words, these offices or departments rarely provide a ready-made academic home.

Thus, communication researchers in medical education environments must be prepared to educate the people with whom they work about what it means, and what it takes, to conduct communication research. While medical educators are likely to be well versed in educational, basic science, or clinical research, they may not be familiar with the perspectives, methods, or timelines associated with communication studies. The goal of coming to a shared understanding is solid

research and high-profile publications that will strengthen the partnership between communication scholars and medical educators.

SUMMARY: DIRECTIONS FOR FUTURE RESEARCH

The topic of this chapter could yield a book on its own and thus has been
necessarily selective. It does not explore links between medical education and
communication research on medical ethics (see Chapter 6), health policy (see
Chapter 8), health campaigns (see Chapter 9) or media messages (see Chapter
10). This chapter does, however, point to a number of viable areas for communication research in medical education. The examples selected to illustrate
directions for future communication research are consistent with my own experience as a communication professor involved in medical education, as well
as a widely distributed and accepted vision for the future of medical education
(American Association of Medical Colleges, 1992). To review, there are opportunities for research in:

1. Intrapersonal communication, focusing on patient narrative regarding the illness experience as well as physician narrative regarding clinical decision making.
2. Interpersonal communication, focusing on communication skills teaching and assessment for physicians-in-training and physicians-in-practice.
3. Small-group communication, focusing on the problem-based learning process and
   training for work in interdisciplinary health care teams.
4. Organizational communication, focusing on the "hidden curriculum" and managing
   curricular change.
5. Communication technology, focusing on computer-assisted learning and telemedicine
   for distance learning.

Turning these opportunities into productive partnerships with medical educators requires familiarity with past efforts, current practice, and future directions in medical education. Toward that end, researchers would do well to read
seminal reports on medical education issued by the Association of American
Medical Colleges (AAMC), the American Medical Association (AMA) and the
Macy Foundation over the past decades:

Medical Education: Final Report of the Commission on Medical Education (Rappleye,
    1932).
Future Directions for Medical Education: A Report of the Council on Medical Education
    (American Medical Association, 1982).
*Physicians for the Twenty-First Century: Report of the Project Panel on the General
    Professional Education of the Physician and College Preparation for Medicine*
    (Association of American Medical Colleges, 1984), commonly known as the
    GPEP Report.
Adapting Clinical Medical Education to the Needs of Today and Tomorrow (Josiah H.
    Macy, Jr. Foundation, 1988).

Educating Medical Students: Assessing Change in Medical Education—The Road to Implementation (Association of American Medical Colleges, 1992), commonly referred to as the ACME-TRI Report.

In addition, there are several journals devoted to medical education. *Academic Medicine*, published by the AAMC, is perhaps the most prominent journal in North America, while *Medical Education*, published in England, has a more international scope. People working at different institutions, not to mention different countries, tend to emphasize different aspects of communication in medical education. Medical educators and communication scholars will both benefit by moving from a parochial perspective, in which they focus solely on their own work, to participating in a national and international dialogue about communication research in medical education. In time, that benefit will extend to medical students and the patients for whom they are learning to care.

NOTE

1. While small groups are the most common format for problem-based learning, this technique can also be implemented on an individual or large-group basis.

3

The Patient/
Health Professional Relationship

Teresa L. Thompson

SYNOPSIS

In an update of earlier reviews of patient–provider interaction written by this author, research published since the early 1990s is outlined and discussed. The major themes identified in the research include examination of information concerns, interactional control, communication skills, empathy, medical terms, gender issues, outcomes of provider–patient interaction, ethical issues, delivery of bad news, patient narratives, emotions, communication about medications, communication issues that pertain particularly to cancer, multicultural concerns, and theoretical models of provider–patient interaction. Changes and trends over the years in this research are discussed. Some notable improvements in the research are identified, and areas still in need of development are outlined.

The interaction between provider and patient has been arguably the most common focus of health communication research. Although an interaction between a health care provider and a patient is certainly not the only context in which health information is communicated (Rootman & Hershfield, 1994), it is the most prosaic and, in a sense, the defining transaction wherein medical care and the processes of consultation, examination, diagnosis, and treatment occur. This transaction is also fraught with potential problems, and increasingly sophisticated medical technology has made provider–patient communication even more difficult (Wertheimer, Bertman, Wheeler, & Siegal, 1985). Many people, especially within the American culture, are notably satisfied with the physical health care they receive, but they are much less sanguine about the communication accompanying that care. The dissatisfaction with provider–patient communication has been so frequently asserted and so well documented that it need not be elaborated here, although it will be addressed briefly later in this chapter. In addition to the dissatisfaction patients feel when their interactions with physicians are flawed, such interactions create the potential for serious tangible health consequences. For all these reasons, a great deal of research has been conducted over the years on the topic of communication between providers and receivers of health care.

The goal of the present chapter is not to review the entire corpus of this research but to update past reviews of such work (Thompson, 1984, 1986, 1990, 1994). This chapter will, then, review research on provider–patient interaction that has been conducted, for the most part, since the early 1990s. Many of the themes of this recent research, however, are similar to those that occur in earlier reviews: information concerns, interactional control, communication skills, empathy, medical terms, gender issues, outcomes of provider–patient interaction, ethical issues, delivery of bad news, and health communication models. In addition, some new themes appear in the more recent literature. These include patient narratives and emotional responses, communication about medication, communication issues pertaining specifically to cancer, and communication in multicultural settings. These newer themes are also addressed in the present chapter. A good starting point is the topic that is both broadest and most frequently researched in the recent health communication literature, namely, the communication of health information in provider–patient interaction.

HEALTH INFORMATION

Research on health information within the provider–patient context looks at the *exchange* of information between both participants. Within health care, patients are communicating information to care providers, and care providers are communicating information to patients. Much research has documented patient dissatisfaction with the quantity and type of information they receive from care providers. For instance, more than 30 percent of hospitalized patients report receiving no information about anesthesia, time in the operating room, return to fitness, or pain (Williams, 1993). Similarly, a national survey of 6,455 patients who had been hospitalized indicated that 44.9 percent claimed they were not told about daily routine and 31.8 percent were not told who to ask for help if it was needed (Cleary, Edgman-Levitan, Roberts, Maloney, McMullen, Walker, & Delbanco, 1991). Women recommended for gynecological surgery judge the care they receive acceptable but report that they receive inadequate information (Haas & Puretz, 1992). Both the parents and care providers of seriously ill infants indicate concern for the provision of understandable medical information to the parents (Able-Boone, Dokecki, & Smith, 1989). Parental satisfaction is negatively related to delays in providing information (Quine & Pahl, 1986).

In addition to dissatisfaction with information, research has documented the *impact* of information from health care providers. Although, in light of low adherence rates (see DiMatteo, this volume), care providers sometimes wonder whether the information they communicate does have an impact on patients, research indicates that patients who do not receive adequate information from their physicians are more likely to adopt nontraditional treatments (Pruyn, Ruckman, van Brunschot, & van den Borne, 1985). An analysis of communication about weight control indicated that only 29 percent of family practitioners provide good information to their overweight patients. Fifty-one percent of the patients could not remember talking with their doctors about such issues. A positive, moderate association was found, however, between information from care providers about weight control and patients' willingness for and success in weight reduction (Himmel, Stolpe, & Kochen, 1994).

Research also indicates patients' desires for information, although those same patients may not explicitly seek information during provider–patient encounters (Beisecker & Beisecker, 1990). Only in interactions that last longer than 19 minutes do patients find time to seek the information they desire (Beisecker & Beisecker, 1990).

Of concern to both health care providers and patients are data about the likelihood that relevant information from patients will be communicated to providers. A 1993 study by Epstein, Campbell, Cohen-Cole, McWhinney, and Smilkstein indicated that patients are typically interrupted by physicians 18 seconds after they begin describing their symptoms. Epstein et al. also reported that, because of this, most patients fail to disclose their most significant concerns. Van Der Merwe (1995) writes that 54 percent of patient complaints and 45 percent of patient concerns are not elicited by doctors, and that in 50 percent of visits patients and doctors do not agree on the nature of the primary presenting problem. Low disclosure has also been documented in chronically ill patients (DeDonder, 1991). Incomplete information from patients is associated with increased testing, cost, risk and the performance of more medical procedures (Franke, 1995).

When patients lack the opportunity to disclose significant concerns early in the interview, they often find themselves able to do so only at the end of the interaction. Beckman, Frankel, and Darnley (1985) noted that patients who are given a full opportunity to describe their symptoms at the beginning of the consultation are significantly less likely to introduce new concerns at the end of the visit. In a detailed examination of medical interview closures, White, Levinson, and Roter (1994) reported that 21 percent of patients introduce new concerns as the physician is attempting to end the conversation. Increased likelihood of this is associated with less information exchange about therapy and fewer orientation statements by physicians. White et al. suggested that physicians may improve communication in the closing phase of the medical interview by orienting patients to the flow of the visit, addressing patient beliefs, checking for understanding, and addressing emotions and psychosocial issues early in the visit.

Information issues in the provider–patient interaction have also been addressed by research focusing on consistencies of perceptions between the two interactants. Even when information is exchanged, it is interpreted differently by providers and patients. Physician–patient pairs are especially likely to disagree about the information that has been communicated when the explanations have not been thorough or understandable to patients (Rosenberg, Gorman, Snitzer, Herbst, & Lynne, 1989). Guttman (1993) reported inaccurate assessments by physicians of patient knowledge levels and suggested that this inaccuracy leads to less information provision by physicians. Guttman looked at interactions between physicians and diabetic patients whom the physicians claimed they knew at least fairly well and with whom they had "good communication" (p. 306). The results indicated that, even with these patients, physicians overestimated their patients' knowledge about nutrition/food exchanges, hypoglycemia, and skin care. If a physician assumes that a patient already has certain knowledge, there will be no perceived need to communicate that information. Similarly, if a care provider believes that a patient already knows the potential side effects of a medication that the patient has taken in the past, the provider is unlikely to mention them.

Physicians and patients also differ in their thoughts and feelings about the communication interchange and its functions (Cegala, McNeilis, McGee, & Jonas, 1995). Among the differing perceptions found between patients and physicians are those focusing on the role of each and the amount of control to be allowed to each.

CONTROL

The asymmetrical nature of the physician–patient interaction has been well documented and described in earlier research (see, for example, S. Fisher, 1984). Movements to share control more equitably, however, have surfaced in recent years. Beisecker and Beisecker (1993) discuss the differences between two metaphors for the doctor–patient interaction: paternalism versus consumerism. They also describe the societal forces moving health care toward consumerism. Most of the writing focusing on this topic in recent years examines the opportunity to integrate patient-centered and physician-centered approaches to care provision, where the patient leads in areas in which he or she is the expert (symptoms, preferences, concerns) and the physician leads in the areas within his or her domain of knowledge (disease and treatment) (Smith & Hoppe, 1991). Smith-Dupre and Beck (1996), too, describe the creation of a climate in which both parties' goals are pursued.

Not all patients, however, desire more control over their health care. Nor are all physicians willing to share control. Overall, physicians who see their relationships with patients as "partnerships" have more satisfied patients than do those who establish more authoritarian relationships (Anderson & Zimmerman, 1993). Patients who express a preference for more involvement in their care also tend to give more negative evaluations of the care they typically receive

(Cleary, Edgman-Levitan, McMullen, & Delbanco, 1992). Looking at the interaction between patient expectations and physician styles, Ditto, Moore, Hilton, and Kalish (1995) concluded that patients who prefer egalitarian relationships with their providers are particularly dissatisfied with authoritarian physicians and are unlikely to follow treatment prescriptions made by such physicians. All respondents in the study, however, preferred egalitarian physicians—even those patients with more authoritarian predispositions. More authoritarian patients, however, were more likely to seek health care.

The impact of patient participation on patient commitment to medical decisions and patient satisfaction was also recently investigated by Young and Klingle (1996). They reported that patients who were more actively involved in the medical interaction were more satisfied and more committed to the medical decisions made during the interaction. Young and Klingle (1996) also examined barriers to such active participation, noting that it is not easy for patients to increase their involvement. The researchers argued that physician feedback is one such barrier. If the physician responds negatively to active patient involvement, such involvement is less likely to result in patient satisfaction than if the physician's feedback is positive. Cultural barriers, to be discussed in a later section, also moderate the likelihood of active patient participation, as some cultural groups are less likely to feel comfortable being assertive with authority figures.

NARRATIVES

Implicit in some of the studies mentioned above is the recommendation that both physicians and health communication researchers listen to patient stories or narratives to provide better health care and to more adequately understand health communication. In an article directed toward family practitioners, Ventres (1994) conducted interviews with patients with whom residents indicated they were having communication difficulties. A team composed of several care providers including the resident interviewed each patient. The interviews were designed to elicit the patients' stories. Although the residents had labeled these patients as ''problems,'' the interviews in each case yielded rich insight about misunderstandings between the patients and the residents and indicated that the residents had not accurately understood the patients' perspectives and beliefs. Ventres presents a strong rationale for the utility of this approach by physicians. This argument is echoed by Epstein et al. (1993), in another piece geared toward family practitioners.

Utilizing the theoretical basis provided by W. Fisher's (1984) narrative paradigm, communication researchers have provided further evidence of the value of listening to people's stories. Sharf (1990) offers a detailed narrative examination of a provider–patient interaction. Her analysis not only illuminates this interaction, but also yields insight into the nature of provider–patient communication in general. Cherry and Smith (1993) elicited the stories of men with

AIDS and, while their work focuses on loneliness, also add to our understanding of provider–patient communication. More recently, Vanderford and Smith (1996) examined the breast implant controversy using a narrative perspective. The stories told by patients who have and have not experienced difficulties with their implants coupled with the stories told by their physicians indicate the central role of communication in the controversy. Vanderford and Smith's analysis suggests that, had communication between patients who began experiencing difficulty and their physicians been characterized by less disconfirmation and more empathy, a much different image of several relevant parties would have emerged in the press. In the press coverage as it did emerge, the reputations of both Dow Corning and plastic surgeons were severely damaged. Thus, the book presents a case for the powerful impact of interpersonal communication between patients and providers as well as for the value of the narrative perspective.

COMMUNICATION SKILLS

The importance of the provider–patient relationship and the communication that creates it is also demonstrated by Ruben's (1993) content analysis of critical incidents in health care. Almost 47 percent of the memorable experiences described by patients focused on personal treatment/care giver interpersonal communication as the key theme. Clinical/technical issues ranked second, accounting for only 27 percent of the experiences.

In perhaps the most thorough attempt to assess the effectiveness of doctor–patient interactions by looking at the communicative behaviors of both interactants, Scherz, Edwards, and Kallail (1995) utilized the Prutting (1982) pragmatic protocol to evaluate 30 behaviors simultaneously. The rating instrument assesses a variety of verbal behaviors (including speech acts, topics, turn-taking, etc.), as well as nonverbal and paralinguistic cues. Their analysis indicated that most of the noted behaviors were rated as appropriate. The most frequent inappropriate behaviors in the resident physicians were interruptions, lack of specificity, or problems with feedback, vocal intensity, fluency, pausing, or quantity/conciseness. Patients most frequently exhibited problems with quantity/conciseness, specificity, intelligibility, vocal intensity, fluency, pausing, interruptions, and eye gaze. Scherz et al. noted, however, that the rating instrument did not seem to include all relevant behaviors, as indicated by the small numbers of inappropriate behaviors.

In light of concerns about communicative effectiveness in provider–patient interaction, several attempts have been described to address the issue. Provider training programs that do appear to increase patient satisfaction have been described (Evans, Stanley, & Burrows, 1992), as has a self-instructional method for improving doctor–patient communication (Mason, Barkley, Kappelman, Carter, & Beachy, 1988). Thomson (1994) tested the effectiveness of consumer assessment of communicative skills of family practitioners and supported the reliability of the technique.

All of these perspectives focus on the care *provider's* communicative skills, which, of course, misses half of the dyad; the perspectives are therefore inherently incomplete. Other research has focused on physician complaints about communicating with patients. Levinson, Stiles, Inui, and Engle (1993) found that physicians most frequently attribute communication problems to the patient rather than to themselves. They identified six primary problems: (1) lack of trust/ agreement; (2) too many problems; (3) feelings of distress; (4) lack of understanding; (5) lack of adherence; and (6) demanding or controlling patients. Taking a somewhat different perspective, Franke (1995) reported that 67 percent of physicians feel less than satisfied with the amount of time they have to spend with patients, 90 percent feel that patients have trouble following their directions and advice, and less than 25 percent feel their medical school training in communication is adequate.

EMPATHY

One particular communicative skill that has been the subject of some research is empathy. Researchers have demonstrated that physician empathy can be improved with training and that there is a positive relationship between empathy and physician–patient communication skills (Feighny, Monaco, & Arnold, 1995). Even violent patients respond with less anger to empathic messages (Lancee, Gallop, McCroy, & Toner, 1995). Participants in this study manifested moderate levels of anger to statements of explanation and higher levels to messages characterized by unempathic limit-setting.

The signal value of empathy in hospice nursing has also been argued. Raudonis (1995) has indicated that empathy may not only enable nurses to intervene more effectively, but also allow them to revitalize their own practices. She details the gradual process of building an empathic relationship. Unlike much other medical writing, Raudonis's perspective on empathy is very dyadic—she looks at empathy *between* both interactants, rather than just at empathy from the care provider to the patient. Her interviews indicated three phases in the development of an empathic relationship. In what is dubbed the *initiating* phase, hospice patients reveal their physical, social, psychological, or spiritual needs to the nurses. In turn, the nurse enters the home of the hospice patient "as a person wanting to help in whatever way(s) the patient's" (p. 64) needs require. Nurses concentrate on talking and listening, in a caring, therapeutic manner, and communicating information about the patient's health status and what is to come. The family's input is also sought. The *building* phase strengthens and deepens the relationship. The nurse becomes a link to the outside world. Patients emphasize perceptions of (1) the competence of their nurses, and (2) the willingness of the nurse to spend time with the patient. Reciprocity begins to play an important role. The *sustaining* phase is characterized by patients feeling secure and less anxious because they are confident of the 24-hour availability of their nurses. They perceive that the nurses behave in ways that go well beyond normal nursing experience. Although the hospice relationship is more intense than that found in many other health contexts, Raudonis's (1995) findings still provide insight into those behaviors that relate to the development of an empathic relationship.

EMOTIONS

Because empathy focuses on a recognition of the other's emotional state, it seems appropriate at this point to turn to a discussion of some of the research that has focused on the role of various emotions in the provider–patient relationship. This is a relatively new area of study within health communication. In the past, little research has examined anything related to *emotions* in the medical context—a context in which emotions are not really seen as appropriate. Researchers have now begun to move beyond this blind spot, however, and a small amount of research is emerging that is beginning to yield some interesting findings. Focusing on physician emotions, Estrada, Isen, and Young (1994) reported that situations that result in more positive affect in physicians lead them to solve problems more creatively and to experience more satisfaction. Physician emotions significantly affect patients, too. When an oncologist appears worried while communicating mammogram results, patients recall less information, perceive the situation as more severe, have higher pulses, and report higher levels of state anxiety (Shapiro, Boggs, Melamed, & Graham-Pole, 1992).

Patient anxiety is also related to other aspects of provider–patient communication. In the dental office, information sharing, particularly through comforting messages, reduces patient anxiety and enhances perceptions of competence and interpersonal attractiveness of the dentist (Hamilton, Rouse, & Rouse, 1994). Anxiety can also be allayed by encouraging patients to disclose underlying concerns and then confirming or discrediting these concerns (Sprecher, Thomas, Huebner, Norfleet, & Jacoby, 1983).

MEDICAL LANGUAGE

Patient anxiety inhibits understanding of information communicated within health care. Sometimes, however, this information is difficult to understand even when anxiety is not a significant variable. Although there are several reasons for this difficulty, patients' unfamiliarity with medical terms is an important one. This is a concern that has been expressed in the health communication research for decades—one that has been echoed in recent years. Hadlow and Pitts (1991) found notable differences in the intended and interpreted meanings of common medical and psychological terms between patients and care providers. The terms used in Hadlow and Pitts's research included many that are commonly used in provider–patient interaction (depression, eating disorder, etc.). Although even physicians are completely correct in their interpretations of the terms used in the study only 70 percent of the time, patients are correct a mere 36 percent of the time.

Results of other studies are consistent with those reported by Hadlow and Pitts. In an update of a 1961 study examining patients' understanding of medical terms, Thompson and Pledger (1993) reported that patients in the 1990s are somewhat more likely to recognize medical terms than had been the case 30 years prior to their study, but the improvement was much less than had been predicted. Not one of the 50 terms was identified correctly by all participants.

Use of technical medical language has some important outcomes in the provider–patient context. Jackson (1992) concluded that use of more technical messages is associated with less cognitive satisfaction, comprehension, and recall, although the amount of information provided to patients does not significantly affect these variables.

These results all indicate that, when interacting with patients, care providers would be well advised to rely as little as possible on technical medical terms and to check for patient understanding when such terms are used. This concern is particularly relevant when the patient is a child. Noting that little health communication research has focused on communicating to children, Whaley (1994) recently looked at suggestions offered to care providers about such communication. These suggestions, based primarily on anecdotes, encourage care providers to use analogies or metaphors to explain medical issues to children. Although they are intuitively appealing, Whaley argues that such suggestions frequently ignore the empirical knowledge about children's cognitive processing of analogy and metaphor. Although the appropriate metaphor can be helpful to a child, the inappropriate one can be devastating. Whaley concludes that much more theoretical development and research are needed before health communicators interacting with children will be confident about metaphor choice.

The metaphorical implications of medical terms have also been discussed by Van Der Merwe (1995) in the gynecological setting. This article urges practitioners to realize the negative implications for patients of such terms as "failed" to dilate, "inadequate" contractions, an "incompetent" cervix, and "hostile" mucus.

COMMUNICATION ABOUT MEDICATION

Other communication difficulties have also received attention from researchers in recent years, some for the first time. In the past little research was conducted on communicating about medication. Only recently has this topic become the focus of much interesting work. For instance, Hargie, Morrow, and Woodman (1993) report a two-year study of interactions between pharmacists and patients that led to the identification of communication skills to be addressed in pharmacy training programs. These skills will become increasingly important now that pharmacists are required by federal legislation (Omnibus Reconciliation Act of 1990) to communicate with patients about medications. Noting that pharmacists and patients may differ in their expectations about pharmacist–patient communication, Schommer (1994) examined the impacts of congruence and incongruence about these expectations on actual pharmacist–patient communication. Congruence leads to longer interactions and the sharing of more information.

Specific aspects of messages designed by pharmacy students have also been examined. Looking at hypertension messages, Lambert and Gillespie (1994) found that patients respond more positively to messages that express understanding, encourage communication with the physician, and describe alternative therapies.

Implicit in Lambert and Gillespie's findings is the acknowledgment of the interrelationships among pharmacist, patient, and physician when communicating about medications. Many patients, especially the elderly, prefer to receive such information from their physicians (Schommer, 1994; Smith, Cunningham, & Hale, 1994). In a detailed examination of this issue, Smith et al. reported that elderly patients did not perceive their doctors sharing decisions about medications with them. Patients, not their doctors or pharmacists, were the ones who initiated communication about medications if such communication occurred. The patients also indicated that they would have liked more discussion of potential side effects.

Other research has indicated that physicians who are trained in the "health belief model" are able to communicate instructions about medications more effectively (Garrity & Lawson, 1989). DiMatteo, Reiter, and Gambone (1994) have described in detail a collaborative system of communicating about medications that increases adherence to prescribed regimens. Two other more descriptive observational studies have also yielded insight into the nature of communication about medication. Makoul, Arntson, and Schofield (1995) reported that patients are extremely passive in discussions of treatments and that physicians most frequently mention only product name and instructions for use. These researchers found that physicians overestimate the extent to which they talk with patients about their abilities to follow the treatment plan, seek patients' opinions about the prescribed medications, and discuss risks of the medication.

In another small-scale but detailed study of 12 interactions, Parrott (1994) found that only half of the physicians mentioned the name of the medication they were prescribing. Only one of the physicians discussed dosage. Medications were minimally described, but no patients asked for further information. Few physicians provided information about side effects, and most of what was provided was implicit rather than explicit. Drug interactions were not discussed, nor were the benefits of the medication or alternative treatments. Only one doctor mentioned cost, and two referred to addictive potential. One-third of the physicians provided explicit information about how to take the medication, and only two referred to the duration of the treatment. No reinforcement of instruction was provided or requested. Both Parrott (1994) and Makoul et al. (1995) provide suggestions for improving communication about medication. For other reviews, see Hammond & Lambert (1994), Hargie et al. (1993), and Schommer (1994).

GENDER

Although research has examined more specific health communication processes such as communicating about medication, notably little health communication research has examined the more pervasive variable of gender (Gabbard-Alley, 1995). In a thorough review of the topic, Gabbard-Alley found that poor research designs render most conclusions that have been drawn about the role of gender in provider–patient communication "suspect" (p. 35). This is interesting in light of differences in male versus female morbidity and mortality—women report more illnesses, but men die earlier. Gabbard-Alley's review does indicate that interactions involving women are characterized by more communication, but their concerns are taken less seriously. There are some nonverbal gender differences, especially in touch. Gender does not seem to affect compliance, satisfaction, or the impact of communication on these variables. Much of Gabbard-Alley's review, then, is consistent with such recent findings as Dunning and Lange's (1993) conclusion of no gender differences in the communication of male versus female dental students with patients.

This is not, however, the case with all studies. Meeuwesen, Schaap, and van der Staak (1991) reported gender differences in how complaints are elaborated. More gender differences occur in the communication of physicians than patients. Male doctors are more imposing and presumptuous, and females are more attentive and nondirective and take more time with their patients. These findings are consistent with those of Hall, Irish, Roter, Ehrlich, and Miller's (1994) analysis of 100 routine medical visits. In addition, Hall et al. found that female physicians make more positive and partnership statements, ask more questions, make more nonverbal vocal responses, and smile and nod more. Patients also respond differently to female physicians, giving them more medical information and making more partnership statements. Hall et al. also report the interactions of patient and physician gender.

Noting some of these differences, especially the point made above regarding women's health concerns being taken less seriously, Malterud (1993) offers strategies for improving the status of women patients in the medical culture. In light of these strategies, she suggests alternative approaches to physician–patient communication.

CANCER

One of the emphases that has emerged in provider–patient research in recent years is the interaction when the patient has been diagnosed with cancer. Four themes are discussed in this literature: (1) communication problems; (2) communication as it relates to adjustment to cancer; (3) communication and pain;

and (4) persuading women to get mammograms. Each of these areas will be reviewed.

Communication Problems

In Morrow, Hoagland, and Carpenter's (1983) overview of improving communication related to cancer treatment, two basic issues are discussed. They discern the lack of readability of informed consent documents and difficulties in communicating complicated medical instructions orally and suggest using shorter words, simple declarative sentences, specific, definite advice, and dividing the information into components rather than attempting to give it all at once. Morrow et al.'s (1983) concerns are similar to those raised by Glimelius, Birgegard, Hoffman, Kvale, and Sjoden (1995), who cite lack of information to cancer patients as a concern in and of itself as well as in terms of how it impacts patient distress, coping, and compliance. Glimelius et al. provided training for oncology staff on communicating information to patients and families. Results indicated significantly lower problem scores relating to interaction with medical staff. They found that patient–staff and relative–staff interaction is strongly associated with psychosocial problems, especially when the focus is communication and control concerns.

Bowker's (1996) metaphorical analysis of cancer and control not only identifies problems experienced by cancer patients, but also indicates that care providers may address a patient's concerns better by attending to the metaphors used by the patient and taking care with the metaphors used by the care provider. Bowker's case analysis provides an interesting qualitative contrast to the quantitative methods most commonly used in health communication research.

Adjustment

Two studies have recently focused on the role communication plays in the cancer adjustment/coping process. Roberts, Cox, Reintgen, Baile, and Gibertini (1994) found that the communication of a caring attitude by a physician is associated with better psychological adjustment to breast cancer. Although the provision of information is also important, it "appears to be valued largely within the context of a caring physician-patient relationship" (p. 336). Specific desired behaviors include expressing empathy, allowing sufficient time for patients to absorb the diagnosis, and engaging the patient in treatment decision making.

Gotcher (1995) examined the effect of patient–family communication on adjustment to cancer. The importance of the research rests in the recognized role that adjustment to cancer plays in the immune system and recovery. Well-adjusted patients communicated with their families more frequently and more honestly, received encouragement from relational partners, and did not curtail discussion of the unpleasant aspects of the illness.

Mammography

Three recent studies have examined techniques that care providers can use to persuade women to get mammograms. Fox and Stein (1991) found that "the most important variable that predicted whether women of all racial groups had a mammogram . . . was whether their doctors had discussed mammography with them. The discussion did not need to be lengthy or complex" (p. 1065). Building on this research, Fox, Siu, and Stein (1994) reported that the physician's enthusiasm for mammography when it is discussed in an office visit is significantly related to women's likelihood of obtaining mammograms. Marshall, Smith, and McKeon (1995), however, reported source, message, and channel preferences among different demographic groups of women for information about mammography.

Pain

Glajchen, Fitzmartin, Blum, and Swanton (1995), concerned about the undertreatment of pain in cancer patients, examined the interrelationships among communication and pain. They concluded that patients perceiving communication barriers with their care providers experience more pain and more difficulty discussing this pain with their families. Glajchen et al. also note several factors that interfere with a patient's ability to communicate about pain, including anxiety, coping style, not wanting to distract the doctor, wanting to look like a "good patient," and being concerned that increased pain signifies disease progression.

Many of these issues related to communication and cancer are also, at least implicitly, ethical concerns—a topic to which we now turn.

ETHICAL ISSUES

Little work has yet looked at the intersection of ethical issues in health care and communication concerns (Jackson, 1994a), although Addington and Wegescheide-Harris (1995) have recently proposed a model for doing so. Four themes are apparent in the recent literature in regard to ethics: (1) informed consent; (2) advance directives; (3) treatment of sicker patients; and (4) delivery of bad news (see Chapter 6).

Although obtaining informed consent is an ethical obligation in health care, physicians perceive that it is an intrusion into the doctor–patient relationship (Taylor & Kelner, 1987). They feel that it leads to decreasingly effective doctor–patient communication and less personalized relationships with patients. Informed consent also requires the transmission of emotion-laden information to patients (Wertheimer et al., 1985). Accordingly, Wertheimer et al. describe a training program to address communication skills as they impact this ethical concern. Such training seems appropriate in the context of observational and interview data by Royster (1990) indicating that physicians are not always aware of patients' knowledge and understanding regarding the issues and some doctors omit key legal elements of informed consent. Royster's data also showed that patients sometimes change decisions based on information disclosed by physicians.

Although discussion of informed consent is not easy, communication about advance directives is even more difficult. Three recent studies have focused on discussion of CPR, Do-Not-Resuscitate (DNR) orders, and other advance directives. This research indicates that only 47 percent of physicians know when their patients wish to avoid CPR and 46 percent of DNR orders are written within two days of death (Connors et al., 1995). Only 30 percent of seriously ill patients report any discussion of treatment decisions with their physicians (Virmani, Schneiderman, & Kaplan, 1994), and these discussions are more likely to be about general life attitudes and feelings rather than specific treatments such as artificial nutrition or ventilation. Physicians find it difficult to initiate such discussions and are likely to delay them, but patients are often grateful if the discussions do take place (Clarke, Goldstein, & Raffin, 1994). Connors et al. (1994) report an ineffective attempt to increase the information provided to physicians about patients to encourage more communication about these issues. Clarke et al. (1994) provide specific suggestions to manage such interactions.

Another ethical concern relates less to legal issues than to a more subtle moral one. Evidence suggests differences in treatment by physicians based on the sickness level of the patient. Hall, Epstein, DeCiantis, and McNeil (1993) reported that physicians like their healthy patients more than their less healthy patients. Similarly, patients with fewer health problems are more satisfied with their care providers (Burton & Parker, 1994). An interesting question arises in regard to the last finding—does satisfaction lead to fewer health problems, or do fewer health problems lead to satisfaction? Finally, Cleary et al. (1992) suggest that sicker patients are more difficult to communicate with because they are likely to be in more pain, to be distracted, and to have difficulty expressing themselves. These patients, of course, are the ones who most need communication. It may, however, be more gratifying for care providers to interact with patients with more encouraging prognoses.

Dealing with a patient with a poor prognosis forces a care provider to encounter another difficult situation—communicating that poor prognosis to the patient. Reviews of research on this topic indicate that physicians have become much more willing to share terminal prognoses with patients in recent years (Klenow & Young, 1987). This increased willingness, however, leads to another problem—many care providers are not at all good at communicating bad news. Research by Girgis and Sanson-Fisher (1995) shows that only 35 percent of medical interns feel competent at interactional skills, including announcing bad news. Both Buckman (1992) and Girgis and Sanson-Fisher (1995) provide suggestions for delivery of bad news in a manner that will do the least harm.

OUTCOMES

Much research now argues that information and communication are related to health outcomes (Baker & Connor, 1994). Summaries by Kaplan, Greenfield, and Ware (1989) and, more recently, Stewart (1995) indicate that "better health . . . (is) consistently related to specific aspects of physician–patient communication" (Kaplan et al., 1989, p. 110). Stewart's meta-analysis of 21 of these studies concluded that "the quality of communication both in the history-taking segment of the visit and during discussion of the management plan was found to influence patient health outcomes" (p. 1423). Outcomes affected, in rank order, are emotional health, symptom resolution, function, physiologic measures, and pain control. Even cardiovascular responses are affected by communication (Garvin, Kennedy, Baker, & Polivka, 1992).

Physician assessments of the overall quality of psychosocial care administered by other physicians are best predicted by communication variables. Benzing (1991) had 12 experienced general practitioners rate 103 consultations between other physicians and hypertensive patients on the quality of psychosocial care. Ratings showed high reliability. On the basis of these judgments, interactions were categorized as high or low in quality of psychosical care. Benzing then had social scientists rate the same interactions on frequently studied communication variables. The variables included affective measures, such as showing interest, giving nonverbal attention, encouraging, and providing verbal statements of empathy, systematic and purposive behavior, such as clarifying, structuring, and purposing probing, and patient-centered behavior, manifested diagnostically and therapeutically. His analysis indicated that the communication variables predicted the categorization of interactions. Nonverbal affective behavior showed the strongest predictive power. Benzing (1991) concluded that, in positively rated consultations, providers show more interest in the patient, have more eye contact, show more empathy, and encourage the patient. In "high-quality" interactions the provider is also more patient-centered, during both diagnostic and therapeutic phases. In a third portion of the study, patients' satisfaction was compared with the other assessments of the interactions. Statistical relationships were lower but were still in the predicted direction. Affective behavior was the most important determinant of patient satisfaction.

Another important outcome of communication in the health care context is the filing of malpractice suits. Although not the first to suggest such relationships (see Thompson, 1990 and 1994 for reviews), Hickson, Clayton, Entman, Miller, Githens, Whetten-Golstein, and Sloan (1994) recently provided empirical evidence indicating that patients of physicians who are more frequently sued (compared to those who are not frequently sued) feel rushed, do not receive explanations for tests, and feel ignored. Problems with physician–patient communication are the most commonly expressed complaints in these patients. This is true even among those patients who do not sue physicians who have been frequently sued by others.

Other researchers have recently suggested another outcome measure for health communication research—quality of life assessment. Raising the question, "quality of life measurement: does it have a place in routine clinical assessment?", Jenkinson (1994) notes an increasing belief among care providers that traditional measures of medical outcomes do not provide a full picture of the impact of health care interventions. He argues that health status measures—subjective patient self-reports—may be able to bring about change at the institutional level, influence treatment and treatment choices, and improve medical consultations. Writing about dealing with patients whose prognosis is terminal, Gregory and Cotler (1994) also note that quality of life considerations may be more relevant than medical outcomes.

MULTICULTURAL CONCERNS

Some of the studies referred to in the various sections above tangentially addressed multicultural populations and racial or other demographic differences. A few other recent articles have addressed multicultural concerns more directly by focusing on provider–patient interaction concerns in other cultural settings. All of these studies are based on the assumption that cultural differences help shape provider–patient interaction and should be taken into account by care providers operating within multicultural settings.

Herselman's (1996) ethnographic study of clinical interactions between Xhosa-speaking patients and Western medical practitioners in South Africa suggests that, in order to effectively deliver health care, care providers need to incorporate knowledge about native language and cultural beliefs that relate to medicine. Writing also about experiences in South Africa, Van Der Merwe (1995) explains how OB/GYNs may use a knowledge of ancestral spirits to achieve holistic healing. Although their perspective is not confined to any particular culture, Burgoon and Hall (1994) urge the examination of myths as health belief systems in their article on "salves, sorcery, and science" (p. 97). Cultural differences in approaches to health care are also reported by Young and Klingle (1996) in their study of differences between mainland Americans and Asian Americans in terms of patient participation in health care. They conclude that patient encouragement toward more active participation in health care may be misplaced in some cultural settings.

MODELS

Several theoretical models of physician–patient interaction have been offered recently. Models such as those developed by Cegala, McGee, and McNeilis (1996), Epstein et al. (1993), Frederickson (1993), Keller and Caroll (1994), and Ong, de Haes, Hoos, and Lammes (1995) need to be tested by health communication researchers before they will be able to provide useful information for health care providers. These models offer much opportunity for useful research, although they vary in direct testability and specificity.

Many of these models begin by reviewing the literature on physician–patient interaction and attempting to provide a synthesis of it. For instance, Ong et al.'s (1995) review focuses on: (1) background variables such as culture, the doctor–patient relationship, types of patients and doctors, and disease characteristics; (2) content of communication, especially instrumental versus affective behaviors; and (3) patient outcomes, including satisfaction, compliance, recall and understanding of information, health status, and psychiatric morbidity. They argue that an appropriate theoretical framework must link these groups of variables. Ong et al. (1995) suggest direct links between background variables and communicative content and between content and patient outcomes, as well as an indirect link from background variables to patient outcomes. Unfortunately, this framework is as yet too broad to lead to the generation of testable hypotheses; it does, however, provide an organizing focus for future development.

Keller and Carroll's (1994) model of physician–patient communication is not as broad as that offered by Ong et al. (1995), in that it focuses almost exclusively on the behavior of the physician when interacting with the patient. Keller and Carroll advocate moving from the "find it–fix it" (p. 134) biomedical model to incorporate communication tasks along with traditional medical activities. The communication tasks on which they focus are engaging the patient, empathizing with the patient, educating the patient, and enlisting the patient. Although Keller and Carroll (1994) provide a useful organizing framework for practitioners, testable hypotheses are also in short supply in this theory.

Building on a musical metaphor, Epstein et al. (1993) advocate "achieving a harmony of understanding" (p. 377) as the goal of physician–patient communication. They describe four schools of thought on the topic of physician–patient communication: 1) the three-function model of the medical interview, which focuses on gathering information, developing a therapeutic relationship, and giving information; (2) the patient-centered clinical method, which emphasizes open-ended inquiry into the patient's concerns and the patient's needs for comfort, information, and being understood; (3) the family systems approach to patient care, concentrating on the patient's embeddedness in a complex social unit and the need to communicate with the family and social networks as well the patient; and (4) an emphasis on physician self-awareness to create effective interaction. After describing these approaches, Epstein et al. (1993) show the similar themes, albeit using different terms, emerging from the various approaches. They advocate a synthesis in light of these commonalities.

Frederikson's (1993) model is also integrative but focuses on information processing. Unlike Keller and Carroll (1994), Frederikson's model includes both the patient and care provider. Frederikson's model includes input, process, and outcome variables. The input concerns focus on frame of reference, motivations, goals, needs, expectations, and personal information for both interactants. Sim-

ilarly, the outcome variables encompass perceptions, compliance, concern, understanding, the relationship, and satisfaction of both patients and providers.
Linked between input and outcomes is process, the main component of which
is information exchange. Other aspects of process include initialization, acknowledgment of the problem, questions, the physical exam, diagnosis, treatment
options, and termination. Specific causal links are suggested among these components of the process, resulting in numerous testable hypotheses. Of the models
described to this point, Frederikson's (1993) appears to be most immediately
amenable to future investigation.

Although the models discussed above are based on reviews of the past research, that offered by Cegala et al. (1996) combines a knowledge of past research with analysis of videotaped physician–patient interactions. Grounding
their work in the concept of communicative competence, Cegala et al. attempted
to identify components of doctors' and patients' communicative competence
during primary care interviews. The physicians and the patients were asked to
rate their own competence and that of the other and to identify the particular
behaviors on which their assessments were based. These behavior descriptions
were then content analyzed. The results indicated that information exchange and
relational development were most directly associated with judgments of communicative competence. Information concerns were key for both doctors' and
patients' perceptions of self- and other-competence. Both interactants agreed that
the major responsibility for relational work during the medical encounter appears
to fall on the provider. Cegala et al.'s (1996) model, too, provides important
hypotheses for future work.

TRANSITIONS

The provider–patient literature has undergone changes since past reviews of
this work (Thompson, 1984, 1986, 1990, 1994). Many of these changes reflect
positive directions for an understanding of the provider–patient interaction. The
development of theoretical models is certainly such an improvement, although
the value of these models cannot yet be ascertained. Examination of important
processes such as communicating about medications and multicultural issues
also increases the value of research being done in this area. Significant in even
those areas that had been the topic of much health communication research in
the past is that they are now being approached in more sophisticated and helpful
ways. There is less bemoaning of problems in provider–patient interaction and
more empirical investigation into the issues. For instance, rather than merely
complaining about care provider use of complicated medical terms by care providers, as was typical in past reviews, recent research empirically investigated
patient and physician understanding of those terms.

Furthermore, the research on provider–patient interaction reflects a more sophisticated understanding of communication than has been found in the past.
There are still some differences between those who focus on the word ''health''

and those who emphasize the word "communication" in the study of "health communication." As would be assumed, health communication research published in medical journals has typically demonstrated a sophisticated understanding of medical issues but a simplistic understanding of communication processes. Conversely, health communication research published in communication outlets has characteristically been less sophisticated in its understanding of medical issues but has provided more adequate conceptualizations of communication. This dichotomy is, however, much less noticeable now than it has been in the past. Communication researchers are more completely accounting for health variables, and medical researchers are demonstrating less simplistic views of communication processes. Medical communication research at one time naively suggested that communication problems could be solved by communicating more.

This does not mean that significant development has been shown in all aspects of this research area, of course. The research on information concerns still spends much time documenting the lack of information given to many patients. This is not new knowledge—the problem has been recognized for some time. Recognition of this problem should, one would expect, lead to proposals and actions to eliminate it. Included within the present review, in fact, are studies that tested methods of addressing the problem. More research is also needed which links communication processes to health outcomes. This is the area in which health communication research is most unique and where communication researchers have the greatest opportunity to make an important contribution.

Some development has also been noted in the research methods utilized to investigate provider–patient interaction. Although little qualitative research has been reported apart from that published in *Qualitative Health Research*, a journal that does not focus specifically on communication issues, the research on patient and provider narratives cited in this chapter reflects a promising trend. The application of qualitative methods in other health communication research could be fruitful and interesting.

This review has, then, discussed some exciting new directions in research on the provider–patient relationship and has indicated research building on some earlier foundations.

4

The Many Cultures of Health Care: Difference, Dominance, and Distance in Physician–Patient Communication

Rebecca J. Cline and Nelya J. McKenzie

SYNOPSIS

Evidence indicates that gender, age, ethnicity/race, socioeconomic status, and education, among other social and cultural factors, influence the patterns of interaction between physicians and patients. This review synthesizes and clarifies the relationships among these variables as indices of ''relational difference'' that point to the value of construing such interactions as intercultural in nature. Viewing the physician–patient relationship as intercultural places the focus of attention on difference. Typically, difference results in asymmetry, and often in stigma, which in turn, explain the patterns of dominance and distance characteristic of physician–patient interaction. This perspective clarifies the particularly frustrating and potentially harmful interaction that occurs when difference is magnified because the physician–patient dyad exhibits differences in cultural factors (i.e., on the basis of difference in gender, age, ethnicity). Research on the effects of the patient's gender, age, and ethnicity is reviewed in depth to highlight the similar influence of the role of difference in physician–patient communication, regardless of the source of that difference.

Eric Cassell introduced his work, *Talking with Patients* (1985), with the following anecdote: ''During the 1930s my grandmother saw a specialist about a melanoma on her face. During the course of the visit when she asked him a question, he slapped her face, saying, 'I ask the questions here, I do the talking' '' (p. 1). Contemporary health care has glimpsed the vision that better communication leads to better health care (as well as the avoidance of litigation) and thus such blatant physical abuse of patients has disappeared. However, the more subtle underlying dynamics of who is in control, who asks the questions, and who does the talking in physician–patient relationships remain largely unchanged. Cassell's grandmother was sharply reminded not just of "her place," but that as a patient she was from a different culture. She had entered the physician's territory and was required to adhere to his values, norms, and linguistic patterns. Understanding the physician–patient relationship as the intersection of cultures accounts for much of the dissatisfaction as well as communication patterns reflecting relational dominance and distance. This chapter explores the physician–patient encounter as "intercultural" with a focus on how various social characteristics (e.g., gender, age, and ethnicity) can be understood as cultures.

THE DOCTOR–PATIENT RELATIONSHIP: A CLASH OF CULTURES

Patients' dissimilarity from their physicians begins with the "patient role," a role so different from that of physician that the two might be said to be from different cultures.

Culture as Difference in Symbolic Meaning Systems

Anthropologists understand culture as a symbolic meaning system in which symbols signal shared meanings among members of a given society (Casson, 1981). Thus, culture can be thought of as a shared "system of knowledge, beliefs, and values." Culture provides "the mental equipment that society members use in orienting, transacting, discussing, defining, categorizing and interpreting actual social behavior in their society" (Casson, 1981, p. 17). Thus, culture is the means by which people know how to enact and interpret "appropriate" social behavior.

The rules of a given culture are subtle and largely unconscious; however, differences in roles and rules are magnified in intercultural interaction. Tajfel (1970) clarifies the relevance of emphasizing "difference" in conducting interpersonal relationships: Social order is created by classifying "we" and "them." We learn that the appropriate attitude is to give favor or preferred treatment to members of the "in-group" and to discriminate against members of the "out-group." In-group/out-group relations often result in mutually devaluing interaction, that is, disconfirmation.

The Doctor–Patient Relationship as Intercultural

The meeting of doctor and patient is the meeting of individuals with discernibly different "life patterns" that arguably can be construed as different cultures. Physicians constitute a relatively homogeneous group by virtue of their education, training, specialized language, and shared territory, as well as by other social characteristics (tending to be white, male, and of moderate to high socioeconomic status). While patients are heterogeneous in many ways, generally they offer a clear contrast to physicians when they meet in a health care context.

Bochner (1982) explicates the doctor–patient relationship as intercultural by virtue of difference. Doctors tend to be middle-class males who are highly educated and speak a specialized language that reflects both expertise and a particular ideology. The intersection of cultures between physician and patient is significant largely because it functions to create the model for the relationship, which in turn, influences the model for health care. One significant result of the in-group/out-group distinction is an imbalance of power that defines the nature of the interpersonal relationship. In this context, the traditional physician–patient one-up/one-down relationship as the standard is not distinctive or surprising. Even when physicians attempt cooperative or participatory models, patients enter the relationship in a one-down position due to several factors. Patients arrive in the relationship out of need; the physician controls the resources to address patients' needs. Illness contributes to patients' tendencies to accept relatively passive roles. Thus, the stage is set for physician and patient to meet in a context that emphasizes difference that influences the resulting discourse.

The Emergence of Dominance and Distance in Physician–Patient Interaction

Disconfirming or devaluing communication patterns between people of difference can be accounted for largely by two concepts: power and stigma.

Physicians have authority, not simply by virtue of their expertise and socioeconomic position, but their power is further accomplished through discourse. Fisher and Groce (1990) contend that the asymmetry in physician–patient discourse functions to "silence the patient" (pp. 226–227). The nature of the talk tends to be technical and bioscientific. Patients, for whom this is a "second language" at best, struggle to use talk to present themselves as competent but are unlikely to challenge the physician's authority directly (Fisher & Groce, 1990). Evidence suggests that when the doctor and patient are from different "cultures," interactional negotiation functions to negate the personhood of the patient while confirming "medical dominance and the hierarchical organization of the medical experience" (p. 244).

Stigma also accounts for the devaluing communication that occurs between people of difference. The very concept of stigma is rooted in undesired difference (Goffman, 1963). Stigma is not limited to physical deformities, but rather includes "blemishes of individual character" (e.g., mental illness, homosexuality, suicidal tendencies) and "tribal stigma" (e.g., race, nation, and religion) (Goffman, 1963, p. 7).

The effects of stigma on interpersonal communication are clear. Lack of acceptance and failure to receive respect and regard are common occurrences in "mixed contacts," when the stigmatized meets the "normal" in a social situation. In anticipation of such discomfort, avoidance is a common ploy. When interaction does occur, it often is distorted and negative (Jones et al., 1984), characterized by psychosocial as well as physical distance (Kleck, 1968, 1969), and talk tends to be briefer and restricted to tasks (Coleman, 1983, as cited by Gibbons, 1986). In short, those with stigma are disconfirmed due to their difference(s), which, when focused upon, create "us" and "them" relationships. The same dynamic may well apply in physician–patient encounters.

Communication Patterns in Physician–Patient Relationships

The asymmetric relationship and stigma characterizing physician–patient interaction result in communication patterns defined by dominance and distance, leading to disconfirmation.

Power in Physician–Patient Interaction. Relational control, the right to define, direct, and delimit the dyad's actions and interactions, is accomplished via specific communication patterns (Millar & Millar, 1976). Physicians achieve relational control by dominating talk time, specifically by using longer talking durations and showing more status markers (Street & Buller, 1988). Question patterns reflect physicians' dominance as they tend to ask more questions than patients (Ford, Fallowfield, & Lewis, 1996, West, 1984a), fail to answer patients' questions (von Friederichs-Fitzwater, Callahan, Flynn, & Williams, 1991; West 1993), and use closed rather than open questions (Ford et al., 1994).

Physicians tend to control the content of the conversation by interrupting patients (West, 1984b), changing topics frequently (von Friederichs-Fitzwater et al., 1991), particularly when patients raise emotional issues, and rejecting patients' topics of conversation. Relational communication analyses show that physicians attempt control twice as often as patients (O'Hair, 1989) and physicians assume control when it is offered by patients. Certainly, patients play a role in defining the relationship as physician-dominated. Patients rarely offer their opinions and often behave in passive patterns (Makoul, Arntson, & Schofield, 1995), accepting a subordinate role.

Distance in Physician–Patient Interaction. Typical physician–patient communication can be understood as distancing as well as controlling. The "right to talk" and responsiveness to one's talk constitute the essence of humane treatment (West, 1984a). In addition to offering patients little opportunity to initiate topics, physicians tend to limit psychosocial discussion (Ford et al., 1996). While patients prefer affiliative physicians, patients rarely verbalize emotions and instead offer indirect clues; physicians tend to ignore both the direct expression of emotion and indirect clues (Suchman, Markakis, Beckman, & Frankel, 1997).

Disconfirmation as the Norm. Cline (1983) argues that while many physicians acknowledge the importance of communicating respect to their patients, nearly all of the commonly observed communication problems between physician and patient that are attributable to the physician involve negating the worth of the patient, that is, disconfirmation. Disconfirmation in this context takes the form of ignoring the patient and his/her attempts to communicate, using a communication style that discourages the patient's participation, distancing oneself from the patient, and using ambiguous language (Cline, 1983).

In summary, the concept of culture clarifies the nature of the physician–patient relationship as a meeting of people of difference. Doctors and patients represent different cultures. Differences, whether due to cultural categorization directly or exacerbated by additional personal characteristics that contribute to asymmetry or stigmatization, result in interaction in which disconfirmation is common, if not the norm (Cline, 1983).

When the In-Group/Out-Group Factor Is Multiplied: Layers of Power, Layers of Stigma

Understanding culture as a shared set of assumptions about interpersonal conduct (Bochner, 1983) suggests the viability of considering social factors such as gender, age, and ethnicity (as well as social class, education, religion) as cultural factors. Evidence indicates that "communication effectiveness decreases as the distance between the respective cultures of the participants increases" (p. 130). Once physicians and patients are recognized as members of different cultures, preferential treatment is predictable on the basis of cultural similarity. Bochner defends doctors as not likely to be deliberately discriminating, but rather as simply more comfortable and less formal with patients who are more culturally similar. In turn, those patients are more confident and talk and listen more and ask more questions than patients who are culturally dissimilar.

Understanding physicians' stereotypes helps to identify populations that are likely to be preferred or dispreferred by physicians. From the viewpoint of physicians, "good" patients are compliant, uncomplaining, and passive, while "bad" patients attempt to gain information and attention (Lorber, 1975). Physicians surveyed about "best," "worst," and "typical" patient characterized the "best" patients as being from their own social class (Jones & Phillips, 1988). "Good" patients gave accurate information and did not expect too much; physicians reported impatience with people who ask questions. In short, physicians "tend to respond best to people much like themselves" (Jones & Phillips, 1988, p. 120). The "typical patient" was characterized as between the ages of 35 and 55, talking about irrelevancies, being occasionally disrespectful, and asking too many questions. The "worst" patients were those who were older, terminally ill, unpleasant looking, complained about their treatment, and were preoccupied with their bill. Furthermore, physicians tend to like male patients more than female patients (Hall, Epstein, DeCiantis & McNeil, 1993) and younger more than older patients (Ford & Sbordone, 1980).

By virtue of their role-relationship, patients begin their interactions with physicians as out-group members. In addition, numerous social characteristics readily can be construed as constituting cultures that magnify difference. Specifically, analysts have identified the following sociodemographic characteristics of patients as those likely influencing physician–patient interaction: gender, age, ethnicity/race, socioeconomic status, and education (Blalock & DeVellis, 1986; Hall, Roter, Milburn, & Daltroy, 1996; Hinckley, Craig, & Anderson, 1990; Lepper, Martin, & DiMatteo, 1995). Hall et al. (1996) also hypothesized that physicians treat sicker patients more negatively. If such stereotypes influence the interaction dynamics, in turn, the process of clinical decision making as well as health care outcomes likely are affected (Clark, Potter, & McKinlay, 1991). At the center of these differences in dynamics is the presumption of cultural difference. In short, physicians generally prefer people like themselves who also accept their preferred relational model; the outcome likely is preferential treatment.

GENDER AS DIFFERENCE IN PHYSICIAN–PATIENT COMMUNICATION

One contemporary theoretical perspective on gender and communication posits that male-female interactions can be understood using a cross-cultural approach (e.g., Tannen, 1990). In essence, men and women grow up in different worlds, experience different socializing messages, learn to talk differently, and have different expectations for interpersonal interaction.

Pendleton and Bochner (1980) argued that gender functions as culture in physician–patient interaction. Stereotypes, expectations, and attributions based on gender likely influence inferences as well as behavioral responses (Hinckley et al., 1990) as physicians expect women to be difficult and demanding (Bernstein & Kane, 1981; Fidell, 1980). In turn, communication processes and, ultimately, health care outcomes likely are affected. However, relatively little research has addressed this issue.

Gender and Communication Patterns

Clearly, physician–patient interaction can be understood as asymmetric; the differences in communication behaviors associated with asymmetry are further exacerbated when gender is factored into the equation (Davis, 1993). The literature on asymmetry in some areas of physician–patient interaction involving women as patients is equivocal (e.g., literature on interruptions, with discrepancies in findings due at least in part to differences in methods). However, the overall pattern of findings supports the conclusion that women are treated as subordinate in communication with male physicians. The greatest asymmetry in physician–patient interaction with regard to gender occurs when female patients interact with male physicians (West, 1984a, 1993).

On the surface, women patients appear at an advantage relative to their male counterparts. Physicians spend more time with women; female patients talk more, ask more questions, and get more information than men (Pendleton & Bochner, 1980; Waitzkin, 1985). A more careful look at the subtleties in the patterns suggests otherwise. Observing mothers' interactions with physicians,

Korsch, Gozzi, and Francis (1968) found that mothers' questions often were ignored, given vague responses, or met with a change of subject. Just as women tend to ask more questions than men in general interpersonal interaction, they do so with physicians.

In communication between male physicians and patients, women receive more explanations than men, but less complete explanations, that is, less technical/medical information (Wallen, Waitzkin, & Stoeckle, 1979). The researchers noted that women they observed appeared considerably frustrated with their interactions with physicians; they attributed this frustration to the fact that the amount of time women spent asking questions was disproportionate to the information yielded (Wallen et al., 1979). When women asked direct questions, physicians gave them shorter answers than they gave men and less information than was requested (which was not true for male patients). These findings can be interpreted as women having to do more "conversational work" in order to obtain the same response; while women received a greater quantity of information, that information is not "volunteered" (Gabbard-Alley, 1995). As Pendleton and Bochner (1980) suggest, physicians may well maintain power by withholding information; women must work harder to overcome that information barrier.

Physicians also control the interaction by controlling the topic. Women as patients tend to operate from a holistic model that accounts for emotional, social, and contextual factors, while physicians tend to respond from a biomedical model (Borges & Waitzkin, 1995). Thus, in the medical encounter, it is not surprising that female patients' issues of greatest concern tend to be marginalized.

Todd (1993) observed physician–patient interactions regarding prescription of contraceptives. The observed physicians controlled the interaction by asking questions and making directives. They controlled the interaction further both by initiating medical topics and by truncating or excluding women's social and contextual topics (e.g., divorce). Furthermore, physicians relied on stereotypic definitions of women's "proper roles" regarding sexual activity, reproduction, and contraception (p. 206). One physician referred to a woman with large breasts as "all girl" (p. 194). Thus, the physician's dominance was social/cultural and not simply medical.

Interruptions are one mechanism for controlling topic. Although it is not clear whether male and female patients differ in the probability of being interrupted, evidence suggests that physicians make more attempts to interrupt female than male patients (Irish & Hall, 1995). In Millar and Millar's (1976) terms, these physicians may not dominate their patients but do engage in greater domineeringness with female patients. More specifically, physicians did not differ in their rate of successful interruptions on the basis of patients' gender, but did use significantly more unsuccessful interruptions (approximately 50 percent more) with female patients.

Topic changes are not simply shifts in emphasis to "the task at hand," but rather function to provide the framework for constructing meaning (Jenks, 1993). To clarify with an example: Paget (1983) explored the case of a woman whose conversation with her physician was characterized as full of disagreements and radical breaks and shifts in conversational topics. Since the woman had had surgery for cancer, her obvious concern was recurrence. The physician framed the woman's repeated symptoms, reports of pain, and anxiety as psychological and diagnosed her as having a case of "nerves." ("I don't think you have a new tumor every place you have a new pain," p. 121.) The physician ignored the patient's implicit primary topic through interruptions, reassurances that the pain was from the previous treatment, shifts in the time frame to the more distant past, and disconfirmation of her reports as meaningful. Her topics were not developed; his were as he controlled the discourse, kept the topic away from her earlier experience with cancer, and ultimately constructed the meaning of her illness as psychosomatic. This pattern was repeated over a series of visits in which the woman was treated with valium and assured of her good health. A post-questionnaire from the patient indicated that she subsequently went to another hospital where she was diagnosed with cancer of the spine.

Although men offer more accounts to physicians for their behavior, justifying their behavior in medical terms rather than excusing their behavior, physicians are proportionately more likely to reject such accounts from women than from men (Fisher & Groce, 1990). Physicians rejected 50 percent of the accounts that women volunteered and were twice as likely to reject women's medical accounts versus their social accounts. The researchers concluded that the communication patterns of the male patients were more like those of doctors than of patients.

Women may be more likely to be heard if they do not upset the asymmetry that the physician expects (Fisher & Groce, 1990); the paradox of sustaining the asymmetry is that their personhood is negated and they may lose a primary avenue for establishing competence and getting information, namely, asking questions. On the basis of gender alone, male patients have a type of solidarity with male physicians that affords them greater legitimacy and acceptance, and have their problems taken more seriously (Fisher & Groce, 1990). In short, through their interaction, male patients with male physicians "enact" their solidarity (p. 246) and become more like status equals.

In summary, the picture of female patients interacting with male doctors is one of a struggle to present themselves as competent. In general, women's concerns appear to be taken less seriously than men's in medical interaction (Gabbard-Alley, 1995). Physicians make judgments regarding patients' participation in medical interaction and decision making based on competency assessments. Women are faced with the challenge of presenting themselves as competent, which they do through question asking, but without challenging the physician's authority directly.

AGE AS DIFFERENCE IN PHYSICIAN–PATIENT COMMUNICATION

Today's elderly possess knowledge and values that set them apart from other age groups. Many of them have experienced economic depression, war, and lack of access to education (Haug & Ory, 1987), and all have experienced historical differences in socialization (Ryan & Butler, 1996). Perhaps more than any other age in the life span, age 65 serves to set a group of persons apart from others in society, physically as well as socially. While lip-service is given to the value of the elderly, as children are taught they should "respect their elders," in fact, older persons are seen as more likely to "take" from society. Specifically, they require greater health resources than other groups in society (Beisecker, 1989; Cook, Coe, & Hanson, 1990), making them less valued than other age groups.

Age 65 is the most commonly used marker for separating older from younger groups; demographers project that the population of the United States will include 64 million elderly (age 65 and older) by the year 2030 (U.S. Congress, Senate Special Committee on Aging, 1985). In the context of national concern for the growing costs of health care, the elderly are disproportionately heavy users (Soldo & Manton, 1985; Waldo & Lazenby, 1984), largely because of their increase in chronic disease (National Center for Health Statistics, 1986). People age 65 and over average eight visits to health providers per year compared to the general population's average of five visits (U.S. Congress, Senate Special Committee on Aging, 1991); overall, they may require as much as two-and-one-half times more medical care than younger age groups (Williams, 1981). Moreover, their double stigma of being old and being ill likely magnifies physician–patient differences in health care interaction (Kreps, 1990b).

Age and Communication Patterns

Communication between physicians and the elderly is a particularly complex task. Elderly patients represent a wide range of health conditions and cognitive and functional abilities (Hodes, Ory, & Pruzan, 1995). Physiologic factors often influence communication with the elderly, including with their physicians, and may enhance the risks of misunderstanding. Although, in the larger perspective, these factors represent minor changes in communication function, hearing and vision impairments, slower information processing, and changes in memory function represent differences and may influence interaction (Bayles & Kaszniak, 1987; Kemper, S., 1994; Nussbaum, Thompson, & Robinson, 1989). The presentation of multiple medical problems, mostly chronic, and therefore many not curable, adds to the complexity (Adelman, Greene, & Charon, 1991). Thus, the elderly are more likely to require combinations of prescriptive medications (German & Burton, 1989), a factor making information processing both more complex and more important to the interaction. In turn, the physician–elderly patient interaction tends to differ substantively from interactions with younger patients (Adelman, Greene, & Charon, 1987).

How physician–patient communication involving the elderly differs from the context in general is based on differences in the behavior of both patients and physicians (Beisecker & Thompson, 1995). Ironically, the elderly's greater willingess to "play by the rules" (Greene, Adelman, Charon, & Hoffman, 1986) may contribute to less effective communication and, ultimately, poorer outcomes. Many elderly patients prefer the physician to be in control, particularly of decision making (Greene, Adelman, & Rizzo, 1996), and are less likely to challenge their physicians or to be assertive (Haug, 1979). Elderly patients learned the patient role in an era when patients were more compliant with physician status and consumerism had not yet emerged (Beisecker, 1988).

The issue of whether age defines people or people define age surfaces perhaps more clearly in the physician–patient interaction than in any other (Coupland & Coupland, 1994). In effect, "acting your age" becomes "talking your age." One feature of elderly patients' interactions with physicians is their many age-telling references, particularly when interacting with younger physicians (Coupland & Coupland, 1994). But far more telling in constructing age are the more subtle features of interaction that indicate differential treatment of the elderly with regard to control, information processes, and supportive communication.

Physicians exert greater control over their interaction with older than younger patients both by controlling the topic and by the manner in which they talk. Physicians initiate the majority of topics (two-thirds) and are more responsive to patients' interactions on the topics that the physicians initiated (Adelman, Greene, Charon, & Friedmann, 1992). When physicians interact with older patients (65 and older), they use more medical and fewer psychosocial topics than they do with younger patients (under 45) (Greene et al., 1986). Patients' social topics regarding family and work tend to be raised marginally, or indirectly, and to be responded to as marginal rather than as central to patients' medical concerns (Waitzkin, Britt, & Williams, 1994). Consistent with expectations regarding what is important to the elderly, physicians are more responsive to patients' topics concerning past rather than present events (Greene, Adelman, & Rizzo, 1996). Older patients and their physicians agree less on the goals and topics for their interaction than younger patients (Greene, Adelman, Charon, & Friedmann, 1989). Although physicians tend to *believe* that older patients report more nonspecific problems in their interactions (e.g., report symptoms like dizziness, incontinence, falls, and issues of memory), research fails to support that belief (Greene et al., 1986).

Physicians take control stylistically as well as topically in interacting with elderly patients. The one-up, one-down relationship is facilitated by elderly patients' tendency to be less assertive than younger patients (Greene et al., 1989). The stereotype of the elderly as infantile is somewhat self-fulfilled in the style of physicians' interactions with their elderly patients. Doctors tend to speak more slowly, louder, in simplified language, and with a patronizing air, while blaming their patients for forgetfulness (Ryan & Cole, 1990). While using simplified language with the elderly (over 65) may facilitate the interaction, as they are less likely than younger patients (45 to 64) to understand technical medical terms (Thompson & Pledger, 1993), other forms of patronizing speech are less defensible.

Forms of patronizing communication observed in physicians' interactions with their elderly patients include being dismissive, inattentive, overparenting, and disapproving (Kemper, 1994; Ryan & Butler, 1996; Ryan, Meredith, MacLean, & Orange, 1995). The pattern of asymmetry in general, and a patronizing style in particular, tend to feed the "second childhood" stereotype of the elderly in health care. Ironically, this stylistic pattern engenders the very sense of declining capability and loss of control that elderly patients most fear (Caporael, 1981; Rodin & Langer, 1980).

One of the primary ways that physicians dominate their interaction is via information control (Waitzkin & Stoeckle, 1976). Evidence indicates that physicians tend to supply less information to older than to younger patients (Greene et al., 1986; Street, 1991). In addition, physicians engage in more active questioning of younger patients and thus are likely to have more complete information for use in diagnosis and treatment (Greene et al., 1986).

In part, younger patients get more information because they ask more questions, talk more about their problems, and are more assertive (Adelman et al., 1991; Breemhaar, Visser, & Kleijnen, 1990), but physicians also offer more and better information to younger patients (Greene, 1987 cited by Greene, Adelman, & Majerovitz, 1996; Greene et al., 1989).

One specific area in which elderly patients would like to receive more information regards medications and potential side effects (Smith, Cunningham, & Hale, 1994). Generally, younger patients tend to get more information regarding medications than older patients (Helling et al., 1987). Although elderly patients identify physicians as their most desirable source for information about drugs (Smith et al., 1994), only 60 percent reported that physicians gave them directions for using their medications (Morris, Grossman, Barkdoll, Gordon, & Soviero, 1984). Moreover, only 3 to 6 percent of patients reported *asking* for medication information from physicians (Morris et al., 1984) and 25 percent of elderly patients failed to discuss their adverse reactions with their physicians (Klein, German, Levine, Feroli, & Ardery, 1984). Research by Hulka, Cassel, Kupper, and Burdette (1976) indicated that 58 percent of elderly patients engaged in errors in medication use (i.e., noncompliance) when they did not know the function of their medication; that is, they were uninformed or underinformed. Physicians usually provide the desired information when patients request it (Smith et al., 1994), but the patients most likely to need it, the elderly, are least likely to ask.

More than information, affective communication seems particularly important to older patients (Nuttbrock & Kosberg, 1980). While the general population of patients tends to prefer a high information/high affect style from physicians, and older patients appear less concerned about style than other age groups, the low information/high affect style is more often preferred by older patients than by any other age group (O'Hair, Behnke, & King, 1983). If affective issues are central to older patients, then their typical communication patterns with physicians likely are disappointing.

Evidence indicates that physicians tend to be less respectful, less supportive, less patient, less engaged, and less attentive with older (65 and older) patients than with younger patients (under 65) (Adelman, Greene, Charon, & Friedmann, 1992; Greene et al., 1986). These behaviors tend to correspond with physicians also being less egalitarian and less likely to share decision making with older patients (Adelman et al., 1992; Greene, Majerovitz, Adelman, & Rizzo, 1994).

One common feature of physicians' interactions with elderly patients is the presence of a third party. Often a spouse, a child, or a hired professional caregiver may accompany an elderly patient for a clinical visit. The presence of a third party may further exacerbate the patterns regarding control and support due to changes in both the physicians' and the patients' behavior. Patients raise fewer topics, are less likely to respond to the topics they raised themselves, are less assertive, are less likely to engage in shared laughter, and are less likely to engage in joint decision making (Greene et al., 1994). Thus, the presence of a third party, although increasing the likelihood of consumerist comments (Beisecker, 1988), appears to reduce further the patient's control and active participation in the interaction.

In summary, the dynamics of a physician who controls both topic and information, while withholding respect, in conjunction with a cooperative ''good'' patient who is unassertive and unchallenging, foretells reduced quality of health care for the elderly.

ETHNICITY AS DIFFERENCE IN PHYSICIAN–PATIENT COMMUNICATION

Cultural factors emerge when a white male upper middle-class physician encounters individuals of differing ethnic or racial backgrounds. Participants must contend not only with professional role differences that represent different cultures, but also with the full array of linguistic and value differences typically associated with racial, ethnic, and cultural diversity that, in turn, shape the meanings of discourse in health care.

Little observational research has focused on the role of ethnicity, race, and culture (in its more traditional sense) in health care communication. While most physicians report that the care they provide does not vary for different types of patients (Drucker, 1974), numerous factors dispute that claim. Ethnicity represents a readily observable cultural difference; the greater the cultural distance, the greater likelihood for interaction based on an ''us'' and ''them'' relationship.

Ethnicity and Communication Patterns

Despite the dearth of direct observations, sufficient evidence of communication problems in this context exists to raise serious concern about the influence of ethnicity and race on health care outcomes. Four examples illustrate: challenges to mutual understanding based on language difference; misunderstandings due to cultural values; differences in cultural values regarding openness and disclosure in health care, specifically with regard to diagnosis and prognosis; and the failure of physicians to provide information to patients regarding prevention and screening on the basis of cultural and racial characteristics.

Most patients face a language barrier in health care interaction, as physicians tend to rely on medical jargon for which patients have limited understanding. In cross-cultural health care encounters, additional language issues arise. More than 31 million residents of the United States do not speak English; thus language differences between providers and clients are common occurrences (Hornberger et al., 1996).

Available evidence indicates the advantages of physician and patient speaking the same language in terms of greater rapport, better explanations of treatment, better understanding of instructions by patients (Shapiro & Saltzer, 1981), and greater recall and more question-asking by patients (Seijo, Gomez, & Freidenburg, 1995).

One response to language differences is the use of a third party to act as interpreter. The options are the use of a person close to the patient (i.e., someone the patient knows and trusts) or the use of a trained interpreter who is likely a stranger. Both solutions create additional difficulties.

Family members who act as interpreters "may be too embarrassed, protective, or indeed defensive when they have to air issues that they think should be kept within the family" (Baylav, 1996, p. 405). In addition, they may be uncomfortable disclosing to the patient what the doctor wishes to know. Family members may be unwilling or unable to convey bad news from the physician to the patient; parents may be embarrassed to report symptoms via their children (Witte & Morrison, 1995).

When translators are not family members, problems can arise when translations are "too literal" or when translators' beliefs influence the translation (Seijo, Gomez, & Freidenberg, 1995). Informal translators may edit messages, making their own decisions about what is medically important and culturally relevant. Many physicians report experiences in which a simple question ("How are you feeling?") results in a lengthy interaction between the interpreter and the patient, but results in a one-word response ("Fine") to the physician upon translation (Fitzgerald, 1988). Furthermore, interpreters who know the language but not the culture may miss significant information in both the verbal and nonverbal messages (Witte & Morrison, 1995).

While language differences account for much misunderstanding in cross-cultural health care interaction, differences in cultural values and beliefs also contribute to misunderstandings. For example, most Haitians in the United States were born in Haiti, have strong ties to their community, and speak Creole (Bibb & Casimir, 1996). But if asked if they speak French (as commonly assumed), they will say they do because speaking French is associated with social mobility and status, enhancing the probability of misunderstandings when assigned to a French-speaking clinician. Moreover, typical communication among Haitians is loud and animated and is misunderstood often as anger by non-Haitians (Bibb & Casimir, 1996). Thus, typical communications styles associated with members of particular cultures may lead to misunderstandings.

Cultural values regarding the nature of the physician–patient relationship itself also influence interaction. In some cultures (e.g., Latinos, Mexican Americans, Middle Easterners), authority figures cannot be disagreed with or challenged (Witte & Morrison, 1995). For example, the Latino patients' value of *respeto* emphasizes tactful and nonconfrontative interaction, making them less likely to engage in interaction that questions authority (Vera, 1996). The controlling demeanor of most Western-trained physicians adds to their already perceived authority and may lead to responses of politeness and agreement even when diagnoses and treatments are not understood or contradict patients' illness experience. Similarly, the Latino value of *personalismo*, which suggests that it is bad mannered to discuss problems or get directly to the task without first engaging in social interaction (Vera, 1996), likely leads Latino patients to be uncomfortable with the task-oriented and direct approach of Western physicians.

A third major area of concern regards disclosure of "bad news." Western medical ethics, further reinforced by law, is rooted in a value for individual autonomy that promotes full disclosure of risks for various treatments as well as openness regarding diagnosis and prognosis. However that value varies significantly by culture. For example, oncologists from various countries differ subtantially in using the word "cancer" in presenting diagnoses (Holland, Geary, Marchini, & Tross, 1987). These findings are consistent with other cross-cultural differences in truth telling in health care. Full disclosure is viewed as burdensome to the patient, and truth telling is opposed in cultures that are family-centered, such as Italians, Greeks, and Hispanics (Dalla-Vorgia et al., 1992; Perez-Stable, Sabogal, Otero-Sabogal, Hiatt, & McPhee, 1992; Surbone, 1992). Withholding bad news is defended culturally as preventing loss of hope and, ironically (relative to Western bioethics), protecting the patient.

Beyond cultural differences associated with geographic boundaries, research indicates that substantial cultural differences exist among Americans of diverse cultural backgrounds regarding disclosure of diagnosis and prognosis (Blackhall, Murphy, Frank, Michel, & Azen, 1995). Specifically, Korean Americans and Mexican Americans were found less likely than European Americans to believe that a patient should be told the diagnosis of metastatic cancer. They were also less likely to believe that a terminal diagnosis should be disclosed to a patient and to believe that the patient should make decisions regarding life-supporting technology. Instead, both Korean Americans and Mexican Americans believed that such decisions should rest with the family. (Interestingly, 90 percent of all groups believed that truth telling between the physician and the family should be the norm.) Further analyses showed that culture rather than socioeconomic status was the primary predictor of these differences.

Similarly, research on Native Americans identifies a contrast in valuing direct disclosure. Conducting qualitative interviews with Navajo informants, Carrese and Rhodes (1995) found that disclosing negative information is viewed as potentially harmful. Such disclosure is in direct conflict with the Navajo concept of *hozho*, the view that thought and language *shape* reality (p. 829). The informants emphasized the significance of both thinking and talking positively. One Navajo nurse reported how the risks of bypass surgery were communicated routinely to her father as part of the informed consent procedure. When he was told that he might not wake up, the man refused the surgery. In this culture, negative words are viewed as harmful. So strong is the belief that 10 of the 22 informants would not even discuss the issue of advance care planning. In conclusion, "full, truthful disclosure may be at variance with cultural beliefs about hope, wellness and thriving of individuals" (Gostin, 1995, p. 844). Furthermore, the focus on individual autonomy may clash with cultures whose values are family-centered.

Finally, while physicians believe that cultural characteristics (e.g., race) do not influence their behavior (Hooper, Comstock, Goodwin, & Goodwin, 1982), evidence indicates otherwise with regard to informing them about preventive and screening measures. For example, research indicates that physicians are less likely to discuss and to follow guidelines for preventive and screening measures, such as mammograms, with their minority patients (Gemson, Elinson, and Messeri, 1988). The difference in practice was accounted for in part by the socioeconomic status of the patient and in part by the character of the physician–patient relationship. Physicians commonly assume that members of some cultures are not motivated to be fully informed or to get preventive care. Contrary to that belief, Naish, Brown, and Denton (1994) found that once non-English speaking minority women were fully informed about preventions (e.g., cervical screenings), they not only accepted but were enthusiastic about them. Thus, differences in health care behavior likely were based on cultural differences.

SUMMARY AND FUTURE RESEARCH

Throughout our literature review, we found researchers apologetic and bemoaning the fact that little is known about the influence of age, gender, or ethnicity, or their combinations, on physician–patient interaction. Relatively few analysts appeared to give thought to the potential for the factors to be related. Often, when they did, they simply referred to them almost as a "laundry list" of sociodemographic characteristics that happen to describe the population. Haug (1996) at least recognized that these factors, when used to characterize the physician–patient encounter, typically set up a relationship in which difference is the norm. Future research needs to focus on the role of difference, regardless of the source of that difference, in health care interaction. As the society grows older and increasingly multicultural, difference is a feature that likely will continue to be characteristic of physician–patient interaction.

Culture: The Inverse Melting Pot of Sociodemographic Characteristics

Clearly, relatively little is known about the role of sociodemographic characteristics in physician–patient communication and the decision-making and health care outcomes that result from that interaction. Researchers addressing each characteristic reviewed here conclude that little is known about that characteristic, be it gender, age, ethnicity, or health care interaction and outcomes. The results have mostly been treated in piecemeal fashion, viewing the role of each characteristic as an independent phenomenon. That trend has been due largely to the failure to develop a theoretical framework that makes apparent the relatedness of the influence of gender, age, ethnicity, and other factors on physician–patient interaction. Viewing gender, age, and ethnicity as cultural phenomena provides guidance for conducting programmatic research into each area as a source of difference that influences interaction. Furthermore, the perspective points to the need to consider the influence of the combinations of these factors when they are joined in the same interaction (i.e., the older minority woman interacting with the young, white, male physician) as a potential inverse melting pot that magnifies difference and its impact.

Conceptualizing Health Care as a Culture

The theoretical framework connecting numerous bodies of literature reviewed here is one focusing on culture in health care. Ironically, few researchers or analysts have conceived of health care constituting a culture of its own which must be adaptive to social, economic, and political change as well as to diverse cultures within the larger society (Greenlick, 1995). In the context of recent major changes in health care, and the anticipation of continuing change, the culture of health care itself needs attention. Evidence of the changing culture of medicine includes the following changes that require changing medical education: the shift from infectious to chronic disease; the shift from treatment to prevention; the emergence of group-to-patient relationships replacing one-to-one relationships in health care; the ''management'' components of managed care; and professional responsibility to the population at large as well as to individual patients (Greenlick, 1995). The role of the rapidly emerging model of managed care in influencing the nature of physician–patient communication needs to be addressed.

Disease as Difference

Although we reviewed some literature indicating that among physicians' yard-sticks for difference is how sick the patient is, we barely had the opportunity to focus on disease and physical disabilities that in themselves mark patients as different and provide an additional source of cultural diversity. Prior to HIV/AIDS, cancer was the most stigmatized disease in our culture. With the onset of the HIV epidemic, patients with this disease are presumed to differ on a number of stigmatizing conditions: sexual orientation, sexual promiscuity, drug use, and race/ethnicity. Each of these factors in itself, as well as having a terminal illness, denotes a likely source of readily perceived difference with physicians that may further influence the nature of the physician–patient interaction as well as health care outcomes. Research needs to investigate "disease" as "difference," disease as culture.

Talking Social Structure, Talking Health Care Outcomes

The focus on sociodemographic characteristics as indicators of the macro social structure helps to substantiate the notion that identifiable groups of people are systematically disenfranchised in the health care system due to difference. However, simply noting outcomes fails to reveal *how* visible, and sometimes not so visible, differences get translated into potentially lower quality of health care and jeopardize medical outcomes. The focus on discourse, on the process of interaction between physician and patient, clarifies the processes by which difference is translated into dominance and dehumanization, control and discon-firmation, as the dynamics leading to potentially poorer quality of health care and predictably worse outcomes. Future research needs to focus on the relation-ship between subtle interaction processes and health care outcomes.

The Physician–Patient Encounter as Transactional

Most research on the social and cultural aspects of physician–patient inter-action has focused on the role of various characteristics of the patient on the interaction; to a much lesser extent, the physician's characteristics have been investigated. Almost nonexistent are studies that focus on the dyad as the unit of analysis. (One modest exception is research that has looked at the gender composition of the physician–patient dyad, i.e., similarity versus difference, in influencing interaction.) Moreover, research generally has focused on linear in-fluences, particularly emphasizing the physician's role in determining the proc-ess. While physicians automatically have greater power to influence those interaction processes, the role of the patients' behaviors in facilitating, yielding to, or attempting to subvert that power needs attention. Physicians are able to talk their control and dehumanization, in part, because patients talk acceptance of subordination and disconfirmation. More attention needs to be paid to the interdependence and reciprocal nature of that interaction as solutions are sought for more widely diffusing the good communication/better outcomes relationship.

5

Promoting Adherence to Courses of Treatment: Mutual Collaboration in the Physician–Patient Relationship

M. Robin DiMatteo and Heidi S. Lepper

SYNOPSIS

Patient adherence to medical treatment is a serious, unsolved challenge in the present-day delivery of medical care. Out of every ten patients who receive medical recommendations, on average at least four of them ignore, forget, misunderstand, or for some other reason fail to follow them correctly. This chapter presents a review of the ways in which nonadherence can be traced to problems in provider–patient communication. We examine the various elements of the communication-adherence connection and the factors that can stand in the way of building trust between physician and patient. A research agenda focused on the value and inevitability of conflict, as well as its resolution through provider–patient negotiation, is proposed and clinical applications are suggested.

Over a quarter century of research demonstrates that across a wide variety of settings, an average of 40 percent of patients in the United States fail to adhere to the recommendations they have received from their physicians for prevention or treatment of acute or chronic conditions (DiMatteo, 1994; DiMatteo & DiNicola, 1982; Epstein & Cluss, 1982; Lin et al., 1995). Nonadherence (also termed noncompliance) can involve such behaviors as patients taking antibiotics incorrectly, forgetting or refusing to take medication for chronic conditions, failing to engage in prescribed self-care behaviors, and persisting in dangerous and unhealthy lifestyles (Rosenstock, 1988). Nonadherence can contribute to serious illness, such as when treatment-resistant bacterial infections develop because antibiotics have been used improperly, or when treatments are altered or misdiagnoses made on the assumption that patients have been adherent when they have not (Joshi & Milfred, 1995; Sanson-Fisher, Bowman, & Armstrong,

1992). Furthermore, nonadherence may guarantee that the time and money spent on the medical visit is wasted (Haynes, Taylor, & Sackett, 1979). For reasons that may have much to do with the structure of the medical interaction, most physicians are grossly unaware of their patient's nonadherence; they do not ask, and patients do not tell (Haug & Lavin, 1983).

CRITICAL REVIEW OF THE LITERATURE

The Provider–Patient Relationship and Adherence

Patient adherence is heavily dependent on the quality of the physician–patient relationship (Hall, Roter, & Katz, 1988) and relies, in good measure, on the patient's trust in the good will of the physician (DiMatteo & DiNicola, 1982). This trust can enhance the patient's positive expectations for healing (Roter & Hall, 1992; Shapiro, 1960) and is built on provider sensitivity and emotional expressivity (DiMatteo, Hays, & Prince, 1986; DiMatteo, Linn, Chang, & Cope, 1985). Trust is critically important in many aspects of enhancing long-term adherence. Following diagnosis, for example, physician and patient need to work together to build patient commitment to a treatment plan. Elements of the environment that pose limitations to patient adherence need to be discussed openly, and barriers to achieving successful implementation of the regimen overcome (DiMatteo et al., 1993).

Pressures on the physician–patient relationship render it difficult to build the trust that is essential to greater adherence, improved health outcomes, and a reduction in the waste of health care dollars. In the following sections we examine these pressures and suggest ways to enhance the therapeutic relationship and resulting levels of patient adherence.

The Traditional Physician–Patient Relationship

Historically, in social science, the provider–patient relationship has been conceptualized as one involving physician authority and patient submission. Sociologist Talcott Parsons (1951) proposed that patients submit to the authority of the physician as part of a social contract because the physician is the gatekeeper of the sick role. This sick role grants the patient exemption from normal social responsibilities of work and family in exchange for full compliance with medical recommendations. Nonadherence can be seen as grounds for doubting an individual's claim to illness and for denying the benefits of the sick role.

In this social contract model, physician authority is supported by the fact that the patient's release from his or her normal role in society depends on legitimization by the physician. A patient who questions or chooses to ignore physician recommendations jeopardizes legitimate entry into the sick role. In Parsons's model, the patient is *expected to trust completely* all of the judgments and recommendations of the physician. The centerpiece of this trust is the "fiduciary relationship,'' in which, as society expects, the physician's foremost concern is the patient's best interest.

Differing Perspectives of Physician and Patient

Although the Parsonian model may have represented the practice of medicine many decades ago, the current, for-profit nature of most medical enterprises sheds some doubt on its legitimacy today (Starr, 1982; Stevens, 1989). Eliot Friedson (1970) and others (Haug & Lavin, 1983) have highlighted the differing perspectives held by patients and providers, and have argued that belief in the fiduciary relationship may be somewhat naive and limited.

Providers and patients necessarily view disease from different perspectives. While disease affects a patient's physical and emotional experience, daily functioning, economic livelihood, and family interactions, disease is primarily an intellectual puzzle even to the most sensitive physician. It is the patient therefore, not the physician, who must live each day with the results of medical choices (Lynn & DeGrazia, 1991).

Research suggests that physicians and patients often have different preferences for medical outcomes and the means by which to achieve them. When given alternatives, patients tend to select more conservative, less invasive, and less expensive treatment strategies than do their physicians (McNeil, Weischelbaum, & Parker, 1978; Wennberg, 1990). They implicitly (if not explicitly) weigh the costs and benefits of adhering to recommendations (Donovan & Blake, 1992), and may view nonadherence as a rational choice. Research also suggests that patients are typically more concerned with quality, rather than with quantity, of life when faced with end-of-life decisions (Emanuel, Barry, Stoeckle, Ettelson, & Emanuel, 1991; Schneiderman, Kronick, Kaplan, Anderson, & Langer, 1992).

Providers and patients differ still further in their search for the meaning of the patient's illness. One example of this difference is the physicians' focus primarily on physiological and biochemical meaning, as opposed to the patients' focus on the psychological and social meaning (Taylor, 1982; Taylor, Lichtman, & Wood, 1984). Shared meaning and perspective depend, to a great extent, on shared experience; unfortunately, most physicians and patients are separated by their socioeconomic and educational experiences (Mechanic, 1992). Gender differences might also be at issue, in that the most common medical interaction today involves a female patient and a male physician, individuals who can be viewed as having two inherently different experiences and perspectives of illness. Merging very different perspectives generally requires some finely tuned and well-practiced communication skills.

Pressures of Modern Medicine

Informed decisions on the part of the physician require full understanding of patients' outcome preferences. Without such information, medical decisions can lead to imperfect outcomes in patient adherence and quality of life (Lincoln, 1982; Lynn & DeGrazia, 1991). The proliferation of technological alternatives in medicine in recent years has made medical decisions more complex than ever. The use of advanced technology may further reduce the amount of time physician and patient can spend thoroughly discussing preferences for outcomes and the best means to achieve them.

The financial incentive structure of medicine further presses toward limiting the talk that may be necessary for physician and patient to understand each other's perspectives. In fee-for-service structures, compensation depends not on talking with patients but instead on maximizing the number of procedures performed (Gambone & Reiter, 1991). One analyst argues that over the past several decades, such pressure has accounted for the skyrocketing costs of unnecessary health care services (*Consumer Reports*, 1992). Attempts to limit costs with managed care and with capitated programs (in which a flat fee is paid for each patient regardless of the use of services) also tend to limit talk between physicians and patients. At the extreme in capitated programs, financial incentives lie in amassing large numbers of patients and spending as little time as possible with each of them. In both structures, as Waitzkin (1985) found, physician income tends to be inversely correlated with time spent talking with patients about their illnesses, their perspectives, and about all the elements necessary to help them to adhere (Dolan, Reifler, McDermott, & McGaghie, 1995).

Technological advances and financial incentives have limited patients' abilities to explain fully their experience of illness and its effect on their lives (Kleinman, 1988). In response, some patients have chosen to make unilateral decisions about their health care (Haug & Lavin, 1983) and to insist that medical care, as an exchange of resources, should work by the same principles that drive other consumer exchanges (Beisecker & Beisecker, 1993). Each of these factors can lead to a medical malpractice litigation when outcomes are unsatisfactory, when the patient has not been fully informed, and when the patient has not fully participated in the decision (Beckman, Markakis, Suchman, & Frankel, 1994; Entman et al., 1994; Levinson, 1994).

The Need for Mutual Participation

Physicians and patients are separated by "the competence gap" (Parsons, 1951) in which the physician typically holds far more technical information about medicine than does the patient. This problem is likely to be exacerbated as a greater percentage of physicians become specialists and as technology for diagnosis and treatment becomes more complex. In response to feelings of intimidation and poor technical knowledge, patients may remain unassertive about their desire for information and involvement in their own care or preferences for treatment and its goals (Brody, 1980). A preponderance of medical information, however, does not make the physician an expert about the outcome preferences of the patient. Decisions about the care of patients made on the basis of assumptions about these preferences cannot be effective and cannot be in the best interest of the patient. Often, such assumptions rely on stereotyped expectations based on characteristics of the individual who is a patient (e.g., Smith & Zarate, 1992).

Szasz and Hollender (1956) developed a model of mutual participation that casts patient and physician, regardless of their differences in social status and medical knowledge, in mutually responsible and supportive roles. They engage in a cooperative venture toward accomplishing their goal of improving the patient's health and quality of life. The foundations of this model are patient involvement in the medical care process, patient responsibility for personal health care behaviors, physician sharing of information with the patient, and physician partnership in decision making with the patient. Mutual participation deemphasizes the paternalistic assumptions of physician authority and physician control over the treatment, and emphasizes physician and patient joint responsibility for the welfare of the patient (Beisecker & Beisecker, 1993).

According to one study, interventions that increase mutual participation can lead to higher levels of patient adherence and subsequent improvements in health status (Greenfield, Kaplan, & Ware, 1985). Some interventions have focused on patients and have involved guidance in reading their medical charts and coaching on question-asking and negotiating medical decisions. Trained patients were found to be more verbally involved, to achieve better physical outcomes, and to function better than those who were not trained. Other research has focused on the physician–patient relationship and on altering the structure of the medical interaction in order to increase and improve joint decision making. For example, one study examined the effects of having patient and physician coauthor the patient's medical record (Fischbach, Sionelo-Bayog, Needle, & Delbanco, 1980). Patients who shared the medical record were found to ask more questions, to provide more information, and to understand better their recommended treatments than those who did not share the medical record (Robinson & Whitfield, 1985).

Research on altering physician behavior has not been as prevalent as that focused on altering patient behavior in the medical visit. One study did find, however, that short-term improvements in a provider's adherence counseling skills could be made with a training workshop (Schlundt et al., 1994) in which health professionals were taught skills relating to relationship building, interviewing, diagnosis of the problem, and behavioral interventions. Follow-up interviews with these trained providers demonstrated good short-term retention of the training in these four areas. Another recent study found that physicians taught communication skills in an eight-hour training Continuing Medical Education (CME) workshop were more likely than those not trained to employ problem-defining and emotion-handling skills, and they did not require additional visit time to do so (Roter et al., 1995). This research suggests that with proper training, physicians can improve communication with their patients within reasonable time constraints.

In sum, empirical research provides evidence that interventions can alter the behavior of physicians and patients, and can increase the likelihood of mutual participation and shared decision making. To reconcile their inherently different perspectives and goals, however, physician and patient need very effective communication methods.

Communication in Medical Care

Communication is the centerpiece of the physician–patient relationship and an essential component of the effective practice of medicine. As Laine and Davidoff (1996) noted, "American medicine is in the midst of a professional evolution driven by a refocusing of medicine's regard for the patient's viewpoint" (p. 152). The patient's viewpoint is learned through effective communication and active listening.

In one sense, communication is a process of sharing meaning. Ideally, an unrestricted exchange of meaning between physician and patient will establish a consensus of attitudes, beliefs, feelings, and goals (DiMatteo & DiNicola, 1982). Unimpeded exchanges between provider and patient typically involve some combination of open verbal and nonverbal communication (wherein meaning is conveyed through body and facial cues). Linguistic, cultural, personal, and educational differences can be impediments to effective communication.

Even if culturally and personally similar, however, physician and patient can still fail to understand each other. Misunderstanding can result from their different perspectives regarding the patient's illness and pain as well as from the patient's anxiety and emotional upset (Kleinman, 1988; Mechanic, 1968). Communication can also be impeded by behavioral barriers imposed by the use of medical jargon (Hadlow & Pitts, 1991) and time limits (Beisecker & Beisecker, 1990). As Barnlund has noted, "the factors that complicate the process of shared meaning are nearly all present in doctor–patient encounters" (Barnlund, 1976, p. 721).

Factors in physician–patient communication can be divided among instrumental (task-focused) talk and socioemotional (care-focused) talk (Ong, DeHaes, Hoos, & Lammes, 1995). Elements of instrumental communication essential for patient adherence to treatment recommendations include medical directives in which patients understand clearly what they have been told (Ley, 1979, 1982, 1988), sufficient skill on the part of patients to articulate their questions (Christy, 1979; Roter, 1984), the opportunity to ask questions, and the chance to learn about and challenge the assumptions their physicians have made about their condition and what can be done to improve it (Haug & Lavin, 1983).

Several studies show that almost all patients (over 90 percent) highly value having as much information as possible from their physicians, and need to know about potential outcomes of and alternatives to treatment recommendations before they can adhere (Blanchard, Labrecque, Ruckdeschel, & Blanchard, 1988; see review, Roter & Hall, 1992). Sufficient information is rarely provided to them, however (Faden, Becker, Lewis, Freeman, & Faden, 1981; Waitzkin & Stoeckle, 1976). Furthermore, enough time for the consultation (at least 19 minutes as suggested in a study completed by Beisecker & Beisecker, 1990) is needed to promote their adherence to recommended courses of action. Adherence requires adequate communication because it serves to enhance patients' belief in and positive expectations for treatment or self-care behaviors (Leedham, Meyerowitz, Muirhead, & Frist, 1995; Stanton, 1987) as well as to recognize and provide solutions for the barriers to adherence (Atwood, et al., 1992; DiMatteo, et al., 1993).

For patients to accept a recommended treatment regimen, their communication with physicians must be based on trust, and they must have a sense that their physicians are operating in their best interest (DiMatteo & DiNicola, 1982). It may no longer be possible to rely on the social institution of the "fiduciary" relationship (Parsons, 1951). Rather, trust must be built through mutual respect, rapport, empathy, understanding, acceptance of the patient's perspective, and recognition of the patient's unique treatment and outcome preferences.

Empathy and understanding of the patients' feelings are essential to promoting patient adherence and positive health outcomes (Squier, 1990). Empathy does not include "emotional involvement" in the patient's life such that the provider is impaired in his or her ability to do the job (Marvel, 1993; Marvel & Morphew, 1993), but it does require the provider to attend not only to the patient's disease but also to his or her suffering (Brody, 1992; Cassell, 1985).

Conflict and Negotiation

Differences between physicians' and patients' interests and perspectives necessitate acknowledgment of the inevitability, and the value, of conflict in the medical exchange (Katz, 1984). Traditionally, conflict has been avoided in medical interactions through the physicians' use of silence. If the patient is given no information about treatment alternatives and is given little time in the interaction to question prescribed procedures, silence is maintained and conflict is avoided. Conflict is, however, a necessary and beneficial element of the therapeutic relationship because it acknowledges the patient's right to information and alternatives, and it allows for a process of physician–patient negotiation that may ultimately lead to the best outcomes for both individuals. A negotiated approach to patienthood and models of shared decision making (e.g., Speedling & Rose, 1985) have supported the value of conflict in introducing patients' preferences into the decision-making process. These models advocate the need for physicians and patients to negotiate their goals and expectations for the outcomes of treatment and the means for achieving these preferred outcomes (Friedson, 1961, 1970; Lazare, Eisenthal, Frank, & Stoeckle, 1978).

Bargaining and negotiation between physician and patient require the physician to accept the possibility that the patient's goals are different from the clinician's, and that the patient has a different idea of at least some of the acceptable methods for achieving those goals. The clinician's flexibility is critical in considering alternative courses of treatment that are in the best interests of the patient, as the patient defines those interests (Brody, 1980). This is not to say that patients should design their own treatments, but rather that they should be actively involved with the physician in identifying preferred outcomes and in assessing the costs and benefits of alternative means for achieving those outcomes. To participate at this level, of course, patients need information (Roter, 1977; Waitzkin, 1985; West, 1984). They must not be discouraged, given ambiguous responses, challenged in their right to ask questions, or limited in the total time (perhaps over several visits) available for discussion (see review, Roter & Hall, 1992).

Physician's and Patient's Points of View on Conflict

Fears of time-consuming visits with patients often prompt physicians to control and limit the amount of information they elicit from and give to patients and the complexity of the issues that they are willing to discuss with them. Physicians accomplish this goal by asking patients serial, closed-ended questions (Hall et al., 1988; Kleinman, 1988; Sankar, 1986). As little as an additional two and a half minutes of visit time (Beckman, Frankel, & Darnley, 1995) in which patients provide additional information by interjecting and volunteering details, however, materially improves the likelihood that physician and patient will arrive at a common definition of the patient's problem (Rost, Carter, & Inui, 1989).

Patients are at a distinct disadvantage in attempting to become active participants in their medical care, in breaking the silence that is so often upheld, and in engendering earnest discussions of the medical condition, its prognosis, and alternative treatment choices. First, patients are most often disrobed and already on an examination table when the medical interaction begins. Unlike normal social discourse, the physician typically directs the conversation by asking questions and limiting the patient's responses (Waitzkin, 1991). Physician–patient interactions are typically conducted in a relatively efficient, if not rushed, manner with the physician controlling the amount of time it will take (Fisher, 1983). Patients are typically deferent in response to this control, partly because of the social power they accord their physician. Patients may be ill and feel dependent on the assistance that they believe only the physician can provide for them; consequently, they may fear abandonment by their physician if they do not behave as a ''good patient'' (Taylor, 1979).

Second, many patients believe that urgency conveyed in the interaction is in response to patient care emergencies, and they may be reluctant to take up time with their questions (DiMatteo, 1993). Office-based medical practice is rarely, if ever, concerned with true clinical emergencies; instead, the perceived urgency revolves around issues related to economics and medical reimbursement (Waitzkin, 1985). Physicians have been found to behave in a hurried manner, such as watching a clock or wristwatch and interrupting patients midsentence (Svarstad,

1976). Moreover, patients often place a premium on being polite to their physicians (Aronsson & Satterlund-Larsson, 1987) and on saving face when physicians sometimes attempt to regain control of the interaction by asserting superiority, and by questioning the patient's stability and normality (Beisecker, 1986).

Third, patients often enter the medical interaction with considerable anxiety and may be in a state of illness and pain. Such limitations can introduce challenges to the management of an already difficult social interaction. In addition, physicians control access to patients' records and test results, limiting patients' use of the information in their personal medical cases (Fisher, 1984). This control of medical information reinforces the social status and power afforded to physicians, maintains their social dominance over patients, and further places limits on patients' attempts to become involved in their care and decision making (e.g., Waitzkin, 1991).

Patient Involvement and Adherence

Therapeutic success depends on patient adherence, which has been shown to depend on sufficient explanation of the condition and treatment options (Carter, Inui, Kukull, & Haigh, 1982; Svarstad, 1976; West, 1984; Wolf, 1988), sharing of opinions (Carter et al., 1982), receipt of adequate information and encouragement (Jackson, 1994b; Roter, Hall, & Katz, 1988), and consensus between physician and patient on the appropriate treatment regimen (DiMatteo, 1994). Mutual exploration of alternatives toward the goal of agreement can help physician and patient to form realistic expectations of various reasonable treatment strategies. Without the opportunity to assert their preferences to their physicians, patients often privately make plans for their own medical well-being, even to the point of making decisions not to adhere to medical regimens (Donovan & Blake, 1992; Hayes-Bautista, 1976; Rodin & Janis, 1979). Nonadherence may even be an active coping strategy on the part of patients to restore a lost sense of control (Rodin & Janis, 1979).

Empirical research demonstrates that patients benefit from taking an active role in their medical care choices (Kaplan, 1991) and experience greater improvement when they and their providers have consonant expectations (Starfield et al., 1979). When patients are involved and active in their care, they express greater satisfaction and have much greater alleviation of their symptoms, better control of their chronic conditions, greater improvement in their overall medical conditions, less distress and concern about their illnesses, and better response to surgery and invasive diagnostic procedures (Egbert, Battit, Welch, & Bartlett, 1964; Johnson & Leventhal, 1974; Kaplan, Greenfield, & Ware, 1989; Roter, 1983; Roter & Hall, 1992).

Patients who are involved in choices about their care, compared with those who are not, feel a greater sense of control over their health and their lives, have more positive expectations for their health, and demonstrate better adherence to the treatment on which they have helped to decide (Speedling & Rose, 1985). Patients who participate in and share responsibility for their health decisions also receive treatments that are more consistent with their preferences (Fisher, 1983) and are less likely to blame their physicians if their outcomes are less optimal than they may have expected (Wagener & Taylor, 1986). When patients are not informed and involved, they give less adequate histories (Waitzkin & Stoeckle, 1972), they tend to delay in reporting important symptoms (Hackett, Cassem, & Raker, 1973), they have less positive therapeutic outcomes (Kleinman, Eisenberg, & Good, 1978), and they may be more likely to litigate malpractice claims (Levinson, 1994).

How Conflict Can Be Managed and Participation Achieved

To arrive at the best decisions for a patient, the therapeutic interaction must be genuinely mutual, and not based on ''pseudo-mutuality'' in which patient and physician act superficially as if they have the same goals. Patient and physician must recognize that they hold divergent perspectives on illness and treatment, and that these perspectives need to be examined and resolved in earnest. Avoidance of meaningful discussion and its inevitable *but manageable* conflicts only preserves the silence that limits the patient's ability to follow through with treatment plans. Because of the traditional power differential between physicians and patients, and the many pressures on their relationship, the recognition of these differences must be made *overt* (Brody, 1992). Physician–patient collaboration in decision making needs to be based on an exceptionally good mechanism for facilitating open, unimpeded communication between physician and patient. One method, the ''conversation model'' (Brody, 1992), has the patient regularly providing to the physician information about his or her values, preferences, and constraints. The physician ''thinks out loud'' about possible courses of action, the recommended interventions, and the possible implications of these for the patient's future in language that is accessible to the patient.

A structured approach, such as the PREPARED™ system, can enhance provider–patient communication and patient self-efficacy and satisfaction (DiMatteo, Reiter, & Gambone, 1994; Gambone & Reiter, 1991; Gambone, Reiter, & DiMatteo, 1994). This system involves a checklist or agenda, which helps to make the medical visit focused and to save time. With PREPARED™ provider and patient discuss seven important elements of care: the recommended procedure, prescription, or other course of health action (P); the reason for the recommendation in terms of the observed or potential harm that is or could be threatening the patient's health status (R); the patients' and providers' outcome expectations in terms of preventing or reversing any harm (E); the probability of achieving those expectations (P); reasonable alternatives to what has been recommended including expectant management or watchful waiting (A); all significant risks associated with what has been recommended (R); and expenses, including direct and indirect costs (E), before making a decision (D). Including patients in the decision-making process using PREPARED™ has been shown to contribute to an overall reduction in the utilization of hysterectomy (Gambone & Reiter, 1991) and hysterectomy for chronic pelvic pain (Reiter, Gambone, & Johnson, 1991). Recent data suggest that in hypothetical decision-making situations, consumers have increased self-efficacy after being trained to use PREPARED™.

Building a Model of Provider–Patient Communication

An effective provider–patient relationship requires joint recognition and examination of disparate goals and collaborative evaluation of the means to achieve them. The process of negotiation between provider and patient involves developing courses of action that the patient finds acceptable given his or her values and preferences, and that also satisfy the clinician's values and preferences. The most effective interaction will occur if physician and patient each fully understands the goals and expectations of the other (DiMatteo et al., 1994) and negotiates an agreement for the course of care.

The best decisions will be reached if the physician develops an empathic attitude in which the patient's internal frame of reference is understood and the situation is viewed through the patient's value system (Squier, 1990). Shared decisions must be made with direct, negotiated discussions. When this is impossible, such as when the patient is very ill, the clinician must make decisions (typically with the family) in the context of considerable knowledge of the patient's personal values, expectations, and goals for treatment (Brody, 1992).

Conflict in the therapeutic relationship is always valuable (Katz, 1984). Without it, physicians tend to assume (incorrectly) that they know their patients' tacit preferences, values, goals, needs, wants, and expectations for care (Brody, 1980). Physicians would do well to *provoke* conflict by exploring patients' assessments and feelings about proposed treatment choices (Brody, 1992; Speedling & Rose, 1985). Therapeutic conversations should legitimate expressions of differences and conflicts and make clear that the encounter is one in which differences can be resolved (Lazare et al., 1978).

Suggestions for Future Research

Studies of patient preferences for involvement in decision making have yielded equivocal and sometimes confusing results (Ende, Kazis, Ash, & Moskowitz, 1989; Strull, Lo, & Charles, 1984). Measurements of patient preferences have been diverse; in some studies, patients are asked about their desire to make medical decisions, while in others patients are asked about their wishes to participate through detailed discussions with their physicians. Lack of commonality in measurement makes it difficult to compare studies. No studies have systematically tracked variations in preferences as a function of patients' demographic characteristics, experience with the disease, and level of disease impairment.

Research on patients' decision-making preferences is in need of strong theoretical underpinning and hypotheses regarding the meaning of patients' preferences, such as the difference between a patient's decision to participate in therapeutic treatment choices versus the preference solely to make such decisions (Clarke, 1986). Patients' preferences to discuss treatment with their physicians likely involve patients' expectations that their physicians will fully understand and take into account their values, preferences, and goals when making medical decisions, but currently modeling of these expectations and decisional processes is lacking.

As patients become involved in their medical decision making, research is also needed on the changes that occur in the physician–patient relationship. Longitudinal studies following patients over time in caring for chronic conditions will advance our understanding of the implications of various degrees of patient involvement for patient care. In addition, intervention studies are needed which explore the role of patient and of physician training in recognizing and resolving conflict. Empirical research is needed on the effects of patient and physician conflict and negotiation on patient satisfaction, adherence, and the outcomes and cost-effectiveness of treatment.

Clinical Implications

An ethical imperative exists that physician and patient have reciprocal responsibility to share in the decision process and that, if the patient is of sound mind, he or she makes the final decision about care (Clarke, 1986; Pellegrino, 1976). Unfortunately, the essence of this mandate can be easily forgotten in clinical practice, as the social power of the physician can dominate the patient's agenda and manipulate the patient's choices. Sometimes, it is only when malpractice litigation becomes the avenue for the patient's expression of anger at an unsatisfactory result that it is clear the patient was not fully informed and was unable to exercise his or her right to consent (Levinson, 1994). The patient's future possibilities always should be the focus for all discussions of medical treatment and for subsequent medical decisions. The patient's complete involvement must be sought continually. Mutual exploration and discussion of all alternative choices increase the chances of achieving the ultimate goal of medical care—life as the patient would choose to live it (Eddy, 1990).

6

The Role of Communication in Medical Ethics

Lorraine D. Jackson and Bernard K. Duffy

SYNOPSIS

The practice of medicine is undergoing an extensive transformation. The ethic of paternalism, whereby medical decisions are based solely on professional authority, is being challenged and superseded by ethical values favoring patient autonomy and lucidity. These changing values have precipitated a communication revolution that has direct effects on doctor–patient relationships and medical school curricula because lucid, autonomous decision making is made possible through effective communication. Health communication researchers have been hesitant to explore ethical issues directly, perhaps because of the erroneous notion that communication and medical ethics are mutually exclusive areas of study. In addition, the conventional belief that nonphysicians cannot contribute to medical ethics might explain why communication researchers have not delved into this area. Health communication researchers can contribute to improving ethically involved aspects of health care, including informed consent, decision making, truthful disclosure, confidentiality, value analysis, and the dissemination of health information.

Traditionally, the physician's *raison d'etre* lies in the prevention of illness, the restoration of health, and the preservation of life. Today, the very *means* available to medical practitioners has called the undisputed *end* of preserving life at all costs into question. There is now a remarkable ability to preserve life through new medical knowledge and equipment—a mother's life for the benefit of her unborn child, an organ donor's for the benefit of the organ recipient, a terminally ill patient's for the benefit of the family. But this ability has forced physicians and patients to reconsider the purposes of the medical profession. Dramatic and expansive transformations in the practice of medicine have occurred in the last half-century. The health care delivery system has been affected by all manner of changes in the external environment. Social movements promoting consumer rights and legal rights, rapid advances in technology, currents of economic change, the dramatic appearance and acceleration of the AIDS pandemic, political wrangling and discussion of health insurance issues, increasing media attention paid to medical advances and treatment options, and a better informed public, all have reconfigured perceptions of health care in the United States and abroad. These forces have had unprecedented effects on the education of medical students, the practice of medicine and preventive care, and the relationship between doctor and patient.

There has been a paradigmatic shift in this relationship whereby an egalitarian consumerism favoring the patient has uprooted the regnant hierarchical paternalism that favors the physician. Beisecker and Beisecker (1993) note pointedly that "traditionally . . . physicians operated paternalistically, like caring fathers, supposedly providing expert judgment and technical skill for the benefit of the patients. . . . Recently, doctors have been viewed more frequently as medical service contractors" (p. 42). A physician writing an editorial in *Newsweek* expressed the irritation his fellow doctors feel at being recategorized as impersonal "health care providers," along with everyone from X-ray technicians to medical social workers (Fleming, 1997).

Simultaneously, significant, even revolutionary changes have been wrought in the area of medical ethics, although such changes have responded to, rather than anticipated, their technological and political impetuses. As Lamm (1993) graphically stated, the current generation is experiencing "an ethical earthquake to existing medical values" (p. 552). In practical terms, medical ethics (and/or bioethics) is the system of making moral decisions regarding health care (Kreps and Thornton, 1984, p. 202). Communication enables the process of decision making and the articulation and implementation of ethical decisions and behavior. Formerly, ethics was based solely on professional authority and, as a practical matter, nonphysicians remained uninvolved in the discussion of ethical issues regarding medicine. Ethical medical practice evolved from the formal and informal consensus of physicians and their professional organizations. Physicians, exercising an extraordinary degree of professional autonomy, determined what they believed was in the best interest of the patient. As long as the doctor was serving the patient's interest, he or she could deceive or coerce the patient with legal impunity and little accountability to nonphysicians (Brody, 1989, p. 67). Between 1965 and 1970, however, traditional values were rapidly reformulated and a "new medical ethics" emerged. Ethics came no longer to be regarded as a "privileged, in-house medical matter," and the principle of patient autonomy (or the right of self-determination) challenged the beneficence model that had defined the status quo (Brody, 1989, p. 67).

A subtle, yet fascinating, example of the far-reaching effects of this shift can be seen in the recent disapproval of the term *noncompliant patient*. Such formerly conventional terminology had been widely and blithely used to describe a patient who willfully or neglectfully did not follow therapeutic advice. As Trenholm (1995) explains, language is dynamic and closely related to thought. When our collective thoughts change, our collective terminology choices also shift to reflect new realities. As a reflection of the changing face of the practice of medicine, the term *compliance* is now being replaced by terms like *collaboration* and *adherence*, because compliance is associated with paternalism, while collaboration and adherence suggest a consensually agreed-upon plan. Holm (1993) offers the reasons for this semantic substitution:

As we slowly move away from the paternalistic conception of the doctor–patient relationship, to a form of relationship where the patient's autonomy and fundamental right to self determination is acknowledged, we should also abandon the present conception of compliance. If it is ultimately the patient who decides, after being duly informed and advised, then [s]he cannot be non-compliant. (p. 108)

A chain of intricate events, and the resulting reexamination of values, shift in power, and questioning of physician authority, have pushed many ethical issues to the forefront of public discussion. Changing values regarding the doctor–patient relationship have also left an impress on the medical school curriculum. The next section examines trends in the teaching of ethics and overviews salient ethical concepts. Following this discussion is a description of the current status and prospective future role of health communication research as it relates to ethics.

CRITICAL REVIEW OF THE LITERATURE

Medical Education and Ethics

One index to the status of medical ethics is whether and how ethics are taught in medical schools. Medical education is a crucial, interdependent component of the health care system and, as is the case in all systems, has been incrementally adapted to resist the forces of entropy. In the course of its adaptation, medical education will shape the ethical practices of the next generation of physicians and future ethical standards in the medical profession.

Until the early 1980s the formal teaching of medical ethics to medical students and residents was not widely accepted and, furthermore, was often viewed as unnecessary. The profession of medicine was seen as inseparable from its ethical practice, and didactic instruction in ethics seemed to call the moral basis of the profession into question. Critics of medical ethics curricula argued that such courses subtracted valuable time from clinical education. Others doubted that ethics could be taught, and some believed that experienced clinicians could teach ethics adequately to residents in the course of providing care (Perkins, 1989). Despite these misgivings on the part of some physicians, in 1983 the DeCamp

Foundation invited leading medical ethicists to a conference for the purpose of defining a core curriculum in medical ethics; in the same year, the American Board of Internal Medicine issued a statement acknowledging that physicians needed to meet high standards of humanistic behavior (Perkins, 1989, p. 262). Shortly thereafter, in 1984, the Association of American Medical Colleges issued a report stating "ethical sensitivity and moral integrity, combined with equanimity, humility, and self-knowledge are quintessential qualities of all physicians (Muller, 1984).

Manifestations of the trend toward valuing and promoting ethical communication are also occurring in other countries. In the United Kingdom, for example, the General Medical Council (GMC) noted a large increase in the number of serious professional misconduct cases (Ramsey, 1993, p. 1165). This trend was partially attributed to patients' increased awareness of their rights. As a result, the GMC is proposing a new medical curriculum emphasizing rehabilitation, primary-care medicine, health promotion, and "communication skills necessary to deal with patients who have a much better understanding of their diseases and their rights than did patients of previous generations" (Ramsey, 1993, p. 1165).

To meet the needs of a public sensitized to consumer rights and the new objectives set forth by various professional associations, medical schools have felt compelled to teach students a solid framework for discussing and solving ethical questions, and formal courses in medical ethics are becoming standard components of the core curriculum. *U.S. News and World Report* (1993) conducted a peer review reputational survey to assess the top comprehensive and research-oriented medical schools, as well as top schools for various specialties. Under the "ethics" specialty, the top schools include the University of Chicago, Georgetown University, the University of California at San Francisco, Harvard University, and the University of Washington.

As an example of one of these top schools, Harvard University requires students to take Doctor/Patient I, II, III courses, which span three years of the medical curriculum. Unlike some courses offered for only one semester, students are exposed to the importance of communication skills and ethical sensitivity throughout their entire medical education. A summary of the "goals section" of the Doctor/Patient courses makes notable reference to the importance of communication in fulfilling the professional responsibilities of the clinician:

Course Goals: By the end of the third year, students should be able to do the following: (a) analyze ethical implications of clinical dilemmas, interview patients in a complete and efficient way using skills of empathy, listening, explanatory models and negotiation; (b) discuss difficult patient problems like death and dying, chronic pain, substance abuse using patient-centered techniques; (c) understand basic ideas from disciplines that study issues related to the patient–doctor relationship (e.g., multi-culturalism, health-care finance); (d) appreciate the relevance of prevention in every clinical encounter and apply principles of health promotion and disease prevention; (e) demonstrate maturation as a clinician by communicating in an appropriate manner to peers and faculty, and sharing relevant observations from clerkships; (f) consider the range of career choices in medicine and develop personal and professional goals; (g) pursue in-depth study of Patient–Doctor curricular topics during 4th year electives or independent study.

To accomplish these goals, various topics are explored. Among the topics considered are the medical interview, childhood interviewing and the patient's experience of illness, interviewing about lifestyle, informed consent and patients' role in decision making, analyzing common clinical problems, truth-telling and the disclosure of information, decisions about the goals and intensity of medical care, risk management and professional liability, chronically ill or dying patients, diversity issues in medicine, difficult patient/doctor interactions, health promotion and disease prevention.

Courses in medical ethics provide forums where students learn how to develop and apply criteria for ethical decision making when confronted with contradictory values. Students are exposed to the numerous influences on the patient–doctor relationship, including issues of status and power, as well as other ambient psychological, economic, social, cultural and legal factors affecting communication. In these courses, values are molded and modeled, both directly and indirectly, and ultimately shape the communication patterns of future physicians.

The Intersection of Ethics and Communication: Salient Concepts in Medicine

Medical school faculty, as well as clinicians, jurists, and ethicists have identified a number of intersections between medical ethics and communication. Fried (1974) regarded an ethical relationship as having four "rights in personal care." He labeled them as lucidity—the right to full disclosure of pertinent information; autonomy—the right to be regarded as a self-determining agent and to be consulted in one's own care; fidelity—the right to service aimed toward one's own interest, and the rejection of conflicting interests; and, humanity—the right to be treated with compassion and to have one's own uniqueness taken into account. Brody (1989, p. 70) notes that effectively Fried's explication of patient rights combines the "new" medical ethics (lucidity and autonomy) with the most desirable aspects of the "old" ethics (fidelity and humanity).

Informed Consent

Although so clearly central to both ethical and legal concerns, informed consent is a recent concept related to the rights of lucidity and autonomy. Discussions of the concept of "informed consent" only began around 1972, in part as a reaction to the ethically questionable medical experimentation involving human subjects in the 1960s (Beauchamp, 1989, p. 175).

Issues concerning consent are often complicated. For example, an article in the *San Francisco Chronicle* (October 14, 1994, p. A22) debates the unsettling ethical implication of the case of a three-year-old child who gave bone marrow to his father. Minors and other ''incompetent'' persons are usually safeguarded through parental consent procedures. However, the right to fidelity discussed by Fried may be jeopardized in cases where the consenting parent is also the recipient benefiting from organ or bone-marrow transplantation.

Although many people might regard a signature on a legal document as an act of informed consent, an authentic (or a so-called quality) informed consent involves: (1) disclosure, (2) comprehension, (3) voluntariness, (4) competence, and (5) consent (Beauchamp, 1989, p. 180). In spite of the honorable ideal to facilitate patient decision making, some critics offer the following caveats:

Indeed, both empirical research and clinical observations indicate that informed consent often becomes an empty ritual in which patients are presented with complex information that they cannot understand and that has little impact on their decision-making. Many see informed consent as directly interfering with the care of patients by wasting valuable time and leading patients to reject medically desirable care. (Lidz, Appelbaum, & Meisel, 1988, p. 1385)

Lidz et al. (1988, p. 1385) contend that the doctrine of informed consent is sound, but its implementation is often problematic. They note that it may be implemented from either (a) the event model, which regards informed consent as a one-time procedure to be completed before treatment to cover legal matters; or (b) the process model, where informing the patient and active patient involvement occur over time as part of routine dialogue regarding diagnosis and treatment.

Issues related to informed consent are complex and are integrally tied to communication. For instance, intricate medical and statistical information may be difficult for laypersons to understand. In light of this complexity, professionals need to understand the decision-making process, the variables that affect it, and the communication techniques that can improve it.

Truthful Disclosure

Related to informed consent is the question of truthfully disclosing ''bad news.'' The radical shift in the value placed on patient lucidity is evidenced by changing perceptions of truthful disclosure. In 1960, 90 percent of cancer physicians favored not disclosing a cancer diagnosis (Oken, 1961); yet in a similar study a mere 20 years later, 90 percent favored full disclosure (Novack et al., 1979).

The most difficult ethical decisions occur when two or more of the personal rights identified by Fried are in conflict. For example, in a recent court ruling, the California Supreme Court determined that doctors must give seriously ill patients enough information to make intelligent decisions about treatment, but are under no obligation to divulge the statistical chances of dying—even if patients ask (Roan, 1993). The ruling was prompted by the case of a 42-year-old patient suffering from pancreatic cancer. After the patient's death, the patient's family sued his doctors because the patient was not told he only had a 50 percent chance of living one year. The family contended that had he known his chances were poor, he would have refused painful medical treatment and would have had time to make appropriate arrangements. In this case, the rights of lucidity and autonomy clashed with the physician's desire to give the patient hope (right of humanity). In addition, there is always an element of uncertainty regarding predictions because survival statistics cannot accurately predict individual outcomes. An ongoing debate in the *Journal of Medical Ethics* concerns whether an important moral distinction exists between lying and forms of deception that do not involve lying per se (Bakhurst, 1992; Jackson, 1991, 1993). As a general rule, communicating the truth to a patient is now deemed important for reasons beyond the self-evident morality of honesty. For example, uncertainty often leads to increased anxiety, and most patients would like to make decisions about how to live in the remaining time, and how and where to die.

But are there special circumstances when telling the truth is not in the best interest of the patient? If a patient requests (or perhaps simply implies) that the physician withhold the truth, one could argue that the patient's wish should be respected. Some courts recognize "therapeutic privilege" as a legitimate reason for nondisclosure. Therapeutic privilege can be exercised in special situations where truthful disclosure will cause undue harm to a patient (Brody, 1989, p. 80). Determining what constitutes undue harm can be extremely difficult. Doctors often anticipate the grief associated with a serious diagnosis. Yet, how individuals will react to a frightening diagnosis is often impossible to predict. What causes one person to lose hope might in another person provide a motivational spark needed to fight a potentially fatal illness. Oncologists often couple bad news with the communication of an action plan designed to help the patient (Roan, 1993). Insensitive handling of a serious diagnosis can lead to problems with long-term adjustments. One study assessing anxiety and depression a year after breast cancer treatment found that women who perceived that the "bad news" interview was inappropriately handled were twice as anxious or depressed as those who were satisfied with the interview (Fallowfield, Baum, & Maguire, 1986). Another study examining HIV positive women found correlations between how the diagnosis was communicated, patient satisfaction with the diagnosis consultation, and later mental adjustment to HIV (Jackson & Selby, 1998). This is particularly important in light of the fact that anxiety and depression can be associated with lowered functioning of the immune system (Bloom, 1988).

Confidentiality

Confidentiality relates to Fried's "right of fidelity" and is valued because of the importance of trust in the doctor–patient relationship. Confidentiality promotes the free exchange of information and protects outside sources from gaining access to sensitive material. How and to whom one chooses to disclose sensitive material is a major issue of control in interpersonal relationships, and changes in the levels of data individuals have about one another define developing relationships (Trenholm, 1991, p. 160). When confidentiality is breached, emotional, moral, and possibly legal consequences may arise. Yet confidentiality is becoming more difficult to maintain. Norton (1989), writing for *Hippocrates*, notes: "Though physicians still swear an oath not to reveal patient information, old fashioned medical confidentiality has become a notion quaint as the house call—gradually eroded by court decisions and a victim of the industrialization of medicine" (p. 54). Various statutes require that health care professionals report gun shot wounds, sexually transmitted diseases, and suspected child abuse cases to government agencies. Unquestionably, there is social value to this policy. Yet, is disclosing confidential medical information to a third party (nongovernment authority) ever justifiable? In some cases, where revealing information would prevent likely harm to a specific, identifiable individual, a relatively strong case can be made for breaching confidentiality. Preventing the transmission of AIDS creates new communication challenges. Some patients do not want to disclose their HIV status to sexual partners. Normally, attempts can be made to convince a reasonable person to disclose information voluntarily. In some instances, physicians have helped patients construct letters describing their HIV status to former sexual partners, thus avoiding the difficult question of whether to violate confidentiality. Recently, California amended its strict confidentiality rules to enable physicians to inform the spouse of an HIV infected individual. However, many practitioners agree that confidentiality should rarely be breached. The burden falls on the physician to demonstrate when exceptions are justified morally and the likelihood that the intended purpose will be achieved (Brody, 1989).

Communication Research and Ethics

In the inaugural volume of the journal *Health Communication*, Smith (1989) invites communication scholars to study questions of bioethics and remarks that "communication researchers could play a leading role in making bioethics more empirically descriptive" (p. 25). It is interesting to note that seven years after this invitation was proffered, a search of *Health Communication* reveals only one article with ethics or bioethics in the article title. Although several of the articles deal with improving doctor–patient interaction and issues that are indirectly related to ethics, such as power (e.g., Beisecker, 1990), participative decision making (e.g., Ballard-Reisch, 1990), patient literacy (e.g., Thompson &

Pledger, 1993), and improving communication (e.g., Evans, Stanley & Burrows, 1992; Jackson, 1992), direct dialogue pertaining to medical ethics in health communication journals is rare.

Addington & Wegescheide-Harris's (1995) theoretical article dealing with communication and the terminally ill represents one exception to this desideratum. In this article, the authors note that two separate bodies of literature deal with ethics and communication. They observe that medical ethicists are apt to ignore communication and that health communication researchers give short shrift to ethics. They propose a model that places communication in an ethical decision-making framework. This model assumes that one can deduce a caregiver's particular ethical orientation from his or her communication and meaningful physical behavior. Pragmatically, monitoring communication and behavior allows one to rectify it with the espoused ethical stance.

A study reported in the *Journal of Applied Communication Research* analyzes HIV patient and physician values before and after a 12-month ethics training program. The results suggested that physician values became more congruent with patient values, and thus physicians became more sensitive to patients' needs for information, confidentiality, individuality, personalized care, and nonstigmatization during treatment. This article provides an illustration of how ethical communication interventions can result in improved physician–patient relationships (Vanderford, Smith, & Harris, 1992).

The paucity of research has made it difficult for editors and authors of health communication books to broach the topic of ethics (e.g., Ray & Donohew, 1990). Communication books to date include a case study adumbrating and defining salient ethical terms (Smith & Harris, 1993) and general discussions of communication and medical ethics (Thornton & Kreps, 1993).

Perhaps one of the reasons why communication researchers have not developed research agendas in this area is that they have treated the domains of physician–patient relationships and medical ethics as separate. The traditional belief that nonphysicians should not interfere with ethical decisions regarding medicine is still influential. In a perceptive and useful article by Wyatt (1991) reporting a search of medical literature concerning doctors' perceptions of physician–patient relationships, medical ethics was intentionally excluded from the search. The author justified the omission on two premises: (1) truthful disclosure and medical ethics deal with legal and medical issues not related to communication, and (2) the large number of articles on this subject precludes adequate coverage. This rationale is indicative of a pervasive belief that ethics is somehow in a category separate from doctor–patient communication. Yet, in examining closely the scholarship regarding medical ethics, it becomes apparent that communication and ethics are inextricably bound, and that physicians often use ethics-related journals as a forum for discussing doctor–patient communication. Although legal, moral, and medical directives do constrain and shape the interpersonal communication that takes place between physician and patient, this observation supports, rather than denies, the conclusion that studying these complex interrelationships is necessary. Furthermore, the existence of a considerable discussion of ethics in the medical literature indicates the importance of the topic. To eliminate medical ethics from the field of communication suggests an unfortunate gap in the comprehension of the communication situations facing health professionals and patients. It might be that social scientists have seen ethics, a traditional subject in the humanities, as outside of their purview or, from a practical point of view, less susceptible to social scientific study than topics where the variables are more concrete. In fact, however, delimiting the study of communication in health settings to those matters that are objectively measurable will also limit the usefulness of health communication research to health professionals who deal daily with vexing questions involving ethics. As Sharf (1993, p. 40) notes, communication researchers could play a part in exploring how discourse can resolve ethical dilemmas, while simultaneously improving health care and interaction. Prominent medical ethicist Robert M. Veatch suggests: "There is no reason to assume that being skilled in medical science will make one an expert in choosing among . . . basic philosophical and ethical positions" (Veatch, 1989, p. iv). Veatch also recommends that an interdisciplinary, critical examination of ethical issues is desirable.

Ethical Considerations in Health Information Dissemination

At first glance, the process of presenting health messages in an effort to promote health related behavior seems to be a worthy goal devoid of any need for ethical guidelines or consideration. Upon closer examination, efforts to influence, persuade, or create behavior change historically have raised ethical questions. For example, gray areas exist between "health education" and "manipulation." As Witte (1994b) explains:

Although health communication researchers and practitioners prefer to call their work public health campaigns or health education interventions, the truth is that their ultimate goal is to manipulate people into practicing healthy behaviors. As health communication research and practice moves into the 21st century, this issue must be faced squarely and directly, and strategies must be developed for the ethical use of manipulation techniques to promote health and prevent disease. (p. 285)

The questions of how and what information should be disseminated to the public have important implications and thus necessitate ethical responsibility. First, health communication specialists and campaign planners typically work with health organizations that have limited resources. Subsequently, they must prioritize or choose which types of health threats are most severe or pervasive. Given a limited budget and given multiple health threats in target groups (such as drug use, sexually transmitted diseases (STDs), poor nutrition, and smoking among young adults), choices must be made about which campaigns to pursue. In addition to using epidemiological data, such decisions often require value judgments. Bias can play a role in this process, whereby certain themes are emphasized over other equally important ones. For example, cardiovascular disease is the leading cause of death among women (Eaker, Chesebro, Sacks, Wenger, Whisnant & Winston, 1993), yet according to Brody (1995), a mere 4 percent of women perceive heart disease to be a threat, whereas 35 percent are likely to actually develop heart disease. Few organized health campaigns have addressed this health threat, and this misconception continues to have costly consequences.

The determination of which health beliefs and behaviors to shape extends beyond the *topics* of health campaigns and includes the campaign's message content and style. Within a single emerging campaign, decisions must be made about how much information to present. By presenting some facts and not others, perceptions are inevitably altered. For example, a 30-second public service announcement promoting condom use as a means of practicing safer sex may not contain information about the failure rate of condoms. Similarly, how the message is framed in terms of word choices, risk information, and the order in which information presented influences persuasion. Witte (1994b) describes the 1993 mabmmogram scare in the United States after a Swedish study found mammograms might cause an increase in cancer. In fact, what the study actually found was that for women under 40 the risk of radiation from mammography could be greater than the risk rates of discovering breast cancer. The message that mammograms are lifesaving in women over 40 may have been lost due to the manner in which this risk information was reported in the media.

Because individuals rely on the media for information concerning a number of health behaviors, clarity and accuracy are important. Unfortunately, a lack of clarity and accuracy exists in many media reports. For instance Moyer, Greener, Beauvais, & Salovoy (1995) studied breast cancer and mammography-related articles in every indexed magazine and four leading newspapers over a two-year period. Of 116 articles, there were 113 citations to scientific studies, 60 of which were traceable to an original source (often a scientific investigation). Out of the 60 traceable citations, 42 content-based inaccuracies were found, including misleading titles, shift in emphasis, treatment of speculation as fact, erroneous information, omission of (a) other important results, (b) qualifications to findings, and (c) important aspects of the research methods, overgeneralization of findings, inaccuracies due to personal communications, and other inaccuracies. Whether errors are the result of unintentional omissions, misleading sensationalism about risks, or genuine controversies about efficacy, errors and problems with clarity result in misinformation and ultimately cause undesirable health effects.

In light of these factors, Witte (1994b) contends that ethical guidelines should be established, and she offers preliminary ideas in this regard. Specifically, the suggestions include (1) identifying a specific goal and designing campaigns to fit that goal and (2) promoting the common good as determined by a community standard. To determine goals for the common good, Witte (1994b) suggests the use of community panels comprised of representatives of relevant interest groups.

Ethics and Small Groups

In addition to the community panels proposed by Witte (1994b), small groups can be used to discuss other ethical issues. Thornton and Kreps (1993) describe the typical ethics committee as consisting of specialists, nurses, administrators, social workers, chaplains, patient representatives, and lawyers. These committees, located in hospitals and other organizations, exist to educate, formulate policy, and conduct proactive and retroactive case reviews. Thornton and Kreps (1993) assert that "the field of health communication could make a major contribution to the small group health setting" (p. 96). Areas that researchers might explore in the future include how these groups deal with conflict resolution while exploring highly reactive topics, how roles emerge, and how status and power differences affect the group's functioning.

The Future of Ethics and Health Communication Inquiry

Interest in medical ethics is likely to unfold rapidly and, with it, the role that communication plays in medical ethics. One area with which communication researchers will undoubtedly become involved is the patient's right to die and active euthanasia (doctor-assisted suicide). Not surprisingly, issues surrounding death and dying are already afforded special attention in the curricula of all medical schools. Both advocates and critics of doctor-assisted suicide value humane, compassionate treatment, yet disagree on the manner in which that goal is fulfilled. Shapiro and Bowermaster (1994) contend that more could be done regarding aggressive pain management, identifying and treating depression, and developing high-quality, hospice, and home care. In addition, after examining the effects of Dutch pro-euthanasia policies, the authors suggest that, despite the euthanasia movement's promise of liberation from the power of medicine, it actually increases physician power and paternalism since it is the doctor who makes the diagnosis, establishes how euthanasia is practiced, and decides whether to report it to civil authorities. Whether the United States follows the path of the Dutch medical community, it is inevitable that there will be a continued dialogue concerning the cessation of life. The role communication researchers might play in refining current practices should focus on issues such as the implementation of living wills and other advance directives that involve communication between physicians, the patient, and family members. At least one study has indicated that advance directives are not used as often as they should be because of the reluctance of some physicians to discuss them with patients (Morrison, Morrison, & Glickman, 1994). Not only must advance directives clearly articulate the wishes of a patient well informed about the consequences of his or her decision, but written advance directives must be carried out after full and complete consultation with all parties. Researchers should also study the efficacy of advance directives to protect patient autonomy and the degree to which they foster communication between patient, family, and physician. These and other issues concerning the compassionate treatment of dying patients ought to be explored.

Conflicts of values will thrust other communication issues to the forefront. Physicians, once seen either as paternal figures or as neutral scientists, are being demystified as a result of such forces as medical consumerism, managed care, and a better-educated public. As this process develops, researchers have observed that physicians' values affect their compassion toward patients with lifestyle-related illnesses such as AIDS (Vanderford, Smith, & Harris, 1992). How physicians communicate their opposing values to patients and how patients communicate the value-laden perception of their lifestyle-related illnesses to physicians plainly affect the physician/patient transaction in ways that researchers will find important to investigate. Other vexing questions have to do with the protection of information about patients and with their perceptions of patient/physician confidentiality. Improvements in the storage and retrieval of patient records coupled with the desire of corporations, insurers, and other groups to gain access to information about patients with contagious and costly illnesses will create a need to study such questions as how the potential for breaches of confidentiality affects the doctor–patient relationship.

Other recent developments augur for an ever widening and deepening concern about communication and medical ethics. Advances in the areas of transplant technologies, computers, and genetic testing bring issues involving the quality versus quantity of life into the forefront. The availability of expensive, life-saving technology, coupled with societal appeals to consider health care as a social right rather than a private commodity, raises a host of difficult questions concerning resource allocation. Health care system reviewers attempt to propose ways to reduce waste in the system, which often involves eliminating expensive treatment at the end of a patient's life, eliminating expensive care when the prognosis is poor, and making other attempts to ration care. Computer-assisted prediction of individual patient prognoses could be indirectly associated with rationing. For example, a recent study of 1,025 severely head-injured patients published in *The Lancet* (Murray et al., 1993) reveals that computer-based predictions of a patient's outcome alter decisions for treatment. Patients who are predicted to have a good outcome experienced an increase in the use of specific aspects of intensive care, while patients predicted to have a poor outcome received a 39 percent reduction in such intensive care. Are computer-based predictions of outcome a helpful decision-making tool (when resources are scarce), or could pessimism lead to premature withdrawal of treatment?

Moreover, breakthroughs in genetic research focusing on predispositions for illness are making it possible to glimpse into a patient's medical future. In the previous year more than a dozen mutations responsible for diseases such as colon cancer, breast cancer, hyperactivity, and Alzheimer's were discovered. Yet as Brownlee et al. (1994) note, "Almost as soon as a gene is discovered, commercial laboratories are ready to offer a genetic test—a pace that threatens to outstrip both physician's and patient's abilities to make sense of the information" (p. 60). This may be particularly true for the breast cancer gene. Estimates indicate that 1 in 200 women carry this gene, and as a result, millions will no doubt request testing. With only 1,200 genetic counselors in the country, there will be problems deciphering test results (Brownlee et al., 1994). This shortage of personnel is compounded by the fact that the means to explain complex statistical risk information to the general public have neither been carefully studied nor tested. At least one oncologist has acknowledged that, while scientists have learned more about genetic testing, knowledge about how to talk with patients about predictive testing has lagged behind. (Brownlee et al., 1994, p. 64).

These are just a few examples of the difficulties raised by complex technology. To meet these and other challenges, interdisciplinary research in health communication and dialogue relating to medical ethics will be necessary. The next section lists questions for communication scholars.

Questions for Communication Scholars

This list of research questions is not exhaustive. The availability of health information and dilemmas is outpacing the strategies for assisting those who must use information, and continued research is necessary. Among questions researchers in communication and ethics should explore are: (1) What specific communication skills promote a quality informed consent, and how can a quality informed consent be verified? (2) What role do family members play in informed decision making? (3) What ethnocultural variables influence the informed consent process? (4) How can complex statistical risk information be explained effectively to laypersons? (5) How can the use of written instructions such as living wills be encouraged? How can advance directives be articulated clearly and effectively? Do advance directives actually protect autonomy? (6) How can patients be supported in their decision making about therapeutic options when the long-term effects of the treatments are not known? (7) Given that increasing amounts of information about an individual's health are available in potentially accessible clinical databases, how can privacy be protected under these circumstances? To what extent do fears about breaches of confidentiality interfere with the doctor–patient relationship? (8) How do physicians communicate their values, attitudes, and biases, and does this affect quality of care for patients with lifestyle-related illnesses such as alcoholism, IV drug abuse, and AIDS? (9) What communication issues are unique to interdisciplinary ethics committees, and how can these important committees function at an optimal level? (10) How can health education campaigns be designed and implemented in an ethically responsible manner?

The relative lack of research focusing on communication and issues concerning medical ethics presents significant opportunities, either to communication researchers to learn more about these issues or to concerned ethicists and physicians to incorporate communication variables into their discussions. An aging population, new medical technologies, a more consumer-oriented public, and a society attuned to the need to explore values in health care compel the study of communication in ethical decision making at all levels. Careful investigation of these issues has the potential to shed light on an area of tremendous practical importance to society as a whole.

7

Organizational Communication and Health Care Administration

Robert D. O'Connor, Shriti Hallberg, and Richard Myles

SYNOPSIS

Health care as an industry has been reluctant to embrace radical change. Today, providers have little choice but to be part of the metamorphosis to an integrated delivery system or face extinction. The radical modification of how health care is paid for and delivered is requiring major revisions in communication methodology among all stakeholders in the field.

Managed care, informational volume increases, cultural transitions, and technological innovations are causing a reexamination of traditional ways of communicating between providers and their new partners and their customers. The decrease in individual practitioners and the concomitant rise in systems of providers has magnified the need for better, faster information in order to meet consumer demand.

Numerous studies are reported that examine the separate parts of the health care industry. What is called for in the future is a broader examination of the requirement that more timely information must be shared and understood by more stakeholders, many of whom do not share the jargon of today's caregivers. The effectiveness of this revolutionary transformation of the American health care industry will be highly dependent on the quality of results obtained by organizational communication researchers.

ORGANIZATIONAL COMMUNICATION AND HEALTH CARE ADMINISTRATION

In the 1990s, health care costs skyrocketed to $942.5 billion, or more than 14 percent of the gross national product in 1993 (Holsinger, 1995). Despite uncertainties in the U.S. economy and finite resources for providing health care, the nation's health care providers continue to provide needed services.

However, the impact of managed care and advances in technology, resulting in a need for closer working relationships with physicians and payer groups, is causing unparalleled change in management styles and communication requirements among health care administrators. As the health care system adapts to meet these challenges, more care is being provided in less expensive sites outside the acute care hospital. Duplicative facilities and services are being reduced. Hospitals are fewer in number but larger, and hospital and physician health care delivery is becoming better integrated. Providers are more concerned with the quality of outcomes and consumer loyalty. The trend is toward regional systems with local facilities providing only limited or urgent care. These changes are demanding extensive improvement in the type, methods, direction, and speed of communication used by executive personnel in health service organizations.

The changes in the health care industry have necessitated an increase in the type of information needed by patients, payers, and health care organizations. Areas such as price discounts among providers, bargaining power in negotiating contracts, and defining competitive markets based on profit potential have an increased focus in the managed care environment.

The types of information collected on a patient encounter or visit has dramatically increased with electronic capture and storage of information. Information resources include:

Medical record information—history and physical, results, admission and discharge summaries, images, emergency department visits

Coverage information—claims processing information, status queries, coverage information and information about the employer and payers

Support information—referrals, directions, treatment compliance, wellness information, satisfaction measurements, followup

Community and provider utilization statistics—quality and outcomes measures are being used by employers, patients, and payers in selecting health care providers

Immunization databases—being kept on certain patient populations such as pediatric programs, schools, and communities

Encounter pattern databases—drug and domestic abuse cases, abuse of services

Pharmaceutical interaction and poison control databases—fairly prevalent in urban settings and kept up to date with information from local and statewide information sources

Reference materials

Surveys—patient satisfaction, service satisfaction

Similar to the increase in types of information gathered and stored, the volume of information has increased exponentially. It is now easier and faster to study aggregate data from any perspective—patient, payer, caregiver, administrators, media, employers, and pharmacies.

The sections that follow examine current health care organizational communication issues from the perspective of business and leadership, professional interpersonal communication, internal and external communication, intercultural communication, and computer technology.

CRITICAL REVIEW OF THE LITERATURE

Business and Leadership Aspects of Communication Issues

Determination of patient outcomes associated with new and return business is a primary objective of the managed care marketplace. In 1994, 65 percent of U.S. workers received their health services through managed care plans (WHY, 1995). This is considerably more influence than managed care has exerted in the past. Many U.S. cities are recognizing that in their health care systems, there is an oversupply of inpatient beds. Some of this surplus can be attributed to the shift to outpatient care, but more recently it can be traced to the influence of managed care.

Managed care reflects a basic change in the way medical services are paid for. Managed care plans cut costs by limiting tests, by limiting surgery, by reducing referrals to specialists, and by not paying for hospital stays considered unnecessary. Managed care plans also pay lower fees, emphasize prevention, and demand cost-effective care (WHY?, 1995). Plans for capitation, a ''one-fee-fits-all'' strategy, will likely proliferate.

All of these changes mean that the caregiver has an increased role in the cost of delivering care for the patient and for setting appropriate time guidelines for achieving desired results. Health care organizations have an increased need to communicate these changes and the effects of these changes to the line worker in an effort to reduce the length of stay, use fewer supplies, and entice quicker turnaround times for procedures.

The New York University Medical Center (NYUMC) developed an easy-to-use communication system that can assist in disseminating information about the organization's position on managed care. The Ready, Aim, Communicate, Evaluate (RACE) communication system is a departure from the center's traditional communication model in that it facilitates not only top-down but also bottom-up communication. Multiple methods (open forums, videos, and panel discussions) are used, and then feedback is gathered to help improve communication. The result of this initiative is an organization prepared to meet the challenges of managed care (Falter & Miniace, 1996).

As provider groups consolidate to remain competitive in the managed care market health care executives will need a different set of skills to manage the emerging integrated delivery system. According to Scheffelin (1995):

An analysis of hospital administrators' roles in the past compared to current roles and expected future roles revealed a dramatic shift from the administration of a single hospital site by a medical professional to the administration of a major managed care health system or center by an equally well-trained business executive.

The data for this analysis were gathered from mailed questionnaires to administrators in 100 hospitals in California and interviews with 18 experts in the health care field. A number of findings were reported, and the major conclusions were:

1. Administrators will be expected to be knowledgeable and competent in the business, financial, hospital information systems, legal, negotiation skills, and human resource management aspects of health care administration.

2. Administrators will be expected to comply with rapid changes in laws, regulations, and guidelines in the operation of their facilities.

3. Administrators will be expected to be well-versed in the art of good communication, oral and written, as well as in nonverbal communication.

4. It is imperative that the administrator gain and maintain the trust of all those with whom he or she associates (Scheffelin, 1995).

In an earlier study Agho (1992) replicated studies performed previously in 1948, 1961, 1963, and 1978. In four of the five studies, "working with medical staff" was one of the four most important problems identified by hospital administrators.

A major paradigm shift is occurring as a result of capitation whereby providers make money by keeping subscribers healthy and out of expensive treatment facilities. Health care systems have realized that it is cheaper to keep a person healthy than it is to treat an illness. For the integrated delivery systems affected by managed care and capitation, an increased number of empty inpatient beds is a positive sign. Emphasis is being placed on primary and preventive medicine. Many hospitals have restructured patient care delivery to meet new needs and demands. The vast majority of new services are for outpatient care followed by restructured specialized services and home care (Deloitte & Touche, 1992).

In an effort to identify other executive skills required in a changing environment, Brooks (1994) examined the relationship between the hospital CEO and the governing board and physicians in Canada. Conflicts that result from the interaction of the three groups are identified. A CEO requires technical, human, and conceptual skills to manage conflict effectively but can be successful with minimal technical or human skills if subordinates with these skills assist.

To lead their organizations into the future, health care leaders must adapt their skills and management styles to function as a transformational leader (Benson, 1994). These new leaders, using new communication techniques, must be concerned with how information is used to make decisions that affect the entire organization (Longest, Darr, and Rakich, 1992). Similar results were obtained by Hudak et al. (1993) from an interview of 50 senior hospital administrators.

Professional Interpersonal Communication

The medical field has always had a lexicon of unique phrases and technical vocabulary. However, the users of this vocabulary become so familiar with the subject matter that an insulating jargon develops. These nomenclature problems present significant barriers to effective communication when people try to formulate and communicate their knowledge to someone outside of their domain of knowledge. This situation can be further heightened when the experience base, environment, and theoretical knowledge base is not shared. Even within the same organization, many departments or teams may be suffering from this problem, which is heightened when the organization has to communicate with other organizations, physicians, patients, and payers. The excessive use of professional jargon is often used as a power mechanism between physicians and administrators, physicians and nurses, information services professionals and clinicians, caregivers and patients, medical and nonmedical personnel and various other pairings.

Unquestionably, health care has a language of its own. Bell (1996) recently reviewed five health care dictionaries attempting to demystify the terminology: Freudenheim's *HealthSpeak*, Rognehaugh's *The Managed Care Directory*, O'Connor's *Health Care Glossary of Terms and Definitions*, Health Economics Solutions and Philadelphia's Thomas Jefferson University Hospital's *A Health Economics Pocket Glossary*, and the 1996–1997 *Integrated Health Care 100 Directory* by St. Anthony Publishing.

Ethnographic methods have been used to examine the sociolinguistic dimensions of nurse practitioner interactions with patients. A specific study by Allen (1993) provided a contextual account of the discursive practices used by female nurse practitioners during routine office visits with other female patients. Nine nurse practitioners and 26 patients participated in the study in both private and public ambulatory care settings.

The four major linguistic patterns that seemed to characterize the talk of the nurse practitioners as they interacted with female patients were as follows: supporting, informing, controlling and professional jargon. Instances of sociolinguistic power were identified in the processes that controlled the pace and direction of the office visits and potentially truncated data gathering. Controlling language, including warning and command statements, and the use of professional jargon were also examples of power embedded in the language of nurse practitioners identified in the verbatim transcripts. Some implications for this study relate to educating nurse practitioners about the transparent power of language, and the potential for untoward outcomes for patients when that power is not recognized. (Allen, 1993)

A shift in duties by caregivers has become evident in the current health care environment. Of all health care professionals, physicians face more changes as the twenty-first century approaches, in terms not only of shifts in income for some specialists and primary care doctors, but also traditional autonomies associated with medical practice.

Nurse substitution for physicians in patient counseling, education, and case management has become more cost effective. A study reviewing the doctor–patient relationship, doctor–hospital relationship, and doctor–nurse relationship was conducted by Hughes (1995). Three years of patient surveys (50,000) in 45 university hospitals provide parallel measures of reported amounts of patient care performed by nurses and doctors, and the percentage of patients reporting they had a physician case-manager. To complement this study, three case studies were also conducted in academic medical centers with widely varying characteristics, interviewing administrators, physicians, and nurses about the key concepts and dynamics of the study.

The data reveal that managed care growth in local markets is related to variations in the inpatient experience of doctors and nurses, and that staffing ratios appear to be a key intermediate variable between managed care growth and the reported division of labor. The more nurses per bed, the more patients perceive what nurses do, and the less they say doctors do; the more housestaff per bed, the less nurses and doctors are perceived to do. (Hughes, 1995, p. 1146)

Nursing culture also appears to mediate expansion of work roles: nursing schools are correlated with expanded nursing roles, while nursing unions are related to more limited nursing roles (Hughes, 1995).

There has been an increased focus on multidisciplinary teams in delivering high-quality patient care. A study was done to compare the effects of an outpatient interdisciplinary health care team (IHCT) versus usual outpatient care (UC) on Veterans Health Administration (VA) health care costs. The sample consisted of 166 aging male veteran outpatients, and the intervention was an IHCT that provided outpatient comprehensive geriatric assessment, care management, and inpatient consultative care. The conclusions showed a lack of significant difference in VA inpatient, outpatient, and total costs between IHCT and UC. This suggests that interdisciplinary care is unlikely to reduce costs in the short term, and in fact the nonsignificant trends point to the possibility IHCT may increase costs in the short term. Data also showed that IHCT inpatient costs may be influenced by level of social functioning and IHCT outpatient costs may be influenced by patient level of anxiety. The study was not specific about the social functioning or patient anxiety, but any health care institution considering using multidisciplinary teams would have to be aware of these ''soft'' issues and address them with increased education and improvement in communication (Engelhardt, 1994).

The requirement that nurse managers write business communications has increased dramatically, but the practice and teaching of nurse management writing have received little attention. A study consisting of an examination of documents written by nurse managers and interviews with 54 nurse managers and 13 nurse educators indicates that nurse managers spend an average of 12.4 to 16 hours in a 40-hour work week writing.

Results showed that writing a variety of business communications is a crucial career task for nurse managers, directly affecting their professional power. However, most nurse managers interviewed believed their undergraduate education had not prepared them adequately for their workplace writing and perceived a need for professional writing instruction in 4-year nursing programs. (Spears 1996)

The spread of asynchronous electronic communication media such as electronic mail, voice mail, and facsimile continues to revolutionize organizational communication practices. Even within an organization, communication systems have evolved into electronic systems so that information can be disseminated faster. Caregivers first had to learn all about electronic mail systems and now about knowledge-based systems. Knowledge-based mail systems (KMS) are basically intelligent electronic mail systems that have been developed to overcome the communications problems inherent in traditional systems. Control, filtering, categorization, and the setting of priority are built into the KMS (Aiken & Motiwalla, 1993). Caregivers are now being asked to master this electronic aspect of their jobs that is somewhat distant from patient care delivery.

The dissemination of these media is a complex evolutionary process in which social practices and technological developments interact and affect one another. Evolutionary economics suggests that communication practices change as people use multiple similar media in substitutable and complementary ways. At an early stage, newly introduced media become substitutes for existing media and are used in traditional ways. Later, after some period of use and experimentation, a new phase begins in which people reinvent communication practices as they substitute new media for others and develop interdependent, complementary uses that involve multiple media (Soe, 1994). The challenge for workers within the health care organization becomes choosing the correct mechanism or the correct combination of techniques for effective, timely, and relevant communication at multiple levels.

A 1993 study dealing with a lack of research-based understanding of communication patterns of critical care nurses examined the nurse–client interaction in a situation where the client is initially almost totally dependent, physically and emotionally, with varying degrees of dependency throughout their illness (Daingerfield, 1993).

Significance of the study—two common patterns were observed in the critical care unit: Adult–Adult and Parent–Child. The former occurred with information exchange and education while the latter maintained the dependent role of the less powerful. Doctors and administrators expressed power through MD–RN and Administration–RN relationships while nurses expressed power in the RN–patient and RN–family relationships. Movement of nurse-communication towards adult patterning enhances the educative relationship and empowers a health care team to effect change towards the client's maximum health potential. (Daingerfield, 1993, p. 1888)

The relationship between doctors and patients in health care delivery has become increasingly more important as patients assume accountability for the cost and outcomes associated with the care they receive. Identification of variables that contribute to both positive and negative patient experience in managed care systems is crucial to their effectiveness. Managed care has exposed consumers to new arrangements and practices. Changes in attitudes and beliefs wrought by this exposure contribute to an incremental process that is now reshaping the American health care system.

Consumers of health care have more choices and are exercising them. A researcher-prepared, self-administered survey was mailed to a representative sample of 3,500 consumers. A total of 2,700 of the surveys (77 percent) were returned and analyzed. The purpose of the study was to determine public views on health care, health care reform, and the future role of managed care. One conclusion of the survey was that managed care will be an active player in health care in the future, but enrollees will not be coerced into joining managed care plans. Consumers and providers will be free to operate outside the system if they have the financial means. The implication of this study for health maintenance organizations and preferred provider organizations is that they need to consider the attitudes of consumers as they develop protocols for their plans if they are to have an operational advantage (Essaw, 1996).

Another study looking at factors influencing selection of caregivers was conducted by Kirkpatrick (1994). This study focused on the attribute preferences of academic medical center employees who had opted to enroll in the institution's managed care plan. The intent of this research was to determine whether choice criteria differ for enrollees selecting nonacademic primary care physicians and enrollees selecting academic primary care physicians. The results of the study suggest three dimensions that underlie the perceptual evaluations of the importance of the various attributes: product delivery criteria, personal costs/comfort criteria, and physical facilities/care access criteria (Kirkpatrick, 1994).

Once again, consumers have the choice, and depending on their needs and expectations, the market sectors have to adjust to gain their share of business. Including the patient in the evaluation of nurse competence is another trend in the health care environment. In the present era of consumerism, the delivery of nursing care by personnel who are competent has become ever more important. A study was conducted on 46 orthopaedic patients (Paletta, 1995) using interview and observation. The patients' perceptions of nursing competence were categorized into three domains: helping, teaching, and knowing. The categories of these domains include respect, relationship/connection, care, comfort, attention/presence, responsiveness, willingness, helpfulness, trust/security, communication, education, encouragement, promoting independence, nursing process, knowing job, and coordination. The helping, teaching and knowing domains were influenced by nurses' attitudes. That is, the patient interprets all of these elements within the context of how the nurses present themselves and how they communicate these elements to patients (Paletta, 1995).

A study by Greeneich (1995) tested the functional relationships between the variables of nurse practitioner attributes and behaviors, patient perceptions of the managed care system, and outcomes of patient satisfaction and their intention to return to and recommend the managed care system. The 86 subjects were primarily female and Caucasian, and had some college education. Both negative and positive experiences emerged. In the positive service experience, nurse practitioner inherent personality characteristics and practice accounted for 35 percent of the variance found in attributes of satisfaction. Attributes of satisfaction explained 22 percent of the variance in the patients' positive perception of the managed care system. In the negative service experience, the inherent personality characteristics explained 25 percent of the variance. A post hoc analysis of variance indicated that a difference in patient perceptions occurred relative to the number of visits during a one-month period. Frequency of exposure to health care personnel attributes and behaviors had an effect on patient perceptions of their managed care experience, and their intention to return and to recommend the system (Greeneich, 1995). Since consumers place more value on the type and frequency of contact with their caregiver, the communication skills of the caregiver are highly consequential.

Even pharmaceutical companies are placing a growing value on communicating with patients directly. Traditionally, pharmaceutical companies have used advertising to inform physicians of the characteristics and benefits of prescription medications. Now, patients, managed care organizations, and government payers are just as influential in prescription drug selection. A study conducted by Basara (1995) looked at the relationship between direct-to-consumer advertising (DTCA) and two measures of effectiveness: new prescription volume and consumer information-search activity. The study involved 1,358 consumers in demographically similar and representative cities of the United States: "Discriminant analysis results suggested that consumers who request information in response to direct-to-consumer advertisement differ only on prescription medication knowledge, such that they perceive themselves to know more than consumers who do not search for information" (Basara, 1995). This study illustrates the growing trend of consumers wanting to know more about any level of care they receive in order to make more informed choices. Once again, communication from the caregiver would be invaluable in helping the consumer make a choice between two medications or two providers of care.

Researchers have recognized for years that patient satisfaction, adherence to treatment, and appropriate utilization of health care services depend largely on the quality of communication between doctors and patients during office visits. As health care delivery and outcomes measurement continue to evolve, evaluating and assessing the impact of effective communications on bottom-line costs will likely become more commonplace. The challenge becomes how to measure the impact of health care provider skills on the outcomes and how to develop interventions that improve the communication process between doctors and patients.

The Roter Interaction Analysis System (RIAS) is an assessment tool developed at Johns Hopkins University that can be used to measure the impact of physician skills on both patients and cost containment. It is now widely accepted as the most effective tool available for evaluating the communication skills of physicians (Gibson, 1994).

Evaluating patient and staff outcomes is another measure used to evaluate quality and customer service orientation by a health care delivery system. Goode (1994) conducted research to evaluate patient and staff outcomes with Hospital Based Managed Care (HBMC) intervention. Caremaps and Nursing Case Management were implemented, and the effects on patient satisfaction, staff collaboration, staff autonomy, and staff satisfaction were determined. The results support the use of the HBMC system for delivery of care. Patients were more satisfied with their care under the new delivery system, and they were particularly more satisfied with their participation in decisions. The multidisciplinary staff that worked on the experimental unit had increased job satisfaction as they worked in the HBMC system of care delivery. Nurses who applied and were selected for Case Management positions had higher levels of collaboration than other nurses, higher levels of job satisfaction with quality of care than other nurses, and their autonomy increased as they worked within the HBMC delivery system. Multidisciplinary team members also had higher levels of collaboration than other multidisciplinary staff on the experimental unit, and their job satisfaction with the quality of care delivered increased under this new care delivery system (Goode, 1994).

With this increased level of participation by the patient and increased interaction and team work by the care delivery team, communication becomes the key once again. To be truly effective at decision making, patients must understand their role in the decision-making process as well as the information being presented. Similarly, the multidisciplinary team members must be able to communicate with each other at a higher level and on multiple levels to make sure the message is correctly delivered.

The qualitative outcomes of certain medications on certain ailments were studied in 90 patients on long-term drug treatments (Fallsberg, 1993). The results indicated that patients do have qualitatively different conceptions about medicines, side effects, and natural products. Within the study group, a specific "thought syndrome" concerning the medication and the patients' expectations of the contacts with health care professionals emerged. Fallsberg (1993) claimed that patients suffering from different diseases or symptoms have to be addressed in ways that take their thought syndromes regarding medicines and medications into consideration.

The present shortcomings in didactic measures in health and medical care may to a large extent originate in the endeavor to accomplish a general way of conveying knowledge. Fallsberg (1993) believes, however, that if everyone is addressed in a similar way, no one will be addressed in an adequate way.

Internal Communication

Internal communication encompasses the information exchange that takes place within an organization and can be formal or informal in nature. Both sorts of communication need to be managed effectively in today's rapidly changing health care environment.

Formal internal communication occurs through recognized and established media within the organization. Company newsletters, memoranda, and formal meetings are the most common methods used to disseminate information within the organization. Much has been written about the need for effective internal communication. KPMG, a "Big Six" accounting firm, surveyed senior executives regarding managing change during corporate restructuring. This study determined that one of the organization's primary concerns should be identifying and developing individual communication strategies for each stakeholder group. This ensures that each group receives the message. The study also determined that the communication process must provide an avenue for feedback, in which the employees can express their concerns, opinions, and make recommendations (Luedecke, 1996). This type of communication is especially important to health care organizations, given the myriad of downsizings and reorganizations occurring in the industry.

The health care field has seen a proliferation in the number of mergers and acquisitions to enhance competitiveness. The management of a company that makes a new acquisition should open the lines of communication with their new employees to help them adjust to the changes. Meetings, newsletters, and focus groups can be effective tools in helping new employees enter the organization and in merging the two corporate cultures (Dilenschneider, 1995).

Increased emphasis on organizational communication is particularly important in view of the results obtained from mergers. The short-term effects of mergers on hospital operations were studied by Alexander, Halpern, and Lee (1996). Three areas of hospital operations were examined: scale of activity, personnel/staffing practices, and operating efficiency. General merger effects occurred in areas related to operating efficiency. Mergers resulted in a slowing of preexisting trends rather than a dramatic improvement in operating efficiency. Evidence was more pronounced among hospitals merging in the later periods of the study.

A recent study completed by E. C. Murphy, Ltd. (Murphy, 1996), in conjunction with the American Society for Work Redesign (ASWD), points to serious problems—including increased levels of morbidity and mortality—with much of the across-the-board downsizing that has occurred in hospitals today. The three-year study, which randomly reviewed the restructuring practices of 281 general acute care institutions, found that

1. Hospitals that underwent 4 percent across-the-board reductions in workforce faced a 200 percent likelihood of an increase in patient morbidity and mortality; a 7 percent reduction equaled a risk of over 400 percent.

2. Hospitals that downsized across-the-board to FTE (full-time equivalent) levels of less than 3.25 per adjusted patient day also stood a 200 percent likelihood of increased morbidity and mortality.

3. Increasing levels of morbidity and mortality were associated more with how restructuring occurred (i.e., across-the-board downsizing) than with case mix, operating margins, or other factors.

4. In hospitals that instituted ''cut or else'' policies, cost savings achieved through cuts were lost within 12 to 18 months due to a ''backfill'' effect that occurred as workers and managers fought back.

5. Forty-eight percent of CEOs in hospitals that cut jobs across-the-board were no longer employed by the institution 18 to 24 months later.

Conversely, a second study performed by Murphy and the ASWD revealed that a data-driven process of work redesign can have positive effects. In a review involving over 170,000 health care workers in more than 300 organizations, including 117 general acute care hospitals, they found that when compared to their counterparts in the previous study, none of the hospitals using a data-driven process experienced any increase in morbidity or mortality, even when workforce reductions of 4 percent or more took place. One year after cost reductions were put in place, 90 percent of the organizations experienced no backfill and 70 percent were able to make additional cuts in operating costs of between 3 and 8 percent. CEOs using work redesign experienced a turnover rate of just 11 percent, and half of the turnovers among CEOs in these organizations were due to promotions or their equivalent (Murphy, 1996).

In a summary of the growing body of research on internal communication, Larkin and Larkin (1995) analyzed ways to improve communication with frontline employees. Based on the numerous studies discussed, the authors concluded that employees consider the supervisor to be the most dependable source of information, while executives are not considered as highly as supervisors. Therefore, it is advisable to rely on supervisors to relate information to the frontline employee.

Communication breakdowns between managers and scientists as discussed by Gaines (1994) may be analogous to those existing between administrators and clinical staff within a health care environment. Breakdowns in communication result from differences in training, psychology, language, and thinking patterns. As health care organizations continue to downsize and competition increases, more executives and managers will need to have a strong business background. Many of these individuals lack clinical knowledge and understanding, resulting in a breakdown of communication with the clinical staff. Professionals in the workplace communicate across organizational boundaries to achieve internal and partnership goals. Problems often arise among professionals when attempts to achieve the internal goals of their unit conflict with the external goals of the organization. One of the more recent studies in this area looks at the concerns professionals might have when they communicate across organizational boundaries, as well as which social and rhetorical strategies, if any, they might utilize (Spilka, 1995).

A recent study was conducted to examine employee motives for communicating with their coworkers and superiors. The results indicate that the primary motivation for females communicating with coworkers is for affection and for male employees it is control. Employees who communicate for affection report high levels of job satisfaction and moderate levels of commitment and satisfaction with their coworkers (Anderson and Martin, 1995).

Formal internal communication is becoming more important in the rapidly changing health care environment. Information needs to be disseminated quickly and effectively. There is currently a lack of research data drawn directly from the health care field. Many studies focus on groups and organizational types that parallel health care organizations, and conclusions from these studies can be helpful. Communication should help employees perform their jobs better and become more productive members of the organization.

The primary medium of informal internal communication networks within a company is accurately called a grapevine. Grapevines are comprised of many overlapping branches that are wide, not linear, in design. There are many articles and studies whose analysis and content deal with effectively managing the grapevine. Good supervisors never communicate through the grapevine but listen to it carefully. The main role of the grapevine within an organization is to reflect the concerns of the employees. A grapevine is most active in the absence of official and accurate communication (Hull, 1994).

A recent survey on office gossip revealed that workers who gossip know more about what is going on in their organizations than those who do not gossip. The grapevine covers topics that are mostly work-related, including business changes and challenges (86 percent) and office intrigues (79 percent). According to 57 percent of the respondents, the grapevine is the only means for them to learn what is happening within their organizations (Did You Hear, 1994). This shows a lack of effective formal internal communication. Only 7 percent of the respondents felt that management communicated effectively (Galpin, 1995). Results such as these add emphasis to the need for timely, accurate, formal communication in health care organizations during periods of unprecedented change.

External Communication

External communication encompasses such areas as interorganizational communication and competition, advertising, and mergers and acquisitions. Among recent studies and trends within these areas, competitor analysis and interfirm rivalry have received a fair amount of attention from the academic world. According to Chen (1996), competitor analysis has been studied by Hamel and Prahalad (1990), Porac and Thomas (1994), Porter (1980, 1985), and Zajac and Bazerman (1991). Interfirm rivalry has been studied by Bettis and Weeks (1987), D'Aveni (1994), MacMillian, McCaffery, and Van Wijk (1985). Chen (1996) then reviewed these previous studies and introduced two firm, specific theory-based constructs: market commonality, developed from the literature on multiple-point competition, and resource similarity, derived from the resource-based theory of the firm. The joint consideration of these two constructs shows the complementarity of these two prominent but contrasting strategy theories. In particular, the study highlights the importance of market and firm volatility in capturing competitive relationships.

Proven and Milward (1995) performed a comparative study of interorganizational networks of mental health delivery in four U.S. cities, leading to a preliminary theory of network effectiveness. Data were collected from surveys, interviews, documents and observations. Results showed that network effectiveness could be explained by various structural and contextual factors—specifically, network integration, external control, systems stability, and environmental resource munificence (adequate funding). A major finding of this study was the important role that state governments play through the power of funding.

Luke, Ozcan, and Olden (1995) examined the formation of local hospital systems (LHSs) in urban markets by the end of 1992. Three characteristics of LHS formation are examined: LHS penetration of urban areas, LHS size, and number of LHS members located just outside the urban boundaries (Luke et al., 1995). The main finding of this study was the effect that rival threats might have on the formation of LHSs. Among the market variables examined, the number of competitors was extremely important. Thus, LHSs are formed by hospitals attempting to improve market position and interorganizational power (Luke et al., 1995).

The health care field has seen a recent explosion in the types of advertising utilized and in advertising spending. The newer media receiving the advertising dollar include television, newspapers, yellow pages, and billboards. The focus on these mass media is due in part to an increase in competition between health care providers and a shift in advertising philosophy. There have been some recent studies concerning the effectiveness of the advertising expenditures and the messages that are being received. A study done in 1993 by the Annenberg School for Communication looked at health care reform advertising. This study determined that on both sides of the issue fear was the most prevalent advertising theme. The researchers also determined that 59 percent of 73 television commercials and 25 percent of 125 print ads used misleading information to present their viewpoint. The advertisements were more likely to invite false inferences than to misstate facts (Schwartz, 1994).

Advertising is also shifting from conventional public relations styles to more aggressive marketing-oriented press communications. The shift is away from the boring product-based press release of the past to a more reactive approach that "features a well organized series of company-initiated information projects that support marketing plans, build a leadership image and create a substantial competitive advantage over time" (Deruyte, 1994).

A national survey sponsored by the Chicago-based Academy for Health Services Marketing found that most medical groups that do advertise have increased their advertising budgets over the past two years. This survey had a sample size of 553 groups, the majority of which had fewer than 25 physicians (Zimmerman, 1994). As in earlier studies, the main reason cited for causing the increase in the advertising budget was increased competition. The most common medium of advertising used by the groups was the Yellow Pages. Newspaper advertising is employed by some of the groups but is not the predominant form of advertising. Other forms of advertising tried by practitioners included direct mailings, coupon books sent to new residents, and billboards. Some industry professionals recommend avoiding these types of advertisements based on the reasoning that they could be sending out the wrong message to recipients. Advertisements such as these could present an image of a physician who is unprofessional or one who cannot attract patients. The location of the advertiser weighs heavily in the decision of how to advertise. Physicians in more traditional markets avoid advertising, while physicians in more competitive markets are more likely to advertise. These types of advertisements can be tracked and their cost effectiveness assessed. Physicians can have office personnel track how many patients use the office services as a result of specific types of advertisement. The revenue produced by the advertisement can then be measured against the cost of the advertisement. This type of system would allow the physician to judge the cost of various advertising media versus other means of gaining new patients (Zimmerman, 1994).

A related analysis found that 35 percent of adults use the Yellow Pages before selecting a physician, and, of those, about two-thirds look at one or more block advertisements. This analysis speculates that the Yellow Pages will continue to be a valuable source of patients because

1. Consumers are more concerned about health care issues and costs.
2. Chronic conditions have replaced acute conditions, allowing the patients to have more time to make health care decisions.
3. Outpatient treatment has increased the patient's role in decision making. (Meyers, 1995)

Another study looked at the attitudes of physicians toward pharmaceutical product advertising. The purpose of this study was to explore the impact of physicians' attitudes toward pharmaceutical company advertising on prescription writing habits and responsiveness to patient requests. A total of 148 physicians participated in the study with a response rate of 59.2 percent. The results showed that physician attitudes toward various pharmaceutical advertising varied widely based on subgroup type. In general, older physicians (those in practice more than 20 years) and internists responded less favorably to pharmaceutical advertising and to patient requests for brand-name drugs. Younger, less experienced physicians were more responsive to patient inquiries and requests for prescription drugs. Physicians in group practices and those in urban settings are also more responsive to patient requests and inquiries. As noted in previous studies, physicians have traditionally viewed advertising with skepticism. While limited, this study may be showing a trend toward a more open-minded physician population (Petroshius et al., 1995).

A recent econometrics study examined aggregate cigarette advertising and its effect on total market sales of the product. This study also looked at the effect on demand of cigarette advertising restrictions, including complete bans. The result determined that aggregate cigarette advertising has had little or no influence on total cigarette demand in the United States in the recent past (Duffy, 1996).

Intercultural Communication

Cultural diversity is becoming an increasingly important factor affecting the growth and development of health care organizations. Efficient communication is an absolute necessity when trying to manage a heterogeneous workforce and provide services to a diverse customer base. Cultural diversity can be the result of a variety of different factors.

The first obstacle that needs to be overcome in a more diverse cultural environment is the language barrier. As the workforce continues to become more diverse, verbal communication becomes increasingly difficult. The difficulties arise when communication breaks down within the organization itself (between organizational members) or between the organization and a market/customer that communicates in a different language. An organization's ability to communicate with a varied customer base in the native language of that customer can be a great asset and will be a necessity as the economy shifts to a global marketplace. Organizations that cannot effectively and efficiently communicate will be unable to compete internationally. This is especially important within the health care setting where efficient communication can be the difference between life and death. Language barriers also exist within the health care organization. The entire staff, including administration and clinical personnel, needs the ability to communicate effectively in a vocabulary that is universally understood within the organization. As the workforce becomes more diversified, individuals who speak a different primary language and who were schooled and trained in different cultural environments are becoming more common. In the health care field, it is important that these individuals communicate effectively and provide high-quality care in spite of their varied backgrounds (Cascio, 1995).

Regional, ethnic, or national culture provides people with an identity and includes family patterns, customs, social classes, religions, political beliefs, clothing, music, food, literature, and laws (Cascio, 1995). Adapting to cultural diversity implies understanding and respecting the cultural backgrounds of others. A lack of knowledge regarding a person's culture can result in misunderstandings, decreased productivity, and loss of trust. Organizations must be willing to learn about and understand different cultures and adapt their present systems to interact with these various cultures.

For example: "Anglo" cultures subscribe to the norm of egalitarianism: "All men are created equal." But many non-Anglo cultures proceed from an understanding that people are not created equal—that relational hierarchies dictate, often from birth, one's place in the family, the clan, the work organization, and society (Vandyk, 1995). Ashley Merritt performed a study analyzing the effects of cultural differences on the interactions and command roles within aviation. This research project involved asking 250 pilots of 36 nationalities (60 percent from Anglo countries) for comments. Among the frustrations mentioned, the first was language. Relationships can become strained or degenerate due to customs conflicts, language barriers, and different humor (Vandyk, 1995). Many of the findings would likely be transferable to a health care setting, for an airplane cockpit and flight crew share many similarities with the hierarchy within a hospital or health care setting. Studies of this type are going to be needed in the health care field as the workforce and marketplace become more diversified. Studies will also be needed to analyze the effectiveness of cultural awareness training.

Health care, like most other major industries, is shifting to a global marketplace. Business will need to learn to communicate and adapt in a globalized environment. This is especially true given the technological advances that are "shrinking" the world. A great deal of attention has been focused on restructuring American corporations. However, international corporations have been restructuring as well. The international corporation is different from the international corporation of previous days. The new corporation has a global viewpoint, transcends national identity, and sees the entire world as its market (Howard, 1995). Studies are needed which consider the effects of the "global marketplace" on health care organizations and how they are changing to meet this new environment. These studies will be especially important as technological advances are made and the economy becomes more international.

Computer Technology

Innovations in technology have traditionally involved medical advances. Increasingly, administrators and caregivers are seeking sophisticated electronic and computerized equipment to enhance their communication.

The new interest in communication technology has stimulated varied research. A study was conducted to see if people tended to use a mix of mechanisms when using electronic communication media. The findings showed that several emergent communication genres were formed by recombining traits from traditional and emergent genres. An unexpected number of voicemail messages were long, technical, and included numbers and jargon. To make voicemail easier to process, people incorporated structural traits from electronic mail into the content of voicemail (Soe, 1994). As these technologies become more commonplace, people use electronic mail, voice mail, and facsimile in increasingly similar ways.

A mail survey explored attitudes toward the use of computer-mediated communication (CMC). The survey was of faculty members in professional organizations related to the study of mass communication, consumer behavior, and advertising and public relations. A 59 percent rate of response was obtained (n = 607) from both users and nonusers. The majority (73 percent) of faculty in the sample used computer mediated communication, and quantitative and qualitative measures indicated that use was likely to increase in the future. Younger age was significantly associated with use of computer-mediated communication. Women in the sample were more likely to use CMC and to use the functions associated with higher productivity. Results suggest that the perception of change caused by the use of computer-mediated communication exceeds actual change. Open-ended responses on the questionnaire indicated a degree of anxiety on the part of users and nonusers alike: users felt they should use CMC to a greater extent, and nonusers believed they would begin using CMC in the future (White, 1995).

Another study related to CMC examined the relationship between CMC and social support. This study focused on patients infected with HIV where social support and information are critical but can be limited by time pressures, geographic location, education, physician mobility, and the ability to act during a crisis. The study had two objectives:

1. To apply a methodology for analyzing CMC systems designed to provide social systems.
2. To examine the relationship between how people communicate in CMC systems and the nature of the social support they receive.

The findings were: first, self-esteem support is positively correlated with confidence in communication by the speaker about the other's experience. Second, either other types of support (appraisal support, belonging support, and tangible support) are irrelevant to CMC systems, or there are no significant relationships between them and the different communication role dimensions (Luarn, 1993).

A further study investigated how people interact with computer technology. Twenty-eight secretaries and support staff were given a word processing test to assess their level of proficiency. Out of this group, four novices and six advanced users were selected for nondirective interviewing. The study found that advanced and novice users shared very different thought worlds about word processing. In addition, it was found that some novices tended to learn new word processing skills only when their work demanded they do so (Chen, L., 1992). This is a direct parallel to the unit secretary who knows very little about a computer but can become an expert at computer order entry if the health care organization requires it.

In addition to tools for the caregiver, tools for the patient have emerged on the market. Patients are still requiring the personal touch but are growing impatient with playing telephone tag or making repeat office visits. Use of technology for more effective communication has increased. For example, in some areas of the United States, patients can get their lab results and follow up instructions by phone. An automated message system allows physicians to tell their patients personally the results of laboratory tests without significant delays. The message on the system is secure and must be retrieved using a code only the patient is aware of. Various reports can be generated by the physician to indicate unretrieved messages and the date and time of retrieved messages. No empirical studies have been done, but interviews with patients using the system have shown positive results (Borzo, 1994).

Other enabling technologies are:

- ISDN (integrated services digital network)—essentially a digital telephone line that sends data without being converted to analog, enabling the sender to send greater amounts of voice, data, and video information.

- ATM (asynchronous transfer mode)—allows the transfer of information worldwide regardless of the "end-system" or type of information. With ATM, the goal is one international standard.

- Videoconferencing—involves the simultaneous interactive (two-way) transmission of sound, full-motion video, images, and textual information between two or more sites. The use of videoconferencing can have a dramatic impact on patient care delivery and the provision of medical training, and can provide a convenient and cost-effective methodology for meetings among the senior management of affiliated providers.

- Wireless voice and data transmission.

- Remote access—provides physicians with access to computer-based information from offsite locations. There is also a potential need for patients to access their records.

- Computer to PBX integration—the PBX server has evolved from merely a voice server to a more enterprise-wide server that will accommodate true voice and data integration.

- Voice/data/video integration and multimedia.

- Local Area Networks (LAN), wireless PBX and video technology—concepts such as computer-based patient records and community health care information networks are dependent on how today's technology can integrate data, voice, and image processing.

- Fax store and forward—a technology that can be deployed through voice mail, LAN, and the health care organization's information system. Depending on the level of integration, message notification can be accomplished through a telephone message-waiting light, PC, stutter dial tone, pager, or through outdialing to another telephone number. Users can mark fax messages as urgent, confidential, return receipt, and delivered at a future time.

- EDI (Electronic Data Interchange)—a fast, inexpensive mechanism that has streamlined the human resources aspect of material management ordering and replaced the use of paper documents as a vehicle for communicating information.
- IVR (interactive voice response)—enables hospitals to decrease time wasted on routine, inbound calls by providing answers to common questions automatically.
- Voice mail/automated attendant—utilizes digital technology to mimic the human voice for storage and routing.

Recent developments in user interface software such as hypermedia have opened up a wide range of possibilities in storing both textual and pictorial data in a medical record system. Since clinicians have to incorporate this electronic record into their caregiving practice, the usability of the system requires an accommodation to the user's background, previous experience with electronic records and previous use of computer usage. (Chen, K. L., 1994).

In a study of an instructional program designed to prepare nurses to use a clinical information system (Renfro, 1995), nurses' knowledge level and attitudes toward clinical systems were measured prior to and immediately after the course. Program evaluation was conducted at the time of the post-test. Participants completed the third and final surveys for knowledge and attitudes four to six weeks after attending the course. Pretest results showed that attitudes were already positive, although their knowledge of system features and functions was weak. Post-test results demonstrated a significant increase in level of knowledge and positive attitudes toward a computerized nursing care planning system. This positive relationship was not sustained from post-test to final survey. At the final survey, no consistent pattern of changes in knowledge and attitude scores was observed. Both prior computer experience and prior clinical experience preparing nursing care plans and nursing diagnoses exerted significant influence on pretest attitude outcomes (Renfro, 1995).

This study is significant when viewed from the organizational communication perspective. The lack of interaction or communication between post-test and final survey potentially reversed the positive effects of the training. Education and communication work hand-in-hand when dealing with new frontiers. Computers in health care are a new frontier, and increased communication about technology, reinforcement, or interaction with technology will be increasingly beneficial.

As more health care organizations move toward electronic medical records, data are collected for research and study of utilization patterns. These data can be used to streamline practice patterns and reduce costs. A study focusing on the efforts of utilization managers to identify on inappropriate patient admissions was done with automatic, daily, concurrent screening of inpatient days of care at a hospital with an electronic patient record. Inappropriate patients are those who can be treated more cost-effectively in an outpatient facility or who are unnecessarily delayed in their care. Research data showed that the automated system was twice as efficient as random sampling in detecting inappropriate days of care, enabling cost-effective daily review of all patients on three nursing divisions. Experimental data support significant projected annual health care cost reduction (Nelson, 1994).

A key piece of the clinical information system is a clinical data repository. A repository, or data warehouse, could help the health care industry by providing an independent platform for storing sanitized data retrieved from legacy systems. These data can be used for research and analysis as well as for sketching a patient's medical history over time. A repository has been characterized as the technological solution that will make clinical information systems a reality, but the market is confused. "Data from a recent poll indicates a 50% growth in the number of hospitals using a clinical data depository. However, developers of data repositories claim they only have 14% of the market while traditional patient-care vendors claim over 63%" (Mathys, 1995).

A study describing the impact of implementing a fully integrated hospital information system was conducted. The study focused on a ward's ordering and communication component, which has the greatest effect on the way nurses deliver and record their care. The study covered the eighteen-month implementation period. Its conclusions are summarized as follows:

Results show that the full potential of the system has not yet been realized and demonstrates the threat imposed by computer technology to the values and norms of traditional nursing practice. The speed of implementation and the inadequate preparation of the nurses are major themes impacting on the way the nurses use the system and their attitudes to particular aspects of it. Although the results show that, in general, the nurses would not wish to revert to manual procedures, problems remain with key areas of their practice and the effect of the technology on the professional role of the nurse. (Hampton, 1994, p. 688)

Health care is both a community service and a competitive product, and the challenge for the organization will be to balance these roles. The vision for the future includes all health care providers having access to the electronic patient record of the entire market. Early adopters of community information sharing and those who successfully incorporate this sharing into their processes will best benefit the community while achieving a competitive advantage.

Community health information networks (CHINs) are an evolving concept. CHINs provide a structure for sharing financial and clinical information among a defined group of entities. Several key infrastructure pieces need to be established, such as what "community" will be included, what technical infrastructure to use, what organization or group of organizations will lead the CHIN development effort, what types of information will be shared, and how to safeguard confidentiality (Weaver, 1995).

FUTURE RESEARCH DIRECTIONS

Based on the current level of information and given the profound changes that are occurring, the need for continued research on health care organizations is clear. Questions about the nature of investigation are relevant because traditional approaches to studying organizations have been based primarily on personal communication with another individual. Understanding the complexities of the health care industry undergoing rapid and tumultuous change will require a deeper analysis of the communication process as more information is shared with more stakeholders.

Wheatley (1992) argues that our organizations are enlivened through the deepening of our relationships with each other and our willingness to put communication at the center of our work. Writing about humanizing the face of health care from Wheatley's perspective, Clark (1996) states:

In a living, learning organization, the essential role of management is to be a beacon of information—communicating the vision of the organization, its purpose and direction, its values and desired behaviors. Such clarity allows employees to answer questions like "what is the meaning of my work?" and to shape their behavior in alignment with the organization's purpose. Wheatley believes that the quality of communication and dialogue is the vital sign of organizational health. (p. 66)

As Bell (1996) observes, "the successful healthcare executive of tomorrow will have to do a better job of communicating with staff, patients and payers, as well as participating in health policy initiatives" (p. 25).

Based on the findings presented here, future health care organizational communication research should address processes of communication throughout the organization, its stakeholders and customers; transitional leadership communication strategies; and the application of technology to improve the quality and speed of information exchange.

Management is communication. The successful transformation of the U.S. health care system may well depend on the effective use of research-based organizational communication practices.

8

Health Communication
and Health Policy

Mary Jo Deering

SYNOPSIS

Health policy and practice are increasingly focused on how to maintain health, encourage the appropriate use of medical services, and promote competition based on value and quality of care. There is a role for health communication in each of these areas. However, the successful application of health communication principles may involve expanded purposes, content, and strategies. In addition to prevention-oriented behavioral risk messages conveyed through mass media and community-based programs, there is now the opportunity to shape individual decisions regarding health and medical care through customized approaches. Managed care can provide broad access to health care consumers. Moreover, new developments in communication technology, including the expanded reach of the Internet, permit a level of interactivity (with other people as well as with intelligent software) that may enhance effectiveness. These concurrent and equally challenging opportunities in both health and communication call for a broad research agenda. This would ideally build on the rich knowledge base about behavior change and diverse communication media. It would explore such issues as how different people seek and synthesize health information; population preferences for different media; the effectiveness of various media for specific purposes and content; and the appropriate design for new media communications.

INTRODUCTION

Developments in health policy and practice offer compelling new opportunities for health communication to contribute to both the nation's health status and the status of the nation's health care system. These trends also have implications for the purposes, content, and approaches of health communication, which in turn suggest a new research agenda.

Critics of the American health care system state that it is not about health, it does not care, and it is not a system. We focus on illness and medicine, say the critics. Decisions are based on financial bottom lines. Health care delivery is fragmented, although the move toward managed care has brought some integration.

Health policy develops across a wide spectrum of interests and actors. Ongoing discussions about health care reform confirm that a broad universe of stakeholders—including the public—must be involved. In the meantime, the health care sector is rapidly restructuring itself.

Financial pressures are behind much of the change. In 1995, health care expenditures reached nearly $1.0 trillion. By 2000, annual spending is projected to reach $1.5 trillion (Burner & Waldo, 1995). The federal government, which pays over 36 percent of all national health care expenditures, shares the concerns of states and private health care organizations about reducing costs. The movement at all levels and in all sectors is toward managed care, which uses financial incentives and management controls to stimulate efficiencies and limit use of expensive medical services. Enrollment in managed care organizations (MCOs) is rising rapidly, from 6 million people in 1976 to 50 million in 1994 and an estimated 100 million in 2000 (Coile, 1995).

Reducing Need and Demand for Medical Care

There is mounting evidence that unnecessary or inappropriate health care utilization can be reduced through innovative programs to prevent health problems and promote sound medical choices (Fries, 1994; Fries et al., 1993; Vickery, 1995). It is estimated that a significant proportion of the need for medical care is generated by preventable conditions (Fries, 1994). Research shows that approximately 50 percent of all deaths are attributable to risk factors such as tobacco use, diet and activity patterns, alcohol and drug abuse, firearms and motor vehicles, and unsafe sexual practices (McGinnis & Foege, 1993; U.S. Department of Health and Human Services, Public Health Service [HHS/PHS], 1991, 1994). Medical care alone has only contributed perhaps 5 of the 30 additional years of life expectancy gained by Americans over this century (Bunker, Frazier, & Mosteller, 1994). Programs that focus on reducing need for medical care employ a range of health promotion and disease prevention interventions, many of which include health communication. Such programs have long been part of public health. What is new is the increased attention of MCOs to these public health approaches based on primary prevention.

In addition, part of the demand for medical care includes requests for services that are unlikely to improve health or may be inappropriate (Fries, 1994; U.S. Department of Health and Human Services, Office of Public Health and Science [HHS/OPHS], 1996). It includes doctor visits for conditions that are usually self-limiting, such as colds, as well as procedures that may be unnecessary or of questionable efficacy in the particular circumstance, such as prescribing antibiotics for the common cold, some hysterectomies, or prostatectomies. Patients' perceptions of need and their preferences can influence their requests for or acceptance of these services. Perceptions are shaped by patients' knowledge of the risks and benefits of medical care, ability to assess the medical problem, perceived severity of the problem, ability to self-treat or self-manage the problem, and confidence in their ability to manage the problem (Vickery, 1995). Information and education are clearly among the variables influencing these perceptions. Patient preferences about treatment options reflect both knowledge and values. Patient preferences have not traditionally been the primary factor in medical decisions. However, there is growing interest in patient involvement as a means of reducing utilization of inappropriate or unnecessary medical services and improving health outcomes. At the same time, patients and consumers have become more proactive in seeking—even demanding—such involvement. In a recent national survey of 37,000 patients, more than a third of hospital patients and 21 percent of patients treated in physicians' offices or clinics reported that they do not have enough opportunity to discuss their treatment. Twenty-eight percent reported that they could not get as much information as they wanted (American Hospital Association & Picker Institute [AHA/Picker], 1996).

Self-management or self-care interventions can result in an improved sense of empowerment and more responsible participation in managing one's own health or that of family members or others in one's care. These approaches are often linked to community-based self-help organizations that can also provide information and support (Ferguson, 1995; Pingree et al., 1994).

The Empowered Health Care Consumer

Research has shown for years that informed and involved patients are more likely to comply with treatment plans and have better outcomes (Greenfield, Kaplan, & Ware, 1985; Joos & Hickam, 1990; Lorig, Mazonson, & Holman, 1993). Involvement can also encourage a healthier life and higher satisfaction with medical care (Deber, 1994a). It may even lower health care costs (Lorig et al., 1993; Vickery, Golazewski, & Wright, 1988; Wagner, Barry, Barlow, & Fowler, 1995). In current health policy discussions, the concept of "the empowered health care consumer" is receiving new attention. This encompasses informed choices about health care plans and providers, patient-centered care, shared decision making, or even self-care. The common element in these approaches is the individual. As Rockefeller (1994) states:

We cannot achieve the goals of health care reform without attending to the way individual decisions are made regarding people's health. This includes the choices people make about the healthfulness of their lifestyles, choices whether or not to consult a health professional, and choices made by patients and providers concerning early detection, diagnosis and management of their illnesses. (p. 4)

Health care plans and providers are developing increasingly effective approaches for engaging their patients (Health Commons Institute, 1995). Kaiser Permanente, for example, has adopted a version of the *Healthwise Handbook*, a self-care manual about staying healthy, treating common problems, managing medication, participating in medical decisions, and generally getting the most out of the health system (Kemper, 1994). Even within hospitals, some model programs are expanding patient participation through enhanced information and education (Giloth, 1990).

Quality of Care

There is also more emphasis on measuring the quality of care. Employers want to hold health plans accountable for the quality of care they offer to their employees; consumers want to be able to judge the quality of the providers available. A number of health care organizations and government entities have begun to gather and publish data that allow corporate purchasers, state agencies, and consumers to compare the performance of competing health plans. These documents are commonly referred to as ''report cards.'' Such report cards are becoming increasingly consumer-oriented, such as the Consumer Assessment of Health Plans (CAHPS) (U.S. Department of Health and Human Services, Agency for Health Care Policy and Research [HHS/AHCPR], 1996) or the Mental Health Statistics Improvement Program (HHS/SAMHSA, 1996). That is, quality is measured not only by objective elements like the delivery of key preventive services, but also by consumer satisfaction. And consumers themselves rank communication as a key factor (see Figure 8.1).

As consumers come to value communication and involvement, their expectations will rise. Report cards that explicitly survey patients on their receipt of adequate information to make informed choices will generate additional pressures on health care providers. However, given the reality of increasing time constraints in the patient visit, it will be very difficult for physicians themselves, or even ancillary staff, like advice nurses, to completely fulfill these communication needs. Health care providers may turn to ever-more sophisticated health information packages to help accomplish this function.

New Media Opportunities

New technologies emerging from the computer and telecommunications industries offer tantalizing prospects for more effective health communication for both health promotion/disease prevention and for demand management (Alemi & Stephens, 1996; Brennan, Schneider, & Tornquist, 1997; Chamberlain, 1996; Deering, 1997; Harris, 1995). Interactive multimedia software is available for

Figure 8.1
Consumers Rate Importance of Communication in Quality of Care (Percentage rating element "extremely important")

1. Physician discusses conditions, options, and outcomes: 80%

2. Physician listens to patient's health concerns: 72%

3. Physician asks questions about patient's general health: 66%

4. Physician discovers and explores patient's beliefs about what is causing the problem and what (s)he believes will help: 55%

5. Physician encourages patient to state treatment preferences: 53%

Source: Bayer Institute for Health Care Communication, in *Managed Health Care News*, March 1966.

use on personal computers in homes, schools, clinics, worksites, and other community settings like libraries. The more highly visual programs are helpful not only for low literacy audiences; those with higher reading levels also show improved learning with graphic and video presentations (Boberg et al., 1997; Pingree et al., 1994; Said, Consoli, & Jean, 1994). Computer-based shared-decision-making programs under development are often tailored to specific conditions that can draw out and integrate patient's individual health risks and personal/family values, and even incorporate the "vicarious experience" of others who have been in similar situations. (Brennan & Ripich, 1994; Kasper, Mulley, & Wennberg, 1992; Pingree et al., 1994; Wennberg, 1995). These decision-making programs may be designed to be used by patients and clinicians simultaneously, facilitating complex decisions in situations of uncertainty (Kasper et al., 1992; National Information Infrastructure Task Force [NIITF] 1995; Wennberg, 1995).

Networked technologies extend these benefits by improving access to an infinitely wider pool of information and, perhaps most important, to other individuals and organizations that can share knowledge and experience about the problems and options at hand. Some networked health communication systems also address both health promotion/disease prevention and demand management/decision-support goals. For example, CHESS (Comprehensive Health Enhancement Support System) has modules for several health conditions. It includes computer-based programs and links to information services, analysis services, and communications services that connect the user to health professionals and peer discussion groups (Boberg et al., 1997) In one controlled study of HIV-positive users, 60 percent of all use was for discussion groups; 27 percent for information services; and just 6 percent for analysis services (Pingree et al., 1994). Other research into networked multimedia education suggests that shared learning in a "virtual" world may be especially powerful for lifestyle issues (Dede & Fontana, 1995). These findings confirm that interpersonal communication, facilitated in this case by technology, remains a channel of choice for many people and problems.

New media also support ''just-in-time'' health information, that is, information that the person needs to deal with a specific health problem, as opposed to ''just in case'' information—the classic health education message delivered at a time and through channels chosen by the health communicator. Recent studies confirmed the very high public interest in consumer health information and the increasing market for health information-on-demand, driven by more health-conscious consumers and more cost-conscious payers and care providers (Deering & Harris, 1996; Find/SVP, 1997). Here, too, networked health information has the advantage over other publishing technology because it facilitates the just-in-time delivery that consumers seek, and it can promote better and wider access to information resources generally. These developments suggest that health communication needs to focus as much on providing channels to sound health information content as on the unidirectional delivery of a targeted message.

The Role of Government

The federal government has played a leading role in shaping the nation's prevention agenda. *Healthy People 2000*, the national disease prevention and health promotion objectives, identify the greatest opportunities for reducing preventable illness, injury, and death (HHS/PHS, 1991). Communication underpins many of the targeted interventions.

The dramatic reorientation of health care delivery is now prompting policy discussions about the role of the public sector in helping consumers address their complex and changing choices regarding personal/family health and medical care. The federal government recognizes that there are new pressures for consumer involvement in health care choices—that health care is becoming more interactive. In a market-based health care system, informed decision making on the part of consumers is important for containing health care costs and assuring high-quality care. To help promote informed decision making about preventive care, the U.S. Department of Health and Human Services (HHS) convened the U.S. Preventive Services Task Force and published the resulting recommendations in the *Guide to Clinical Preventive Services* (HHS/OPHS, 1996). The scientific findings about appropriate care by age, gender, and risk factors are published for the layperson in the *Personal Health Guide* (HHS/OPHS, 1997b) and the *Child Health Guide* (HHS/OPHS, 1997a). An *Adolescent Health Guide* will also be published. These booklets help an individual or parent know what preventive services are needed, when, and how often. They are intended to be used interactively with health care providers—to stimulate discussions about and requests for appropriate preventive care.

HHS recently launched a collaborative consumer health information web site, *healthfinder*, to help people find reliable information on the Internet more quickly and easily. The *healthfinder* site (www.healthfinder.gov) has been appreciated as a gateway to a wide range of credible resources in the private as well as the public sector. It includes sections on wise health consumerism, pointing users to reputable sources of information about health care quality. (Figure 8.2 outlines the responsibilities of the various offices within HHS.)

Within HHS, the Centers for Disease Control and Prevention (CDC) plays a major role in informing and educating the public about preventable health risks. CDC has embarked on a comprehensive effort to enhance health communication capacity throughout the agency and to promote health communication research. The National Institutes of Health also translate research findings into public information and education products and services, such as the Cancer Information Services (1–800–4–CANCER). The National Library of Medicine houses the largest collection of biomedical literature in the world and also produces MED-LINE and Internet Grateful Med, which bring the vast electronic databases of professional information to lay audiences as well as health professionals and researchers. The Health Care Financing Administration (HCFA), which manages Medicare and Medicaid, is developing new communication initiatives for the beneficiaries of these programs. HCFA has recently been charged by Congress to enhance information both about specific preventive services benefits and about disease prevention and health promotion. The Agency for Health Care Policy and Research conducts research on the effectiveness and outcomes of health services and publishes the findings for both professionals and consumers.

Agency for Health Care Policy and Research

The mission of the Agency for Health Care Policy and Research (AHCPR) is to generate and disseminate information that improves the delivery and quality of health care. AHCPR supports the development of objective, scientific infor-mation about the value of clinical procedures and health practices. One of the highest priorities is helping consumers make informed decisions about their own personal health and select the highest quality and most appropriate health care services. Toward that end, AHCPR's research agenda includes studies of con-sumers' information needs and preferences and new information resources for consumers. In 1996, AHCPR and the Kaiser Family Foundation sponsored a survey about consumers' interest in information on quality of care to help select health plans and services. The survey showed that a large majority thought that specific information about quality of care was ''very important,'' yet only about 40 percent reported seeing any information comparing quality among health care plans, physicians, or hospitals. About three-quarters said that the federal gov-ernment has a role in making sure that information is available so people can make judgments about quality themselves (Kaiser Family Foundation, 1996).

Implications of Health Sector Trends for Health Communication Theory and Practice

Shared decision making is information-based, but its purposes and content are quite different from those of classic health communication. It focuses on

Figure 8.2

Health Communication and Health Policy: Department of Health and Human Services Diagram (see following chart)

1. *The Secretary*: sets broad policy and priorities.

2. *Assistant Secretary for Health*: coordinates activities and health issues that cut across departmental components and provides leadership in selected areas. The national disease prevention and health promotion objectives, health communication, and consumer health information are among these areas of coordination and leadership.

3. *Assistant Secretary for Planning and Evaluation*: advises Secretary on policy development issues and provides leadership and coordination in strategic planning, policy research and evaluation, and legislative and budget development.

4. *Assistant Secretary for Public Affairs*: oversees media relations for the Secretary and coordinates external communications for the department.

5. *Administration for Children and Families (ACF)*: provides and promotes economic and social services to children, families, individuals, and communities.

6. *Administration on Aging (AoA)*: provides and promotes social and health services for older persons, including information about aging and care options.

7. *Health Care Financing Administration (HCFA)*: manages Medicare and Medicaid, with increasing emphasis on beneficiary information and education.

8. *Agency for Health Care Policy and Research (AHCPR)*: supports research to improve the quality and effectiveness of health services; informs and educates practitioners and consumers about health care.

9. *Centers for Disease Control and Prevention (CDC)*: the lead prevention agency, working closely with state and local agencies and other community organizations; supports health communication research and programs for behavioral risk reduction.

10. *Agency for Toxic Substances and Disease Registry (ATSDR)*: leads efforts to prevent or reduce human health risks from environmental hazards; provides leadership in risk communication practice.

11. *Food and Drug Administration (FDA)*: ensures safety and efficacy of food, medicines, and medical devices; informs the public about safety and efficacy issues.

12. *Health Resources and Services Administration (HRSA)*: provides primary health care to underserved and vulnerable populations; promotes primary care education and practice.

13. *Indian Health Service (IHS)*: provides health services to American Indians and Alaska Natives.

14. *National Institutes of Health (NIH)*: leader in biomedical research and the communication of biomedical information, including the prevention and treatment of specific diseases and conditions.

15. *Substance Abuse and Mental Health Services Administration (SAMHSA)*: promotes quality services, develops new knowledge, and leads in community-based and other communication efforts regarding prevention of substance abuse.

132

The Secretary

Food and Drug Administration (FDA)

Health Resources and Services Administration HRSA)

Indian Health Service (IHS)

National Institutes of Health (NIH)

Substance Abuse and Mental Health Services Administration (SAMHSA)

Administration for Children and Families (ACF)

Administration on Aging (AoA)

Health Care Financing Administration (HCFA)

Agency for Health Care Policy and Research (AHCPR)

Centers for Disease Control and Prevention (CDC)

Agency for Toxic Substances and Disease Registry (ATSDR)

Assistant Secretary for Health

Surgeon-General

Office of Disease Prevention and Health Promotion (ODPHP)

Assistant Secretary for Planning and Evaluation

Assistant Secretary for Public Affairs

133

individual health and medical decision making beyond lifestyle choices, in order to optimize the patient's use of health services. The goals of shared decision making are to increase knowledge about the risks, benefits, and appropriateness of medical care and to improve ability to assess a problem and self-manage it where appropriate. "Decision and self-management support systems [are used] to enable and encourage consumers to make appropriate use of medical care" (Vickery & Lynch, 1995).

While programs that seek to reduce behavioral risks and demand for inappropriate care share the goal of sound decision making, there are some important differences for health communication. Demand management programs are not principally delivered to collective audiences through mass media. They do not seek to persuade a person to do one thing, except to make (and accept responsibility for) an informed decision. There is no "message" in the classic health communication sense of the term. There is no "expert" or "authority" with a single prescription. Instead, such programs seek to educate individuals, sometimes viewed as health care consumers, about a range of potential decisions and to help them reach the decision that is best for their specific circumstances. They may acknowledge that there is no single best choice for any one person. The communication needed for such purposes must be highly customized and interactive. It must often be multidirectional, with the individual receiving and giving information from and to many sources, before reaching a personal synthesis that may include family values and preferences. The individual is not a "target audience" but an informed participant in a shared decision-making process. The burden of educating and getting educated is thus much heavier for all parties.

At the same time, since reducing need is increasingly recognized as good for both public health and cost containment (Fries et al., 1993; Fries, 1994; HHS/ PHS, 1994), the value of effective health communication with traditional purposes and content regarding lifestyle choices for wellness and prevention is more widely appreciated in managed care.

Implications of Health Sector Trends for Health Communication Professionals

Clearly, health communicators have the opportunity to work on new issues and new arenas. The focus, content, and audiences for their work are expanding. So are their potential employers. While prevention-oriented health communication has largely been supported by public and not-for-profit organizations, this same work is of increasing interest to health care organizations under the guise of need reduction. But communication principles, skills, and techniques can also play a greater role in the conception, development, and implementation of demand management/decision-support efforts than they have done in the past. Formative communication research could help refine strategies and content. Social marketing approaches could help tighten the links between communication interventions and desired outcomes (namely, more informed participation in managing health problems and the appropriate use of health care). Programs based on interactive multimedia could benefit even more from the perspectives and skills of health communication professionals.

While many demand management programs have been the product of innovative interdisciplinary teamwork, health communication professionals are not always involved. They need to understand the implications of managed care so that they can make their full contribution to health communication in the evolving health care age.

Communication Research Needs

There is a broad spectrum of research needs in health communication. However, because health communication research is a relatively small field, a well-focused research agenda will be required to meet the challenges and opportunities presented by changing approaches to health and medical care. One major challenge to developing a well-focused research agenda is the lack of primary responsibility for such an agenda among federal government agencies and the private sector. In addition, with the advent of new media technologies, it is clear that two traditionally disparate groups of researchers—health communicators and information technology specialists—will need to closely collaborate. Major focus areas for additional research include:

Risk communication. Different treatments for the same condition have different risks and benefits. Patients' personal profiles and their own value judgments also affect the outcomes of specific treatments. Clearly, if they are to be involved in decisions, they must be able to synthesize complex information in the context of their own preferences. We need to know more about the optimum content of the information and what information may be counterproductive. Among other questions researchers might pose are: How much weight would they give to information from other patients so that they can vicariously experience the consequences of various choices? How should the wide uncertainty regarding various treatment options be characterized?

Communication of information about quality of care. While there has been a significant investment in research about the kinds of quality of care measures that should be reported by health care plans and services, researchers are only beginning to explore the sorts of information on health care quality consumers want and use in making health care choices. Questions to be explored in greater depth include: What are the most effective formats for providing quality information to consumers? How can certain population groups with special information needs be best served? What about differences in language, income and education levels, or disability status? Who should provide information to consumers and help them understand health care choices? How do emerging technologies such as the Internet affect the kinds of quality information consumers use?

Information seeking and information processing patterns. There is relatively little investigation to date on how people use complex information to make choices and how this process is affected by different circumstances. What demographic or other variables influence these patterns? When is interpersonal communication optimum; when can interactive technologies using video or Internet exchanges be effective? The latter two areas are important in light of findings from a small body of research showing the potential value of communication approaches that encourage interactive exchanges between people or between a person and a computer-based program.

Appropriate media for different purposes/content/messages/audiences. It is likely that the effectiveness of specific media will differ depending on the intended function, the message, and the audience. It is possible that a single medium or a combination of media are indicated in specific situations. For example, highly sensitive content may suggest one medium (e.g., a brochure, CD-ROM, or anonymous web access rather than an employer network), while a goal of creating new awareness may suggest mass media. Research is needed to help develop a matrix covering the wide array of communication needs and analyze the strengths and weaknesses of text, visual/video, audio, and interactive multimedia. With rapid developments in communication technology delivery channels, it is difficult to evaluate a specific technology platform (e.g., CD-ROM, interactive video, interactive TV, etc.) which may be superseded or changed regardless of the research findings. It becomes more important to frame the evaluation carefully, so that lessons learned may be valid for new or enhanced delivery modes. As the Internet and World Wide Web expand their reach and attractiveness, we need to better understand their optimum use for communication about health and medical care.

Appropriate design (content, format, degree of interactivity) for new media communications. New technologies are emerging and being applied with more enthusiasm than discernment. Little attention is being paid to the optimum components of an Internet-based health communication product/service, interactive video, CD-ROM, kiosk and so on. Limited research into how they can be tailored to different audiences suggests that this customization increases effectiveness. Given evidence that many people prefer (and may learn most from) interpersonal communication, how can such exchanges be supported through new media? What relative role should such exchanges play in comparison with other functions like access to information databases? Little is known about individual and group-specific differences in interacting with various technologies and the impact of these differences on the effectiveness of the application. Additional research is needed to examine how communication programs should account for these differences in their design and evaluation. A central issue is the development of practical frameworks for evaluating new media-based applications. Research is needed to identify approaches and tools that allow stakeholders with varying responsibilities, knowledge, and skill levels to evaluate the utility and effectiveness of these applications. The U.S. Department of Health and Human Services has convened a Science Panel on Interactive Communication and Health that is charged with developing a comprehensive evaluation framework and tools. The panel's work, including a web site, will be available in the Spring of 1999.

Health communication, which has long been central to disease prevention and health promotion, is becoming an integral component of our health care system. The trends cited above are likely to accelerate this process. The suggested health communication research agenda is only preliminary. It is certain to be reshaped by developments in the field. Equally certain, health communication research findings can in turn shape how health care evolves over time.

NOTE

The views expressed in this chapter are those of the author only and do not represent policy of the U.S. Department of Health and Human Services (HHS). The author acknowledges helpful comments and suggestions from Tom Eng, Terry Shannon, and Christine Williams of HHS.

9

Health Communication Campaigns

Maria Knight Lapinski and Kim Witte

SYNOPSIS

Health communication campaigns are generally aimed at a large number of individuals, conducted during a specified time period, and consist of organized, planned, communication activities. There has recently been an emphasis on the use of theory to guide campaign development. Campaign designers commonly employ a number of micro- or individual level theories, including the health belief model, theory of reasoned action, social cognitive theory, stages of change model, models of risk communication, elaboration likelihood model, and inoculation theory. In addition, a number of theories take a large-scale or "macro"-approach to information campaigns and focus on sociocultural factors that influence the effectiveness of health communication campaigns such as the social marketing approach, diffusion of innovation theory, and so-called community empowerment approaches.

[T]here has been more progress in designing and conducting [health] campaigns in the past 20 years than in the [previous] 125 years.
—William Paisley, in Pfau & Parrott, 1993

Health communication campaigns, which are more numerous, sophisticated, and effective than ever before, advocate health promotion and disease prevention behaviors through the mass media, face-to-face interaction and other communication channels. Although there are a number of ideological models of health education and promotion (cf. Tones & Tilford, 1994), *preventive* health behaviors most frequently have been the targets of health communication campaigns

(Scherer & Juanillo, 1992). Effective health communication campaigns (a) produce changes in knowledge, (b) influence or clarify values, (c) bring about changes in attitudes, beliefs or behaviors, and/or (d) facilitate skill acquisition (Tones & Tilford, 1994).

Health communication campaigns typically are aimed at a large number of individuals, conducted in a predetermined time frame, and consist of organized, planned communication activities (Rogers, 1996; Rogers & Storey, 1987). Obviously, campaigns designed to educate the public about health issues are only a small portion of the health-related content that people are exposed to each day. Talk shows, advertisements, news, and other sources provide individuals with information that often contradicts or refutes the information disseminated by public health campaigns. Unfortunately, mixed messages about health behavior abound in the media, and often, the media provide a tutorial on how to live an unhealthy lifestyle (Wallack, 1990). What differentiates health campaigns from these conflicting media activities is that health campaigns *intentionally* attempt to bring about healthy behaviors or attitudes through some organized and planned set of communication activities.

Campaigns characteristically use multiple communication channels and can range from small to large-scale operations. Large-scale campaigns often rely on television and radio to disseminate information and messages about a particular health issue. Large-scale communication campaigns are commonly conducted by agencies or groups that either have funding from, or are members of, powerful groups such as government agencies, large corporations, or other organizations that have social power, legitimacy, resources, and access to the mass media (Salmon, 1989). In contrast, small-scale campaigns often rely on posters, brochures, videotapes, and booklets to communicate health information.

How does one determine what type of health-related information to disseminate to the public? The debate over which type of information is "pro-social" or in the "public's best interest" and who should make this determination has been discussed at length by several authors (e.g., Downie, Fyfe, & Tannahill, 1990; Salmon, 1989). Historically, various forms of health communication campaigns were evident in the United States in the early 1700s (Scherer & Juanillo, 1992). These campaigns were concerned primarily with either convincing individuals to be immunized against smallpox or to discontinue the use of alcohol. The earliest large-scale health promotion campaigns were related to the temperance movement; by 1839 there were a number of journals dedicated to educating the public on the evils of alcohol (Scherer & Juanillo, 1992). Many health campaigns in recent years, however, have focused on uncontroversial issues such as cardiovascular disease (CVD) prevention. By the late 1980s, there were at least 10 community-based CVD prevention programs operating internationally (Winett, King, & Altman, 1989). A more controversial health-related debate has recently emerged over whether or not teenagers should be educated on how to use condoms to prevent sexually transmitted diseases (STDs) or pregnancy. Campaigns to promote needle exchanges among drug users to prevent human immunodeficiency virus (HIV) infection are often criticized as well. To disseminate health communication messages effectively, particularly when dealing with such controversial issues as those previously noted, it behooves campaign designers to consider the politics, context, and social consequences of their campaigns. By involving various constituent groups in the design and development of campaign themes, health educators can focus on distribution of the message, instead of worrying about the political fallout from a well-intentioned campaign. Once campaign designers are able to focus on message dissemination, they must consider the role of theory in designing and implementing a campaign.

An essential aspect of an effective health communication campaign is that it be driven by theory. Theories help health communicators identify and understand seemingly different behaviors and their influences. Theories also provide the tools for affecting knowledge, attitudes, and behaviors in a wide range of circumstances (Hochbaum, Sorenson, & Loring, 1992). Health educators can use theories to aid in message design, channel selection, campaign structure, methods of dissemination, and audience targeting issues (Flay & Burton, 1990).

Although theories increase the chances of campaign success (because one has guidance about what does and does not work), a number of researchers criticize the usefulness of many commonly employed theories (Freudenberg, Eng, Flay, Parcel, Rogers, & Wallerstein, 1995; Hochbaum et al., 1992). The dominant health behavior change theories have been criticized for (a) their focus on the individual and exclusion of social and environmental factors, (b) their emphasis on the one-way flow of information without consideration of the interactive nature of communication, (c) a lack of either political, administrative, or fiscal feasibility, and (d) limited applicability to unique populations (Hochbaum et al., 1992; Meyer & Dearing, 1996). Some have criticized the tendency to use or test only parts of theories in health communication campaigns instead of examining an entire model (Kirscht & Joseph, 1989). However, although there is wide room for criticism, the importance of using theory in campaign development cannot be denied. Studies have shown repeatedly that the use of theory to guide campaign message development results in a more effective and more efficient (in terms of both cost and time) campaign.

This chapter discusses a number of theories and approaches commonly utilized in health education campaigns. Examples and applications of these theories and approaches will be discussed as well. Given that each of the theories is explained in detail elsewhere in the literature, this chapter will simply provide an overview of the components of the approaches and models. This chapter is not an exhaustive review of the health behavior change theories; rather, it encompasses those theories that are employed predominantly by campaign designers. The first section of the chapter will discuss micro-level theories utilized in health communication campaigns, including the health belief model, the theory of reasoned action, social-cognitive theory, fear appeal theory, the elaboration likelihood model, and inoculation theory. The second section will discuss macro-level theories and approaches, including social marketing, diffusion of innovation theory, and community empowerment.

MICRO-LEVEL THEORIES OF ATTITUDE AND BEHAVIOR CHANGE

Although health communication has been primarily a practice-based field, recently there has been an emphasis on the use and development of theories of behavior change to guide campaign design and implementation. These micro-level theories, generally founded in social psychology, focus on changing an individual's level of knowledge, attitudes, or behaviors related to some health promotive or disease preventive action.

Health Belief Model

The health belief model (HBM) (Janz & Becker, 1984; Rosenstock, 1974) is one of the most commonly used models of health behavior change and is probably the most frequently taught model in health campaign courses. Many have used it to guide the development of health campaigns and interventions, and its influence on health communication research is enormous. It was developed by a group of social psychologists in the early 1950s (Janz & Becker, 1984) as an overarching framework on how to promote preventive behaviors. In brief, the HBM emphasizes the role of certain beliefs in stimulating preventive health actions. The model suggests that preventive health behavior is influenced by five factors: (a) perceived susceptibility to a health threat; (b) perceived severity of a health threat; (c) perceived barriers to performing the recommended response; (d) perceived benefits of performing the recommended response; and (e) cues to action.

Perceived susceptibility refers to an individual's subjective evaluation of the probability that he or she will experience a health threat. People often evaluate the likelihood that they will experience a harmful outcome of a certain action before engaging in that action. For example, before wearing a bicycle helmet people often evaluate whether or not they are likely to fall off their bicycle and hit their heads. If they feel that there is a likely chance that this event could occur, then they will be more likely to wear a bicycle helmet. *Perceived severity* refers to a person's beliefs about the magnitude of the health threat. That is, is the health threat serious? For example, to determine perceived severity of a threat one might ask whether or not one perceives skin cancer, car accidents, or measles to be serious. The severity of a health threat can be evaluated in terms of physical/medical harm (e.g., disease, illness) as well as social harm (e.g., stigmatization).

Demographics and prior experiences are said to affect the four variables just described. For example, if one person knows someone who died of skin cancer while another person knows someone who simply had a cancerous mole removed, then the former is likely to have stronger perceptions of severity toward skin cancer when compared to the latter.

The *perceived barriers* are the potential "costs" of performing a recommended response, while *perceived benefits* are the degree to which the recommended response is seen as feasible and effective in reducing the health threat. The HBM suggests that an individual weighs the potential benefits of the recommended response against the psychological, physical, and financial costs of the action. For example, a mother may realize the benefit of having her child immunized against childhood diseases, but she may lack the transportation, access, or the financial means to realize this benefit. In this case, the barriers would outweigh any benefits, and the child would probably not be immunized.

"Cues to action" is the least studied variable in the HBM. According to the model, cues to action are necessary to trigger the decision-making process. Cues can be external (e.g., public service announcements or brochures on the hazards of smoking) or internal (e.g., symptoms of a condition, such as a bleeding or unusual-looking mole). The model suggests that external cues, such as mass media campaigns, increase individuals' perceptions of threat, which in turn, cause the individual to engage in the recommended response.

Rosenstock (1974) has noted that the combination of perceived susceptibility and severity provide the motivation for action, and the comparison of perceived benefits to perceived barriers provides the means or pathway to action. Thus, the stronger the perceptions of severity, susceptibility, and benefits, and the weaker the perception of barriers, the greater the likelihood that health-protective actions will be taken. One particularly potent example of how strong perceived susceptibility, severity, and benefits beliefs can overcome perceived barriers is illustrated by the case of infant immunization by the Masai women in Kenya. These women have seen children die of childhood diseases (severity), know that anyone's child can be stricken (susceptibility), and believe that immunizations prevent childhood diseases (benefits). Therefore, they willingly walk many miles in hot, dusty weather to rural health clinics several times during the first year of their children's lives (barriers) in order to have their children vaccinated.

The HBM has been empirically tested as the basis for educational campaigns on a number of health behaviors, including bicycle helmet use (Witte, Stokols, Ituarte, & Schneider, 1993), vaccination for infectious diseases, adolescent fertility control (Eisen, Zellman, & McAllister, 1985), and risky sexual practices (Vanlandingham, Suprasert, Grandjean, & Sittirai, 1995). Overall, perceived barriers have been the strongest predictor of whether or not individuals engage in health-protective behaviors, followed by perceived susceptibility (Janz & Becker, 1984). Janz and Becker (1984) found that the perceived severity component was the weakest predictor across studies employing the HBM.

The HBM may be viewed as the precursor of most modern health communication theories. As such, its variables and principles can be seen in many of the other models to be discussed in this chapter.

The Theory of Reasoned Action

Often, messages created for health education campaigns are based on intuitive appeal rather than on sound methodology (Fishbein & Ajzen, 1981). Even if a theory is used to develop messages, campaign designers tend to use the variables in the theory as guidelines to determine what topic to address, without giving special consideration of the actual content or words in a message. For example, campaign designers might address the severity of a health threat and the audience's susceptibility to that health threat—the theoretical variables—in a message, but the actual words or images used to address these variables are not systematically chosen. Fishbein and Ajzen (1981) go so far as to conclude that "the general neglect of the information contained in a message and its relation to the dependent variable is probably the most serious problem in communication and persuasion research" (p. 359).

Fishbein and Ajzen (1975, 1981) suggest specific message construction techniques based on their theory of reasoned action (TRA). In the TRA (Figure 9.1), Fishbein and Ajzen (1975) propose that a person's behavior is predicted by their intentions, which in turn, are predicted by their attitudes toward the behavior and subjective norms. Attitudes are predicted by behavioral beliefs and evaluations of those beliefs. Subjective norms are predicted by normative beliefs and the motivation to comply with those normative beliefs. Fishbein and Ajzen (1975) state that two sets of beliefs must be altered prior to behavior change: (1) beliefs about the consequences of performing a certain behavior and the evaluation of those consequences (attitudes); and (2) beliefs about what other people or referents think about the behavior to be performed and the motivation to comply with those referents (subjective norms). Only when a message targets the salient beliefs of these variables do attitudes and subjective norms, and subsequently, behavioral intentions and behavior, change.

Table 9.1 illustrates how the TRA may be used to analyze a specific audience's behaviors in terms of bicycle helmet use. Table 9.1a indicates one person's hypothetical attitude toward bicycle helmet use. Recall that attitudes are comprised of one's beliefs toward the attitude object (in this case bicycle helmet use) multiplied by the evaluation of the individual beliefs (whether these beliefs are good or bad). This person believes that bicycle helmets are uncomfortable, prevent injury, look unattractive, and are expensive. These are his or her salient beliefs about bicycle helmets. The strength of these beliefs (from .00 to 1.00) is indicated in the second column, and the evaluation of these attributes [ranging from −3 (unfavorable) to +3 (favorable)] is indicated in the third column. These belief strengths and evaluations are multiplied individually and then summed to create the overall attitude toward bicycle helmets. For example, this person strongly believes that wearing bicycle helmets looks unattractive (.90) and this unattractiveness is evaluated unfavorably (−2). In addition, s/he does not believe very strongly that wearing bicycle helmets prevents injury (.3), but anything that

Figure 9.1
The Theory of Reasoned Action

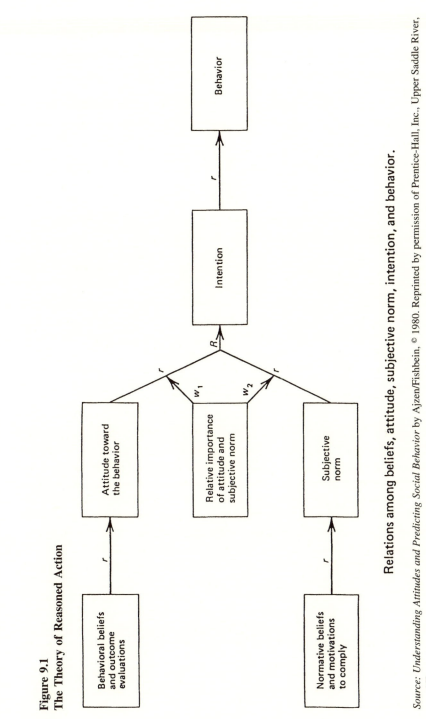

Relations among beliefs, attitude, subjective norm, intention, and behavior.

Source: Understanding Attitudes and Predicting Social Behavior by Aizen/Fishbein, © 1980. Reprinted by permission of Prentice-Hall, Inc., Upper Saddle River, NJ.

Table 9.1

Hypothetical Attitudes and Subjective Norms Toward Wearing Bicycle Helmets

a. Hypothetical Attitude Toward Wearing Bicycle Helmets

Beliefs	Behavioral Beliefs	Evaluations	Beliefs x Examinations
Uncomfortable	.70	−3	−2.10
Prevents injury	.30	+3	+0.90
Looks unattractive	.90	−2	−1.80
Expensive	.10	−1	−0.10
		Attitude =	−3.10

b. Hypothetical Subjective Norm Toward Wearing Bicycle Helmets

Referents	Normative Beliefs	Motivation to Comply	Beliefs x Motivation to Comply
My girlfriend	−1	+2	−2
My best friend	−3	+3	−9
My coach	+3	0	0
My father	+1	+1	+1
		Subjective norm =	−10

prevents injury is evaluated very highly (+3). It is clear, however, that the predominant attitude toward wearing bicycle helmets is negative at −3.10.

Table 9.1*b* is a hypothetical example of a teen male's subjective norm toward wearing bicycle helmets. His salient referents include his girlfriend, his best friend, his coach, and his father (the people who are most important to him, and who are most likely to influence him). His normative beliefs reflect what *he* thinks each of these specific referents believes about whether he should wear a bicycle helmet [ranging from −3 (should not wear) to +3 (should wear)]. His motivation to comply with each referent is indicated on a scale from 0 (not at all) to 3 (strongly). In each case, the normative belief and the motivation to comply are multiplied to yield a product. The sum of these products is his subjective norm toward wearing a bicycle helmet. The attitude and subjective norms are sometimes weighted according to their importance, and then combined, to influence intentions, which are hypothesized to then influence behaviors. This person's scores suggest that he would not wear a bicycle helmet because both his attitude and subjective norm toward bicycle helmets are negative, resulting in negative intentions to wear helmets and negative helmet-related behaviors.

Fishbein and Ajzen (1981) argue that to change a behavior, the *total set* of *primary* (or salient) beliefs must be changed or shifted. In the examples of behavioral and normative beliefs (Table 9.1), note that if only one belief changed, the attitude or subjective norm probably would not change. Fishbein and Ajzen (1975) state that salient beliefs must be altered to effect change because they are, in essence, what ultimately cause behavior.

When constructing persuasive messages, Fishbein and Ajzen (1975) note that it is crucial to choose the "right" target variable. What is the specific goal of the persuasive message—to change attitudes, intentions, or behaviors? Exactly which behaviors are to be targeted for change? Similarly, there must be precise correspondence in specificity between the persuasive message and the targeted goal. For example, a message arguing that AIDS should be prevented will only persuade people that AIDS should be prevented. However, more often than not, practitioners will use such a message focusing on AIDS prevention when their goal is to persuade people to use condoms to prevent AIDS. The presumption is that people will infer that condoms prevent AIDS, simply because this is stated in the end of the message. Note that there is a lack of correspondence between the message (attitudes toward AIDS) and the behavioral goal (attitudes toward use of condoms).

Overall, TRA is one of the few theories to offer a systematic approach to constructing the content of a health campaign message. It has been applied to a number of health-related behaviors, including the impact of health risk messages about tap water (Griffin, Neuwirth, & Dunwoody, 1995), sexual practices and AIDS related-behaviors (Fishbein & Middlestadt, 1989; Fishbein, Middlestadt, & Hitchcock, 1991; Vanlandingham et al. 1995), childbearing intentions (Crawford & Boyer, 1985), testicular cancer prevention (Brubaker & Wickersham, 1990), exercise in schoolchildren (Ferguson, Yesalis, Pomrehn, & Kirkpatrick, 1989), alcoholism (Fishbein, Ajzen, & McArdle, 1980), cigarette smoking (Norman & Tedeschi, 1989), and many others.

Social Cognitive Theory

Bandura's social cognitive theory (sometimes called social learning theory) has been used in a wide variety of health-related campaigns. It was used in the Stanford 5-Cities project to prevent heart disease (Flora, Maccoby, & Farquhar, 1989) and more recently has been used in several AIDS-prevention projects (Bandura, 1989). The focal point of the theory is *perceived self-efficacy*. Self-efficacy is defined as "people's beliefs that they can exert control over their motivation and behavior and over their social environment" (Bandura, 1989, p. 128). In other words, perceived self-efficacy is what you believe about your capability to perform a certain action (your perceived self-effectiveness). Bandura (1977a, 1982) views self-efficacy as the driving force of human behavior. "Efficacy expectations are a major determinant of people's choice of activities, how much effort they will expend, and of how long they will sustain effort in dealing with stressful situations'' (Bandura, 1977a, p. 194). Bandura (1977a) states that an individual's self-efficacy perceptions are developed from four sources of information: performance accomplishments, physiological states, verbal persuasion, and vicarious experience.

Another important construct in Bandura's theory is *outcome expectations*. Outcome expectations refer to an individual's belief that a certain behavior will lead to a certain outcome. For example, ''I believe that if I get a polio vaccination, I won't get polio'' is an outcome expectation. It is what you think will happen if you take a certain action. Outcome expectations are different from efficacy expectations in that the latter is a person's belief about whether he or she is able to ''successfully execute the behavior required to produce the outcomes'' (Bandura, 1977a, p. 193). For example, even if outcome expectations are high (e.g., ''If I get a polio vaccination I won't get polio''), efficacy expectations may be low (e.g., ''but I'm not capable of getting a polio shot because needles scare me''). In short, according to social cognitive theory, a person can believe that certain actions lead to a particular outcome (outcome expectations), but this individual may doubt his or her ability to perform the action (efficacy expectations). Thus, it is the self-efficacy perception that causes behavior.

According to Bandura (1977a), only when efficacy expectations are high will people perform the advocated behaviors. Efficacy expectations can vary on dimensions of magnitude (level of difficulty of task: people may have different efficacy expectations for simple tasks than for difficult tasks), generality (specific to general), and strength (weak to strong) (Bandura, 1977a). Many health communication campaigns promote long-lasting and stable health behaviors by increasing people's perceptions of self-efficacy toward performing a recommended response. For example, one way to promote condom use to prevent HIV infection is to let individuals role-play romantic encounters where they gain practice and experience on how to negotiate condom use (and thereby increase their perceptions of self-efficacy). One potential element missing from social cognitive theory is a motivational factor. The model seems to assume that if people have high levels of self-efficacy and outcome expectations consistent with the recommended response, then they will be motivated to act. Many people have confidence in their ability to perform certain actions (e.g., fasten a safety belt) and expect that the performance of that action will lead to a desired outcome (e.g., prevention of harm if there were to be an accident), yet they fail to do the action (i.e., they still do not wear safety belt). However, aside from this issue, it is clear that self-efficacy and outcome expectations are key variables that must be addressed in effective health communication campaigns. Numerous studies have demonstrated the importance of self-efficacy in health communication campaigns, including examinations of addictive behaviors such as smoking and drinking (cf. DiClemente, 1986) and AIDS-related behaviors (Bandura, 1989).

Stages of Change Model

One of a number of stage models of behavior change, the transtheoretical model allows communicators to determine the stage in which the majority of their target audience members can be placed, along a continuum of no action to consistent action (DiClemente & Prochaska, 1985). The model, also referred to as the stages of change model (SOC), suggests there are five stages in the performance of a behavior: Precontemplation, Contemplation, Preparation, Action, and Maintenance. In the *Precontemplative* stage, persons do not intend to change their behavior. They may not realize they are engaging in risky behavior, or they may deny that their behavior puts them at risk for harm. For example, an individual may be at high risk for a heart attack but may not realize or may deny the fact that a high cholesterol diet is increasing his or her risk of experiencing a heart attack. In the second stage, however, this risk becomes apparent to the person. *Contemplation* is the stage in which individuals begin to think about the behavior that is putting them at risk and to contemplate the need for change. In this stage, for example, a person recognizes that eating foods high in cholesterol is increasing his or her risk for a heart attack. He or she also realizes that a change in the diet would be a good idea. The next stage is the stage in which individuals begin to change beliefs. In this third stage, *Preparation*, one makes a commitment to change and takes some action to prepare for the behavior change. The individual at risk for a heart attack may request a low cholesterol diet from a physician and rid his or her house of high cholesterol foods. It is in the *Action* stage that individuals perform the new behavior consistently. In this stage, for example, the at-risk individual may regularly eat only low cholesterol foods and continue other changes in diet to reduce the risk of heart attack. In the *Maintenance* stage, the final stage of the SOC model, the new behavior is continued, and steps are taken to avoid relapsing into the formerly risky behaviors. For example, a person might join a support group to avoid falling back into former unhealthy eating habits.

The SOC model is useful to health communicators and campaign designers for several reasons. First, individuals in different stages exhibit distinct behavioral characteristics (Weinstein, 1988). Thus, researchers can effectively analyze and segment a target audience according to that audience's different stages of change. Practitioners, then, can design messages strategically to move individuals through the stages (Maibach & Cotton, 1995). For example, if health communicators wish to design a heart-healthy campaign and they determine that the majority of the members of the target population are in the Contemplation stage, they can design messages to systematically move audience members through the Preparation, Action, and Maintenance stages. Similarly, if the majority of the target audience is in the Maintenance stage, communicators can provide messages that reinforce and support the healthy behavior.

This model has been empirically tested with a number of health topics, including smoking cessation, sunscreen use, addictive behaviors, pregnancy prevention, and risky sexual behaviors (e.g., Grimley, Riley, Bellis, & Prochaska, 1993; Prochaska, DiClemente, & Norcross, 1992).

Risk Communication/Fear Appeals

Most health education campaigns either unintentionally or intentionally raise anxiety or fear in audiences, because the campaigns focus on a health risk. In most health promotion/disease prevention campaigns, campaigners are attempting to prevent a certain harm or health threat from occurring and do so by outlining the terrible things that will happen if a recommended response is not followed. Two streams of research are useful in identifying how to channel fear or anxiety into productive behavioral action. The literature on both risk communication and fear appeals can help clarify the relationship between the emotion of fear and the behaviors resulting from that fear.

The risk communication literature has focused on how laypersons and experts differ in how they perceive risks (Douglas, 1985; Kishchuk, 1987; Slovic, 1987). For example, experts tend to view health risks in a very scientific, rational manner—"there's a one in a million chance that you'll get disease X." In contrast, laypersons tend to evaluate risks in terms of whether or not they are controllable, familiar, voluntary, necessary, catastrophic, personally relevant, or representative (Kishchuk, 1987; Slovic, 1987). Slovic and colleagues (1987; Fischhoff, Slovic, Lichtenstein, Read, & Combs, 1978; Slovic, Fischhoff, & Lichtenstein, 1982) have demonstrated that these and other qualitative risk dimensions cluster into two main factors: (1) dread-common and (2) unknown-known.[1] Dreaded risks are characterized by "perceived lack of control, dread, catastrophic potential, fatal consequences, and the inequitable distribution of risks and benefits" (Slovic, 1987, p. 283). Unknown risks are characterized as being "unobservable, unknown, new, and delayed in their manifestation of harm" (Slovic, 1987, p. 283). Thus, experts may evaluate the risk of dying in an airplane crash as low because it is a quantitatively rare event, while laypersons may evaluate the same risk as extremely high because it is an unknown and dreaded risk, with great catastrophic potential.

When risks seem unacceptably high to laypersons, these risks tend to generate fear. The fear appeal literature offers guidelines on how to develop health risk messages that motivate behavior change instead of inhibiting it. Fear appeals are defined as persuasive messages that frighten an audience into adopting a recommended response. The first part of a fear appeal typically focuses on the health threat by emphasizing the *severity* of the threat (i.e., its magnitude of harm) and the *probability* that the threat will occur (i.e., the audience's likelihood of experiencing that threat). Fear is aroused when a threat is perceived as relevant and significant. The second section of a fear appeal usually focuses on the efficacy (e.g., effectiveness) of the recommended response in (a) averting or minimizing the threat (*response efficacy*) and (b) messages that increase perceived *self-efficacy* by increasing one's perceived ability to perform the recommended response. Such an increase in self-efficacy is attained by outlining specific and easy steps to avert the threat. The fear appeal may be thought of as the "cue to action" in the health belief model.

The research into fear appeals has shown them to be potent persuasive devices but only in certain conditions. The most recent fear appeal theory, the Extended Parallel Process Model (EPPM), is based on Leventhal's danger control/fear control framework and is an expansion of previous fear appeal theoretical approaches (Janis, 1967; Leventhal, 1970; Rogers, 1975, 1983). Readers will note similarities between the Health Belief Model and fear appeal theories. Fear appeal models can be thought of as experimental variants or explanatory (as compared to descriptive) versions of the HBM. Clearly, fear appeal research and the EPPM (Witte, 1992a, 1998) grew out of the HBM.

According to the EPPM (see Figure 9.2), the evaluation of a health threat initiates two appraisals, which result in either danger control (i.e., a cognitive process) or fear control processes (i.e., an emotional process). First, persons appraise the threat of the hazard by determining whether they think the threat is serious (e.g., "skin cancer can be deadly") and whether they think they are susceptible to the threat (e.g., "I'm at risk for getting skin cancer). The greater the threat perceived, the more motivated individuals are to begin the second appraisal, which is an evaluation of the efficacy of the recommended response. When people think about the recommended response, they evaluate its level of response efficacy (e.g., "Does sunscreen prevent skin cancer?") and their level of self-efficacy (e.g., "Am I capable of using sunscreen?"). When the threat is regarded as trivial or irrelevant (perceived as low), there is no motivation to consider the threat further; the efficacy of the recommended response is evaluated superficially—if it is evaluated at all—and no response is made to the health threat. If people do not feel at risk or do not feel the threat to be significant, they simply will ignore it.

Danger control processes will dominate, and people will act in ways that prevent the threat, as long as perceptions of efficacy are greater than perceptions of threat (e.g., "I know that skin cancer is a terrible threat that I'm at risk for, but if I have my physician screen me annually, I'll be able to prevent my dying from it"). When danger control processes dominate, individuals are motivated to control the danger by thinking of ways to protect themselves. Danger control processes are primarily cognitive processes where individuals (a) realize they are at risk for a severe danger (high threat) and become motivated to protect themselves, (b) believe they can effectively deter the threat (high efficacy), and (c) deliberately and cognitively confront the danger (e.g., "I'm going to call my physician right now and request a skin cancer screening"). The cognitions or thoughts occurring in the danger control processes elicit protection motivation, which stimulates *adaptive* actions such as attitude, intention, or behavior changes that control the danger. Thus, when persons perceive themselves to be vulnerable

Figure 9.2
The Extended Parallel Processing Model

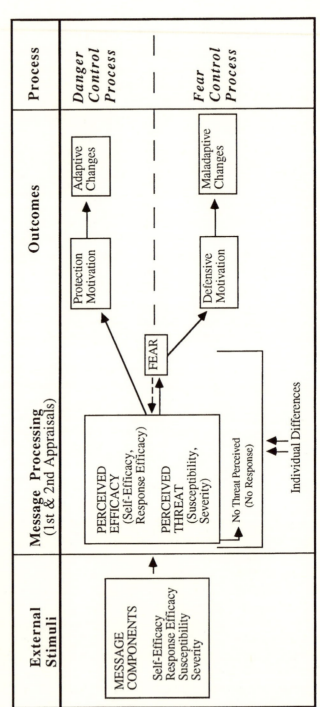

to a serious risk, *and* they believe they can do something to avert that risk effectively and easily, then they protect themselves against the health threat.

At some *critical point*, however, when persons realize that they cannot prevent a serious threat from occurring, either because they believe the response to be ineffective or because they believe they are incapable of performing the recommended response (e.g., "Skin cancer is a terrible disease that I'll probably get, and I don't think there's anything I can do to keep from dying from it"), fear control processes will begin to dominate over danger control processes. Fear control processes are primarily emotional processes where people respond to and cope with their fear, not with the danger. Defensive motivation is elicited by heightened fear arousal, which occurs when perceived threat is high and perceived efficacy is low, and produces responses that control one's fear such as defensive avoidance or reactance. Studies have shown that fear appeals with high levels of threat (e.g., "Skin cancer is a severe disease that you are susceptible to given your history of sun exposure") and low levels of efficacy (e.g., "Sunscreen used now can't undo past skin damage due to overexposure from the sun; therefore you cannot totally prevent skin cancer") result in message rejection. Thus, when persons believe themselves to be vulnerable to a significant threat but believe that the threat is uncontrollable and unavoidable, then they deny they are at risk, defensively avoid the issue, or lash out in reactance. In this case, fears about a health threat inhibit action, and health risk messages may backfire.

In short, according to the EPPM when people are faced with a health threat, they either control the danger (i.e., the actual health threat) or control their fear about the danger. They weigh their risk of actually experiencing the health threat (i.e., getting cancer) against actions they can take that would minimize or avert the health threat (i.e., "Does sunscreen really work? Can I really use it every time I'm in the sun?"). Health risks that are seen as controllable (i.e., people believe they are able to effectively avert them) are dealt with in a protective manner no matter how frightening the health threat. In contrast, health risks that are seen as uncontrollable or unavoidable cause so much fear that people plunge into potentially maladaptive coping strategies where the health threat is denied or defensively avoided.

In terms of a health communication campaign, therefore, the audience must first believe that the health threat is relevant to them and that it is a significant and serious threat. Strong perceptions of threat motivate action. It is important to note that one can have high levels of perceived severity toward a health threat but low levels of perceived susceptibility. The classic example of the relationship among these variables involves perceptions about AIDS. Many people have very strong perceived severity toward AIDS (they believe it leads to certain death), but very low levels of perceived susceptibility toward AIDS (e.g., because they believe their partner is "safe"). Alternatively, one can believe they are susceptible to harm from a threat (e.g., getting skin cancer) but believe the threat to be minimal (e.g., "I'll just have the dermatologist burn off any moles").

Therefore, it is important to promote both perceptions of severity of the threat as well as perceptions of the susceptibility toward the threat. In addition, it is critical that the message promote strong perceptions of both self-efficacy and response efficacy. Recall that threat motivates action—any action—and that perceptions of efficacy determine whether the action controls the danger (which is a health-protective response) or controls the fear (which inhibits health-protective behavior). Therefore, high threat messages *must* be accompanied by high efficacy messages. If it is difficult or impossible to promote strong perceptions of efficacy, then one probably should not use fear-arousing messages because they may backfire. For example, a study on the Trans-Africa Highway in Kenya showed that commercial sex workers had extremely low perceptions of self-efficacy and response efficacy toward using condoms (Cameron, Witte, Lapinski, & Nzyuko, 1996; Witte, Nzyuko, & Cameron, 1996). They felt that they would not be able to convince their partners to use condoms, and even if they did, they did not believe that condoms actually prevented HIV transmission. Because this population group had low perceptions of self- and response efficacy, any perceptions of threat would be likely to push them into fear control, where denial of the threat, defensive avoidance, or reactance would occur. Therefore, the best health communication campaign for this group would be one that focused on increasing self- and response efficacy perceptions toward positive behaviors.

Overall, health risk messages using the fear appeal approach have been shown to be effective in a variety of domains, including skin cancer prevention (Stephenson, 1993), pregnancy prevention (Witte, 1997), radon awareness (Witte, Berkowitz, McKeon, Cameron, Lapinski, & Liu, 1996), tractor safety (Witte, Peterson et al., 1993), nutrition programs (Wunsch, 1996), and breast self-examination (Kline, 1995). With a moderate amount of pilot testing, it is fairly easy to determine an audience's existing perceptions of threat and efficacy and then target campaign messages to produce high levels of threat and efficacy, which should lead to danger control actions.

Elaboration Likelihood Model

Petty and Cacioppo's (1986) Elaboration Likelihood Model (ELM) deals with how information is processed and interpreted and how this process leads to behavior change. Given the same message, two people may process the information in very different ways because of their cultural background, prior experiences, personalities, mood states, and so on, and come up with very different decisions (i.e., behavioral intentions). The ELM suggests there are two distinct routes to eventual behavior change: the central and peripheral routes. The "central" processing route is the most mindful and effortful processing route, whereby people draw on knowledge and experience to evaluate the information provided. The issue must be of great concern to the individual, and the person must be motivated *and* able to carefully examine the message or information

(Petty & Cacioppo, 1986). According to the ELM, information processed in this manner results in attitudes that are persistent over time, predictive of behavior, and relatively resistant to change.

The other processing route postulated by the ELM suggests that when motivation or ability to process information about an issue is low, then individuals will utilize the "peripheral route" when processing messages. In the peripheral route, simple associations, inferences, or heuristics may influence attitude change, but this change is effective for only short periods of time and is less resistant to subsequent contradictory messages. Communication campaigns that encourage processing through the peripheral route are those that utilize celebrity endorsements, inducement of positive affective states, and heuristic cues—all of which become associated with the recommended response. For example, "I usually agree with people who are like me" is a heuristic device that takes relatively little cognitive work and is an efficient way to make a decision. To promote long-term and stable behavior change, most health communicators want to promote central processing of a health-related message. That is, they want people carefully to consider a message and thoughtfully make decisions about their health. Involvement in an issue is the key to promoting central processing: a health issue must be relevant, pertinent, and important if people are to process the message centrally. For those unwilling or unable to process a message centrally (due to language barriers, literacy problems, fatigue, etc.), then peripheral cues such as credible sources or celebrity endorsements may be useful in promoting healthy behaviors.

The ELM has been employed less frequently by health communicators than other models, but the information processing notions of central versus peripheral processing are useful concepts for health communicators to consider. Other information processing models offer similar distinctions (e.g., Chaiken's systematic/heuristic model, 1980) and have refined the predictions offered by the ELM.

Inoculation

While many micro-level theories and models seek to change attitudes, beliefs, or behaviors, the inoculation approach offers lessons in how to promote resistance to unhealthy attitudes and behaviors. McGuire (1964, 1968) adapted the biological concept of inoculation to persuasion by attempting to "inoculate" individuals against certain unhealthy attitudes or behaviors. To accomplish inoculation, he exposed individuals to a threat (defined as a challenge to existing attitudes), which caused them to develop and strengthen arguments as to why they held a certain attitude. He found that by strengthening healthy attitudes and behaviors, individuals were more resistant to subsequent persuasive messages or challenges that tried to persuade them to engage in unhealthy behaviors.

Inoculation has been used most recently in smoking prevention projects with teens. Pfau, Van Bockern, and Kang (1992) sought to provide teens with inoculation against trying cigarette smoking. They found that when teens with low self-esteem (those at greatest risk for smoking initiation) were forewarned and were able to practice resisting messages, they were better able to withstand the pressure to begin smoking and were, in fact, less likely to initiate cigarette smoking. The application of inoculation theory to prevent people from ever engaging in risky behaviors (e.g., smoking, drug use) appears promising. However, more research using innoculation theory as a base is needed in the health arena in order to better understand the predictive value of the approach.

MACRO-LEVEL APPROACHES TO HEALTH COMMUNICATION

Health communication campaigns have often been based on the promotion of individual behavior change. However, a number of theories suggest that social circumstances may make behavior change difficult. These macro-level theories maintain a scope beyond that of individual-level behavior change and attempt to account for essential influences in the sociocultural environment. Macro-level theories focus on the "big picture" of health behavior change, but each theory examines this "big picture" via differing methods. Social marketing, for example, suggests a specific marketing approach for disseminating a health attitude or behavior, while diffusion of innovation theory investigates how large numbers of people adopt a new idea or product. The community empowerment approach seeks to understand factors at the level of the social system and how various components of a system can work together to provide a social and political environment that encourages healthy living. Each of these approaches will be discussed briefly below.

Social Marketing

One macro-level approach to health communication campaigns that has been widely used by health communicators in both the public and private sector of social marketing. Social marketing involves the design, implementation, and control of campaigns aimed at altering the level of acceptability of the social ideas or behaviors of a specific target group or groups (Kotler, 1984; Kotler & Roberto, 1989). Social marketing involves the application of for-profit management and marketing technologies to pro-social, nonprofit programs (Meyer & Dearing, 1996). Wallack (1989) suggests that one of the keys to this approach is the reduction of psychological, social, economic, and practical distance between the target of the campaign and the behavior.

Kotler and Roberto (1989) outline five basic steps in the social marketing management process. The first step is an analysis of the social marketing environment immediately surrounding the particular campaign. Next, the social marketer must research the target-adopter population and segment the audience into groups with common characteristics. The third step involves the careful design of the campaign's objectives and strategies. It is in this step that the social marketer must consider four concerns basic to every campaign—the factors that campaign designers refer to as the four "P's."

The four "P's" are product, price, promotion, and place, or what has been termed the "marketing mix." The product is the behavior to be changed or the product that the target audience is encouraged to adopt. Campaigns have promoted a number of health behaviors as "products," including condom use, contraception, and others. For example, in the Stanford Heart Disease Prevention Program (SHDPP), the "products" promoted were regular exercise, smoking cessation, dietary changes, and stress reduction, in order to prevent heart disease. The second "P" in the marketing mix refers to price and includes any physical, social, or psychological cost related to compliance with a campaign. In the case of the SHDPP's Smokers' Challenge (one facet of the large-scale program), the costs of joining the challenge included the money and energy expended in accepting the challenge, as well as the psychological costs of giving up smoking. The third component of the marketing mix, promotion, deals with how the product can be represented or packaged to compensate for the costs of adopting the recommended response. The Smokers' Challenge attempted to promote the contest by removing or reducing the financial cost of the program in order to make it more appealing to target audiences (Lefebvre & Flora, 1988). Place is the final component in the marketing mix and involves the availability of the recommended response. The designers of the Smokers' Challenge attempted to make access to information about the program as simple as possible. For example, they mailed information on how to quit smoking to individuals in the households participating in the study.

The final step in the management of the social marketing process involves the planning, organization, implementation, control, and evaluation of the social marketing program. Researchers have noted the difficulties inherent in this task for community-based health communication campaigns (Lefebvre & Flora, 1988). Meyer and Dearing (1996) suggest that the final step is differentially important, depending on the resources of the organization conducting the campaign and the type of population that is being targeted. Many programs have utilized some aspect of the social marketing approach inadvertently, through the use of principles such as audience segmentation and evaluation. For example, Rogers (1996) suggests that many of the HIV/AIDS prevention programs in San Francisco are based on the principles of social marketing, although few of the designers acknowledge it. Overall, social marketing has been widely used in health communication campaigns. The most compelling application of this approach can be found in developing nations where social marketing has been used to promote family planning, infant health, and condom use to prevent HIV transmission (Rogers, 1996).

Diffusion

Diffusion of innovation theory (Rogers, 1995; Rogers & Shoemaker, 1971) examines the ways in which new ideas, practices, or objects are communicated through certain channels over time among members of a social system. This theory has seen application in a large number of health communication campaigns. Rogers (1995) outlines four major elements in the diffusion process, described below.

An *innovation* is the belief or practice that is perceived as subjectively new by an individual or group. The potential adopter of the innovation will be more likely to make the decision to adopt if the innovation is seen as advantageous, compatible with the adoptees' values, noncomplex, trialable, and if it provides observable results. For example, this approach has been utilized to promote both products (e.g., condoms) and ideas (e.g., it is essential for one to wear a condom each time one engages in sexual intercourse) related to safe sexual practices. Svenkerund, Singhal, and Papa (1996) examined the use of diffusion of innovation concepts for AIDS education programs in Bangkok, Thailand. In the programs examined, they found that the economic advantages and compatibility with the values of the target were the aspects of the innovation most frequently emphasized.

The *communication channel*, or the means by which a message is transmitted from one individual or a group to another, is a second element of the diffusion model and one that was also viewed as important by HIV/AIDS educators in Thailand. The channels through which information about the innovation is disseminated can be face-to-face, electronically facilitated interpersonal interaction, or mass media-based. The selection of channel is contingent on the target group—some channels may be differentially effective depending on the characteristics of the target group. For example, some groups have less access to mediated channels, such as television or radio, and would be reached most effectively through posters or flyers.

The most frequent transfer of ideas occurs between two individuals who are similar or homophilous (Rogers, 1995). Homophily is an important factor in the diffusion of ideas. It involves the degree to which two people consider themselves similar to one another along a number of dimensions. More effective communication occurs if the potential adopter feels that he or she is similar to the source of message. Some heterophily is effective in the diffusion process if this difference between the sender and the potential adopter is due to the sender's level of expertise regarding the innovation. It is expected, for example, that the outreach worker in an HIV/AIDS information center would have a greater level of knowledge about the disease than that worker's potential clients.

The third major element in the diffusion process is the *time* dimension, which is important for the innovation-decision process, the innovativeness of the target adopter, and the rate of adoption of the innovation. When the target receives the information about the innovation, the target engages in an innovation-decision process that involves a sequence of points relating to the acceptance or rejection of the innovation. The rate at which the target usually adopts new ideas relative to other members of the social system is also an important element. The adopter categories include innovators, early adopters, early majority, late majority, and laggards. The innovators are individuals who are likely to seek and adopt new ideas first; the other categories of individuals follow respectively. Another element related to the time dimension is that of an innovation's rate of adoption. Typically, when the number of individuals adopting an innovation is plotted over time, it results in an S-shaped curve (Rogers, 1995).

The final element in the diffusion process is that of the *social system*, which Rogers (1995) defines as a set of interrelated units engaged in joint problem-solving to accomplish some common goal (p. 23). A social system can be a small farming community in a developing country or a group of medical doctors at a hospital. Social systems are structured in various ways, have differing norms, make different decisions about innovations, and place emphasis on different opinion leaders. The opinion leaders in a social system are those who are consistently able to influence other members' attitudes and behaviors while playing an important role in the adoption decision.

Diffusion of public health information has typically revolved around two areas—the diffusion of new drugs and health information to health professionals, and the diffusion of health information (usually related to family-planning methods or decreasing risky sexual practices) to clients or patients. Svenkerund, Singhal, and Papa (1996) found that the elements of the diffusion process that were utilized most frequently by the most effective communication and outreach programs included homophily, opinion leadership, and the innovation-decision process.

Community Empowerment

A third macro-level approach to the design and implementation of health communication campaigns is that of community empowerment. The concept is based on Freire's (1973) writings in "Education for Critical Consciousness." The recent emphasis on community empowerment (although it is hardly a "new" concept) and the examination of sociocultural factors that influence health behavior appears to be a response to the frequent use of micro-level theories of behavior change in health communication. Several authors have likened this emphasis on the individual to "victim blaming" (Tones & Tilford, 1994) and argue that health communication should be based on the idea that the cultural, historical, social, economic, and political contexts in which the individual exists must be recognized (Israel, Checkoway, Schulz, & Zimmerman, 1994, p. 153).

Israel et al. (1994) make the distinction between three levels of empowerment—individual, organizational, and community. They argue that the concept of empowerment is meaningful only if these three levels are viewed as parts of a whole. Individual or psychological empowerment is similar to self-efficacy (Bandura, 1977a) and deals with the ability of an individual to make decisions and to have control over her or his own life. Organizational empowerment encompasses organizations that empower the individual, are democratically managed, emphasize cooperative decision making, and allow members to play a role in goal design and attainment. Community empowerment involves empowerment on *both* the individual and organizational level. Individuals and organizations utilize their skills and resources in a collective manner to "provide enhanced support for each other, address conflicts within the community, and gain increased influence and control over the quality of life in their community" (Israel et al., 1994). Community empowerment is not only a process, but also an outcome (Eisen, 1994; Israel et al., 1994). That is, the success of a health campaign or intervention can be measured by determining whether or not an increase in power and control is a result of the process.

One recent application of the community empowerment approach is the Boston Healthy Start Initiative (Plough & Olafson, 1994), a federally funded infant mortality-reduction program. The program was evaluated in terms of whether or not it resulted in community mobilization, governance, and capacity-building strategies. The program met these goals in part, but not without a great deal of conflict. Plough and Olafson (1994) suggest that for an empowerment program to work there must be a willingness to reinvent standard practices, hard work, and willingness on the part of the participants. The approach has also been used in diverse areas by attempting to empower a wide range of communities from rural Chinese women and grassroots workers (Wang & Burris, 1994) to pregnant homeless women (Ovrebo, Ryan, Jackson, & Hutchinson, 1994) (see Eisen, 1994 for a review).

DIRECTIONS FOR FUTURE RESEARCH

There are several obvious directions for health communication campaign design. Theoretically based campaign development frequently results in more effective campaigns. There is a need for those who develop and test theories and approaches and those who utilize these theories and approaches to meet on some common ground. Current approaches and theories must be applied, or new theories must be developed, that are politically, socially, and fiscally efficient. The theories presented above are not without flaws and can benefit from continual examination and refinement. The practical use of theory, however, must include the use of entire models, not just certain components of models, and should utilize theory in the planning process as opposed to a post hoc explanation for events.

A call for multidisciplinary work is hardly original, but nowhere is it more necessary than as a solution to national and international health problems. The SHDPP (cf. Flora, Maccoby, & Farquhar, 1989), one of the most frequently discussed examples of theoretically based campaigns, was a collaborative effort between cardiologists, communication scholars, and public health specialists. Bringing individuals together with differing areas of expertise can only serve to increase the effectiveness of health communication campaigns. It is necessary, however, to allow the experts to develop their areas of expertise. Individuals trained in theoretically based campaign design should be the primary architects of the messages and promotional material as opposed to those who are experts in medicine.

Given the changing face of the U.S. population and the shrinking globe, there is a growing need to determine the most effective methods of disseminating information to individuals other than those in "mainstream" Western societies. Many of the theories and approaches discussed above have not been tested with multicultural or international samples, but attempts are often made to apply the principles to these populations. There are potential problems with such an approach. For example, the focus on individual accountability for health behaviors, which is common in many micro-level theories, may not be realistic in cultures where an individual's well-being is a function of other people in their collective (e.g., extended family).

One final area for health communicators to examine is the role of new (or fairly new) communication technology in health education campaigns. Clearly, what is "new" varies by culture and will impact the dissemination of health messages differentially. In many areas in the United States, for example, the World Wide Web provides both communicators and audiences of campaign messages with a wealth of health-related information at their fingertips. For example, many HIV/AIDS resource centers use the Internet to supply their clients with the most current information on treatment and prevention of HIV (Lapinski, 1997). The use of health communication campaigns in this medium is just emerging as an important area of research and will be the "state of the art" in future examinations of campaign effectiveness.

As Paisley noted in the opening quotation, health comunication campaign research, theory, and practice has come a long way in the last 20 or 30 years. With effort, more will be achieved in promoting health and preventing disease as the twenty-first century begins.

NOTES

Portions of this chapter are drawn from Meyer and Witte, 1995; Witte, 1992a, 1992b, 1994, 1998. (Material from Meyer and Witte, 1995 is used with the permission of Hayden-McNeil Publishing. For permission to photocopy this section, please contact Hayden-McNeil Publishing.)

The authors would like to thank Charles Atkin and Kenzie Cameron for their advice and comments.

1. Originally, the two factors were labeled "technological risk" and "severity" (Fischoff et al., 1978). In later work by the same authors, the factor structure was reformulated, resulting in the shifting and renaming of dimensions.

10

Health Images on Television

Nancy Signorielli

SYNOPSIS

The media are a major source of information about health for most Americans. This review describes television's images about health and the medical community, sex and sexuality, alcohol and drugs, and nutrition. Health is a prevalent theme in entertainment programming, but television's images often are not very accurate or helpful. Doctors are overrepresented on television and, until recently, were presented in very positive roles. Television's messages about sexuality and sex exist on several levels (physical attractiveness, interpersonal relationships, specific sexual behaviors) but provide a considerable amount of misinformation. Similarly, while many characters drink alcoholic beverages on television, few are actively involved in using either "legal" (prescription) or illegal drugs. Finally, television provides very problematic and potentially harmful messages about food and nutrition, especially for younger viewers. Overall, most of the images about health on television are in serious conflict with realistic guidelines for health, nutrition, and medicine. More importantly, research on how these images contribute to what people know about health and medicine, although somewhat scarce, consistently indicate that those who spend more time with the media, particularly television, may have beliefs about health-related issues that are in conflict with the things that should be done to remain healthy or improve the current status of their health.

In the past 10 to 15 years, interpretation of the concept of health has changed from a focus on being "sick" to a focus on being "healthy" (Lunin, 1987). In this light, society has come to acknowledge the importance of cultural influences, particularly the media in imparting both heath information and misinformation and thereby affecting the nation's health. The Surgeon-General's 1979 report, *Healthy People: The Surgeon General's Report on Health Promotion and Disease Prevention*, found that as much as half of U.S. mortality could be accounted for by culturally sustained behavioral and lifestyle factors that affect both physical and mental well-being (Lunin, 1987). In the early 1990s, J. Michael McGinnis, M.D., noted that 40 to 70 percent of all premature deaths and a third to two-thirds of all disabilities could be prevented by controlling fewer than 10 health risk factors, including lack of exercise, poor diet, use of drugs and tobacco, and alcohol abuse (U.S. Department of Health and Human Services, 1991).

This shift in health priorities to cultural factors highlights the central role of the media, especially television, in socializing individuals and stabilizing lifestyles. The success or failure of education and information campaigns depends largely on the broader cultural context into which they are injected. Few campaigns can succeed without taking these cultural factors into account. Since media images, particularly television images, may run counter to good health practices, it is imperative to know what messages and images television and other mass media discharge into the mainstream of common consciousness.

For the majority of Americans, the media are a major source of health information. Almost one-quarter of daily newspaper stories are related to health (DeFoe & Breed, 1991). Health-related magazines, such as *Prevention*, and more narrowly cast cable programming focusing on health, targeted to specialized audiences, have proliferated in the past 10 to 15 years. Broadcast television is yet another important source of health-related messages. Daytime serial dramas (soap operas), in particular, are very effective vehicles for both overt and embedded messages about health (Walsh-Childers, 1991). Although there is some concern about how accurately newspapers report health and science news (Molitor, 1991), health-related themes in network television's dramatic programs typically are portrayed very accurately (DeFoe & Breed, 1991). In short, while the average American may visit a doctor one or two times a year, she or he probably reads a newspaper or magazine article about medicine (or health) a few times a month and may watch several television shows featuring a medical problem each week (Sandman, 1976).

The mass media play an important role in the lives of most people. Each day, in the average American home, the television set is "on" for almost seven hours and watched by individual family members for approximately three hours a day. Children and older people watch the most; adolescents the least, but even their viewing averages 20 or more hours each week (Nielsen, 1990). Most Americans report that they read a daily newspaper, and television is often cited as the major source of news and information. Among sources of health information, television is typically cited, after "doctors and dentists," as the main source of information about health (Lunin, 1987; Yankelovich, Skelly, and White, Inc., 1979), and television news is seen as an important source of information about children's health (Prabhu, Duffy, & Stapleton, 1996).

Television is our most common and constant learning environment. Its world both mirrors and leads society. Television is first and foremost, however, a narrative instrument and, as such, is the wholesale distributor of images that form the mainstream of popular culture. In the West, children are born into homes in which, for the first time in history, a commercial institution, rather than parents, church, or school, formulates and unfolds the stories that shape culture.

Television viewing, however, is relatively nonselective. Many people watch by the clock rather than by the program or continue to watch, often repetitively changing the channels to find something of interest. Delivery systems, such as cable and VCRs, provide even more opportunities for viewing and channel surfing.

The world of television is, for the most part, a stable and repetitive world of drama, game shows, talk shows, news, information, and commercials designed to attract (and sell) the largest possible public at the least possible cost. Its entertainment programs and commercials, with potential health (and other) messages embedded in them, reach tens of millions of viewers each day. More importantly, these messages reach viewers who would otherwise not expose themselves to such information and do not fully realize that these messages may affect them. This chapter will briefly describe how four topics are presented on television—physical health and the medical community, sex and sexuality, alcohol and drugs, and nutrition. It will also explore, to the extent possible, how these images may be related to what people know about these topics and how television may contribute to unhealthy lifestyles.

HEALTH AND ILLNESS ON TELEVISION

Scholars and critics have noted for more than 30 years that health is a prevalent theme in both entertainment and news programming. Often, however, what audiences see is not helpful or very accurate. Smith, Trivax, Zuehlke, Lowinger, and Nghiem (1972) examined 130 hours of programming broadcast during one week in 1970, evaluating all items (entertainment, news, commercials, etc.) relating to mental or physical illness, doctors, dentists, medical treatment, smoking, or health. This analysis revealed that while health-related content appeared in 7 percent of the programming, less than one-third was useful information. In fact, 70 percent of the health material was inaccurate, misleading, or both. Messages urging the use of pills or other drug-related remedies outnumbered messages against drug use or abuse by 10:1. In this week of programming, major health problems such as cancer, heart disease, stroke, accidents, hepatitis, sexually transmitted diseases, mental health, and sex education were practically ignored.

An analysis of the 10 top-rated prime-time fictional series broadcast in the 1979–1980 season (Heeter, Perlstadt, & Greenberg, 1984) found more than five medical and health-related scenes each hour. These episodes typically involved current health problems of older adults, young children, and women, and were mentioned; rather than featured, in the story line. The depictions were not very informative. The treatment provided by the physician and his or her overall concern were mundane rather than heroic, and patients were rarely shown interacting with their doctor. In addition, the cost of medical care was never mentioned; characters sought and received the best medical care with no apparent thought of financial consequence.

An examination of trends in 17 years of network dramatic programming (Gerbner, Morgan, & Signorielli, 1982; Signorielli, 1987) found that 40 percent of programs and 8 percent of the major characters in prime-time programs were presented with illnesses or injuries that required medical treatment. Illness and injury seem to affect heroes and villains, males and females, young and old, and other groups of characters quite similarly.

Turow and Coe (1985), in an examination of 14 days of network programming (morning news, soap operas, evening news, prime time, and commercials), detected little similarity between television medicine and current issues in U.S. health care (e.g., the importance of chronic illnesses, rising costs, hospitals' desire for frugality, competition for patients whose ability to pay is unaffected by declining federal and state payment policy). One-third of illness-related coverage was discovered in commercials for pharmaceutical products, especially cold and pain remedies; prime-time network programming accounted for another third of coverage, daytime serials made up almost a fifth, news magazines more than a tenth, and evening news broadcasts less than one-twentieth. No matter in which program illness appeared, however, it took center stage: almost 9 out of 10 interactions involving ill people revolved around their maladies.

Turow and Coe (1985) also learned that almost none of the television portrayals presented the illness as chronic. Television focused on acute illness that could be cured (even if the doctor had to go to heroic ends). Moreover, attempts to deal with the illness focused on biomedical-, pharmacological-, or technological-related cures rather than on its interpersonal or psychological entailments. In addition, the hospital was the location for the professional treatment of illness; medical personnel aside from physicians and nurses were ignored; and medical care "was portrayed as overwhelmingly appropriate, nonpolitical, and an unlimited resource" (Turow & Coe, 1985, p. 47)—a far cry from the reality of health care in the United States.

The world of the daytime serial drama, the soap opera, consistently incorporates themes relating to illness and injury and may be a very important source of medical advice (Lunin, 1987; Gerbner, Gross, Morgan & Signorielli, 1981). Katzman's (1972) analysis of a week-long sample of daytime serials found six cases of mental and psychosomatic illness, five cases of physical disability, four pregnancies, three successful medical treatments, and two instances of important medical research. Cassata, Skill, and Boadu (1979), using a year's issues of *Soap Opera Digest*, studied all daytime serials broadcast in 1977 and found that sickness, injury, and medical treatment were important and pervasive problems involving nearly half of all characters. Characters had psychiatric disorders, heart attacks, pregnancies, automobile accidents, attempted homicides, attempted suicides, and infectious diseases (in that order). The principal killers were homicides, car accidents, and heart attacks. Similarly, Heeter, Perlstadt, & Greenberg (1984) found that health problems and conditions were recurring themes in two top-rated serial dramas broadcast in the 1979–1980 season. Pregnancy is especially problematic in the soap operas. Cassata et al. (1979) found that half of the pregnancies resulted in miscarriages and 16 percent in the death of the pregnant woman. Olsen (1994) in an analysis of two composite weeks of network daytime serial dramas, counted 118 discussions or depictions of pregnancy (about one per hour) and determined that pregnancy-related health problems appeared frequently.

Television Doctors and Nurses

Even though characters are seldom physically ill on television, the world of television is populated by a disproportionately large number of doctors and nurses. An analysis of major characters in samples of programming broadcast between 1973 and 1985 found 103 physicians, 13 psychiatrists, and 28 nurses for 228 physically ill and 88 mentally ill characters: a ratio of one doctor for almost every two patients. Health professionals (doctors and nurses) dominate the ranks of professionals on television, numbering almost five times their real-life ranks. Only criminals or law enforcers are more numerous in television entertainment (Signorielli, 1993).

Doctor shows on television have typically fit a tried and true formula—a strong white male physician in a large urban teaching hospital or small-town private office (Turow, 1989). Nurses play roles similar to those of most women on television—secondary characters who are not very important to the overall story line.

Physicians probably have fared better in television portrayals than any other occupation on television. Compared to other professionals, they are good, successful, and peaceful. Less than 4 percent of television doctors (major characters) are evil, which is half the number of other professionals. Personality ratings used to assess television doctors reveal them to be a bit more fair, sociable, and warm than most other characters. Doctors, in comparison to nurses, are rated smarter and more rational, stable, and fair (Signorielli, 1993). Nurses, on the other hand, are often presented with negative stereotypes, and their roles are often underplayed (Kalisch & Kalisch, 1982, 1984).

McLaughlin (1975) found that physicians symbolize authority, power, and knowledge; they dominate and control the lives of others. In addition, doctors are easily accessible to patients, command nurses (who rarely disobey their orders), advise each other, but rarely receive advice from patients or orders from superiors (and, when they do, they often disregard them). Yet they are also honest, courageous, kind, ethical, and responsive to the requests of their patients.

In the early generation of medical programs, television doctors often risked status or prestige to perform an unusual or dangerous treatment; they also disobeyed rules and conventions, always succeeding against odds to treat or cure some disease or settle some crisis.

The most current crop of medical programs (*ER, Chicago Hope*), however, may be tarnishing this image. Today's programs not only show physicians in their traditional role of diagnosing and treating patients but also show that television's doctors may be uncertain about their diagnoses, and may make mistakes when treating patients. Some even have unflattering personalities—they are arrogant, greedy, and may commit adultery (Pfau, Mullen, & Garrow, 1995).

The very positive image of doctors on television probably contributed to their very high approval ratings in public opinion polls conducted during the 1950s, 1960s, and 1970s (Jeffe & Jeffe, 1984). In addition, Jeffries-Fox and Signorielli (1978) found that adolescents' conceptions about doctors and what they do was consistent with how this group was portrayed on television. Recently, however, there is some evidence that the less positive portrayals in the current doctor programs (*ER, Chicago Hope*) influence how physicians are perceived by the public, particularly among those individuals who watch more medically oriented programs (Pfau, Mullen, & Garrow, 1995). The results of a survey of 600 adults in a midwestern county revealed that the general public perceived physicians as very personable, physically attractive, and powerful but as lacking character. They were seen as less moral, more selfish, less good, and less honest. These authors expressed concern that these recent, less flattering depictions of physicians on television could erode public confidence in doctors.

SEX AND SEXUALITY

The role of the media, particularly television, in sexual socialization constitutes an area of considerable concern. In the past, the commonly held assumption was that information about sex and sexuality should be transmitted within the family, which strove to maintain consistent moral values and understanding. In reality, however, many parents are reticent or even embarrassed to talk to their children about "the facts of life." Thus, adolescents are caught in the dilemma of wanting to know about sex—what is happening to their bodies, how to have a relationship with someone, how to know when they are "in love," and just what sexual activity entails. They often turn to and rely on their peers, who are often equally misinformed about sex (Strouse & Fabes, 1985).

The media, particularly television, because of its indirect nonthreatening, storytelling style, are important sources of sexual information for children, adolescents, and even adults. Until recently, the media have also contributed to the climate of little or misinformation because their primary agenda is to attract and maintain an audience. Consequently, media images are crafted not principally to inform viewers but to attract them; sexuality is one of the ways the media, particularly television, attracts and holds their audience. Until recently, the media have also been reticent or perhaps unable to mention teenage pregnancy or sexually transmitted disease and to offer information that might help combat these problems because viewers might be offended.

The media's message of sexuality exists on several different levels. It is present in models of physical attractiveness, in the way romantically involved characters interact with each other, and in the specific sexual behaviors that are either seen or alluded to on television, in the movies, and in magazines. Sexuality and sexual attractiveness are traditional lures used in commercials and magazine advertisements to help sell products. Consequently, we must ask how often adolescents (and adults) buy certain products because they are "supposed to" make them more sexually attractive. Soley and Reid (1985), in an analysis of advertisements in *TV Guide* also found that sexuality is used to promote television itself. Commercials for new as well as ongoing series often highlight sexual tension as well as sexually attractive actors and actresses.

The amount of specific sexual content on television has risen steadily since the mid-1970s and is now an integral part of many television programs (Franzblau, Sprafkin, & Rubinstein, 1977). Signorielli (1987) found that since the late 1970s the amount of sex on prime-time dramatic programs has remained at consistently high levels, occurring in 9 out of 10 programs. This analysis of eight annual week-long samples of prime-time network dramatic programming revealed that sex was incidental to the plot in 60 percent of these programs and a major or a significant plot feature in 35 percent of the programs. One-quarter of all sexual references on television were light or comic in nature, and sexual references were especially prevalent in situation comedies.

Sapolsky and Tabarlet (1991) noted slightly more sexual language and behaviors in a week of prime-time network programming broadcast in 1989 (a mention every four minutes, or about 15 per hour) compared to a week of programming broadcast in 1979 (once every five minutes, or about 12 per hour). There were very few mentions of sexual responsibility. Similarly, in a sample of network programming broadcast in 1992, sexual behaviors occurred at a rate of about 12 each hour in programming with an additional five per hour in program promotions (Shidler & Lowry, 1995). As with the Sapolsky and Tabarlet (1991) study, there were very few mentions of negative outcomes—AIDS, STDs, or pregnancy. Sexual topics now seen or discussed on television cover a wide variety of issues. MacDonald and Macdonald (1994), in samples of network prime-time programming broadcast between 1989 and 1993, found that the depiction of actual sexual behaviors declined slightly but that issues such as child molestation, homosexuality, and rape were discussed in more depth and with more candor.

Sex on prime time is related to program genre (Smith, 1991). Situation comedies treat sex with humor; they include sexual taboos, innuendo, and ironic humor. The nighttime soap operas examine the consequences of sexual activity and typically link sex with power. Action-adventure programs and detective shows have yet their own brand of sexuality, often focusing on sex as related to criminal investigations and the sexual underworld.

Daytime serial dramas have traditionally relied on sex and sexual liaisons, intricacies, and disillusionments as part of their continuing story lines. A number of studies have found that sexual relations were most likely to occur between partners who were not married to each other, and that sexual acts and references occurred quite frequently (Greenberg, Adelman, & Neuendorf, 1981; Lowry & Towles, 1989b). While Lowry and Towles (1989b) found that the level of sexual behavior remained about the same between 1979 and 1987, Olsen (1994) noted fewer depictions of explicit sexual behaviors in a sample of soap operas broadcast in the 1989–1990 season.

Although there are still many instances of premarital sex in daytime serials, the tendency in recent years has slightly favored depicting such activity in monogamous relationships. For example, Larson (1991), in one year of episodes of *All My Children*, found that premarital sex typically took place in a committed relationship. Moreover, if deception played a role in the relationship there were negative consequences, and, the greater the deception, the more severe the consequences. Similarly, Olson (1994) found that even though unmarried partners were still shown in sexual behaviors, the ratio of sexual behaviors between unmarried partners to the ratio of such behaviors between married partners was smaller than in previous studies.

Music videos have emerged as a medium designed almost exclusively for adolescents and young adults. Sherman and Dominick (1986) found that sexual activity, much of it adolescent and titillating, appeared in three-quarters of the videos at a rate of almost five acts per video. Sex in the videos was seldom overt and usually traditional: most of the sexual acts were flirtations and non-intimate touching. Similarly, Baxter, DeRiemer, Landini, Leslie, and Singletary (1985) found that sex in music videos was understated and adolescent in nature, focusing primarily on attracting the opposite sex with images relying on innuendo rather than overt physical behaviors. More recently, Sommers-Flanagan, Sommers-Flanagan, and Davis (1993) found that women were involved in more implicit sexual behaviors and were more likely to be the object of sexual advances.

Contraception and Sexually Transmitted Diseases

Contraception and sexually transmitted diseases are topics that have been ignored in entertainment media. Broadcast television does not adequately focus on the negative aspects of sexual behavior—unwanted pregnancy, sexually transmitted diseases (STDs), or AIDS. In the daytime serials, sex continues to be the norm for unmarried partners, with little thought given to the consequences. No one ever contracts or has a sexually transmitted disease. AIDS, in particular, is rarely mentioned because it would be a particularly thorny issue in that the sexual histories of most characters are extremely intertwined. Nevertheless, Olson's (1994) recent analysis of sex on the daytime serials found some discussion of the consequences of unprotected sex in a sample of the serials broadcast in 1989–1990. Interestingly, Logan (1993) described how two characters in a serial were tested for AIDS before they became involved sexually.

Similarly, there are few references to contraception or STDs in prime-time dramatic programs (Lowry & Towles, 1989a; Sapolsky & Tabarlet, 1991). In short, as Planned Parenthood has noted, television provides a national sex misinformation (rather than information) campaign (Lowry & Towles, 1989b).

Effects of Sexual Imagery on Television

These sexually explicit messages on television may influence viewers', particularly teenagers', knowledge about sex. Teenagers, for example, rank television after parents, peers, and school, as a source of information about birth control and sex (Planned Parenthood, 1987). Adolescents also believe that television is more encouraging and supportive of having sex than their friends (Newcomer & Brown, 1984).

A few surveys have examined how adolescents' behaviors and beliefs were related to television viewing. Strouse, Buerkel-Rothfuss, and Long (1995), using survey data from 13- to 18-year-old adolescents, found an association between reported viewing of music videos and permissive sexual attitudes and behaviors, especially for girls. Another study found that adolescents who took part in potentially risky behaviors (drinking, smoking cigarettes, smoking marijuana, sexual intercourse, etc.) watched music videos and movies on television and listened to the radio more than adolescents who engaged in fewer risky behaviors (Klein, Brown, Childers, Oliveri, Porter, & Dykers, 1993).

A number of experimental studies discovered relationships between viewing sexually explicit materials and accepting less stringent views about sex. Greeson and Williams (1986) noted that after seeing less than an hour of videos on MTV, adolescents in the seventh and twelfth grades were more likely to approve of premarital sex than their peers who had not seen the music videos. Zillmann and Bryant (1988), in studies of male and female college students, determined that exposure to nonviolent sexually explicit films was related to the acceptance of promiscuity and sexual infidelity.

There have been few studies focusing on the relationship between television viewing and initiation of sexual intercourse. Peterson, Moore, and Furstenberg (1991) found, among a panel of adolescent boys, a relationship between viewing programs high in sexual content and the subsequent initiation of sexual activity. They did not find, however, a similar relationship for the girls. Brown and Newcomer (1991) learned that those adolescents who watched television programs that were "sexy" were more likely to have had sexual intercourse in the preceding year. Brown, Childers, and Waszak (1990) note that this study could not answer the question of whether viewing led to sexual behavior or whether being sexually active led to the viewing of more sexually explicit materials. Overall, these studies point to a relationship between viewing sexual materials and being more sexually active.

ALCOHOL AND DRUGS

References to alcohol and drinking have appeared consistently on television. Signorielli (1987) found, over the past two decades, a steady increase in the number of references to alcohol (talking about, showing characters drinking). While the percentage of programs mentioning the harmful effects of alcohol increased from less than 5 percent to 25 percent of the yearly sample, the number of alcoholics remained about the same (1 to 2 percent of the major characters in each yearly sample). Similarly, Wallack, Breed, and Cruz (1987) found that 80 percent of prime-time programs in a sample of 1984 programming contained one or more appearances of alcohol and that alcohol was actually ingested on 60 percent of the programs. In this sample of television dramas, most drinking took place at the rate of 11 specific acts of drinking per hour. Wallack et al. concluded that a regular viewer of dramas would be likely to see more than 20 specific acts of drinking during an evening's viewing.

Drinking is also a regular and frequent occurrence in the daytime serial dramas; drinking levels, however, are substantially below those isolated in analyses of prime-time programming (Greenberg, 1981; Wallack, Breed, & DeFoe, 1985). MacDonald (1983) found that, in soap operas, alcohol was the most frequently mentioned "drug" and that, contrary to statistics on the U.S. population, more women than men were portrayed as alcoholics or problem drinkers and that most of the alcoholics belonged to the upper-middle class rather than working class.

How much drinking actually takes place on television? Some studies have found that drinking on television usually is not a casual affair of one or two drinks. Breed and DeFoe (1981), for example, analyzed 233 scenes about alcohol in prime-time drama and found that 40 percent consisted of five or more drinks and 18 percent involved chronic drinkers. More recent evidence, however, shows declines in heavy drinking (Wallack, Grube, Madden, & Breed, 1990). Nevertheless, the rate of drinking per hour in 1986 (eight drinking acts per hour) was higher than in 1976 (five drinking acts per hour).

Not only do alcoholic beverages outnumber other beverages consumed on television, but also the pattern of drinking is opposite to what occurs in daily life. On television, characters drink alcohol twice as many times as they drink coffee or tea, 14 times as frequently as soft drinks, and more than 15 times as frequently as water.

Signorielli's (1987) analysis revealed that more than one-third of the major characters in prime-time programming are social drinkers. Men and women are equally likely to drink. Those who drink are more likely than those who do not drink to be involved in a romantic relationship. Alcoholics, on the other hand, while small in number, differ considerably from the typical social drinker on television. Alcoholics are more likely to be men, are much more likely to be involved in violence, and tend to have negative personality traits.

Breed and DeFoe (1981) found that characters seldom refused a drink or disapproved of drinking. If and when disapproval was expressed, it was usually mild, ineffective, came from women, and was directed at women and teenage drinkers. Breed and DeFoe also found that while drinking was seldom rationalized or excused in dramas, it often was in situation comedies. In situation comedies intoxication and hangovers usually were treated humorously. The most frequent reason for drinking on television is a personal crisis. For the most part, the harmful effects or consequences of drinking are rarely presented adequately (Signorielli, 1987).

Daytime serials, however, present a more realistic picture of alcohol as a potentially harmful and problematic substance (Greenberg, 1981; Wallack, Breed, & DeFoe, 1985). Wallack et al. (1985) found that one serial drama, *All My Children*, accurately portrayed drinking problems, presented a number of good role models for social drinking and abstinence, and frequently presented negative reinforcement (and even positive interventions by other characters) for characters who took part in heavy or high-risk drinking.

Analyses of commercials for alcoholic beverages reveal that those for beer predominate. Atkin, Hocking, and Block (1984) summarize research indicating that many of the commercials for alcoholic beverages imply that alcohol can be consumed in great quantities, few commercials suggest moderation in drinking, and none mention any harmful effects. Commercials for alcoholic beverages, particularly beer, outnumber commercials for any other beverage on sports programming. The images in these commercials typically are at odds with safe use practices, and there are few, if any, messages for moderation (Madden & Grube, 1994). Finally, in an analysis of programming broadcast on ABC, CBS, NBC, and CNN between 8:00 A.M. and 11:30 P.M., commercials for alcoholic beverages were shown to outnumber messages (news stories, public service announcements, etc.) about illegal drugs by 39 to 1 (Fedler, Phillips, Raker, et al., 1994), while messages about alcoholic beverages outnumbered public service announcements about illegal drugs by 45 to 1.

Effects of Messages About Alcohol

A nationwide survey of 1,200 respondents between 12 and 22 years of age revealed that alcohol advertising appears to contribute to certain forms of problem drinking. There is a moderate positive correlation between exposure to advertisements for wine, beer, and liquor and excessive consumption of alcoholic beverages as well as drinking in hazardous situations, such as automobile driving (Atkin, Neuendorf, & McDermott, 1983). In a similar study, teenagers were asked about their exposure to TV and magazine advertising for beer, wine, and liquor (Atkin, Hocking, & Block, 1984). The results revealed significant relationships between exposure and drinking behavior, especially for liquor and beer. These authors also found that peer pressure seemed to play a larger role in wine and beer drinking, while advertising had a greater contribution to liquor consumption.

There is some evidence, however, that warnings about the dangers of alcohol can decrease confidence in erroneous beliefs about the risks of alcohol. Slater and Domenech (1995) found that subjects who viewed beer advertisements with warnings about the dangers of drinking had less confidence in their beliefs about the benefits of beer. On the other hand, those youngsters who saw the advertisements without the warnings expressed more confidence in their beliefs about beer.

Finally, even though this review has not examined the large body of literature relating to health campaigns, one campaign deserves mention because it illustrates how images on television can make a difference. The Harvard Alcohol Project (Winsten, 1994), was a successful media campaign conducted in collaboration with the television industry. This campaign worked with writers and directors to introduce the designated driver as part of a story line. Specifically, in a social drinking situation one of the main and popular characters in an ongoing series explicitly stated that they were the designated driver for the evening. By legitimizing the nondrinker's role in television programs, this strategy attempted to take the onus from the nondrinker in society.

While images relating to drinking and alcohol abound on television and in other media, images relating to drugs and drug abuse are relatively rare. Research by numerous investigators (e.g., DeFoe, Breed, & Wallack, 1983; Gerbner et al., 1981a; Greenberg et al., 1979, 1980) indicates that illicit drug use and abuse seldom occur in entertainment programming. Depictions typically focus on the illegal nature of drugs, and the action often revolves around "catching" the drug pushers.

FOOD AND NUTRITION

Information about nutrition is received from a myriad of sources. Advertising, particularly television commercials, plays an important role in helping the public find out what foods are health and unhealthy. In particular, there is considerable concern about the types of nutrition messages found in programming geared especially for children because it is filled with commercials for nonnutritious foods.

The number of minutes allocated to commercials in an hour has remained more or less constant for the past 10 to 20 years and is now regulated by the Children's Television Viewing Act of 1990. Children today, however, see more commercials than they did in the 1970s because today's commercials are shorter. Condry, Bence, and Scheibe (1988) estimate that children see more than 40,000 commercials each year, 30,000 of which are for specific products.

Food products dominate commercial messages on children's programs except for the 8 to 12 weeks before Christmas when programs are saturated with commercials for toys. Cotugna (1988) as well as Ogletree, Williams, Raffeld, Mason, and Fricke (1990) found that about 6 out of 10 commercials on Saturday morning programs are for food-related products. These commercials tend to advertise sugared cereals as well as nonnutritional snacks such as candy bars and other sweets; few are for nutritious foods (Barcus, 1980). In addition, commercials promote fun and tend to be fast-paced with enchanting music, jingles, fantasy, humor, and appealing characters (Barcus, 1980; Goldberg & Gorn, 1978). Most do not mention sweetness or make nutritional claims, but one-fourth mention premiums associated with the product (Atkin & Heald, 1977).

Kunkel and Gantz's (1992) analysis of advertising in a multichannel environment concluded that toys, cereal and breakfast foods, and sugared snacks and drinks accounted for 74.6 percent of the advertisements across all television stations. In addition, they noted that healthy foods made up only 2.8 percent of all advertising directed to children. Moreover, when advertising healthy foods, most advertisers used themes such as fun and happiness over appeals to health and nutrition.

There has been little change in the types of products advertised to children. Kotz and Story (1994) as well as Taras and Gage (1995), in separate analyses of children's television programming, determined that a large portion of children's viewing time is filled with commercials for unhealthy foods, especially sugared cereals. Almost half of the commercials sampled were for foods, almost all of which were high in sugar, fat, or salt, with low nutritional value.

Food commercials also predominate during prime-time viewing hours. In examining prime-time and weekend-daytime commercials (Gerbner, Gross, Morgan & Signorielli, 1981a) learned that food advertising accounts for more than a quarter of the commercials. Furthermore, food-related activities (including a mention of food or drink) occurred in more than 40 percent of the commercials. Sweets, snacks, and nonnutritious ("junk") foods made up nearly half of food commercials. Nutritional appeals were noted in only 9 percent and stressed in another 7 percent of food commercials.

Similarly, Story and Faulkner (1990) concluded that commercials for food (typically fast-food restaurants) made up more than one-third of the commercials aired in a sample of the 15 top-rated prime time programs. Commercials for fast-food restaurants did not advertise salads or salad bars. There were only three commercials (in a sample of 261) for fruit and none for vegetables. Fruits and vegetables were, however, part of advertisements for other products. For example, illustrations of fruit are often found in advertisements for candy. Commercials typically stressed that the food products were "fresh and natural" and that they "tasted good." The only nutritional claims were for unsweetened breakfast cereals (nutritious, high in fiber, low in fat and sodium).

Wallack and Dorfman (1992) analyzed 654 commercials in 20 hours of programming randomly selected over a three-week period. They noted health messages (usually a claim of good nutrition) in three out of ten spots. Health messages occurred in four out of ten of the public service announcements in this sample.

Commercials are not the only venues for television's messages about food. Numerous messages relating to food, eating behavior, and body image are aired during the programs. Kaufman (1980), for example, analyzed the 10 top-rated prime time programs of 1977 and the commercial messages in these programs. She found more references to nonnutritious foods than nutritious foods in both the programs and commercials. When television characters were in the presence of food, they usually seemed happy. Also, television characters rarely dined alone and snacked frequently. Food, for the most part, was used by characters to satisfy social and emotional needs rather than hunger. She discovered that television characters are seldom portrayed as obese and that overweight characters are characterized less frequently than average and thin body types. In addition, Peterkin (1985) showed that the foods that make up the major portion of the diet in the television world did not meet dietary recommendations such as maintaining a desirable weight and avoiding too much fat.

Gerbner, Morgan, and Signorielli (1982) studied the portrayal of eating, drinking, nutrition, and safety in a week-long sample of prime-time and weekend daytime (children's) programming broadcast in 1979 and found that eating, drinking, or talking about food occurred about nine times an hour. More than three-quarters of all dramatic characters, about 25 each night, eat, drink, or talk about food, often more than once. Children's programs present an additional 84 instances of eating and/or drinking, or nearly four each hour, less than half the prime-time rate.

Nutrition during prime-time programs, however, is anything but balanced or relaxed. Grabbing a snack (39 percent of all eating-drinking episodes) is virtually as frequent as breakfast, lunch, and dinner combined (42 percent). In weekend-daytime children's programs, snacks are even more prevalent (45 percent of the eating/drinking episodes) with fewer regular meals (24 percent); "other meals" make up the rest of the episodes. Healthy snacks appear infrequently; fruit is presented as a snack alternative in only 4 or 5 percent of these episodes.

There has been little change in these images over the past decade and little recent research on this topic. For example, an analysis of 15 top-ranked situation comedies and dramas broadcast during the summer of 1988 (Story and Faulkner, 1990) found that references were made to food about 10 times each hour. Six out of ten of the references were for low nutrient beverages (e.g., coffee, alcohol, and soft drinks) and sweets; three-quarters of the food was eaten between meals. Less than 1 in 10 food references was for fruits or vegetables. Although there were 24 episodes involving meals, in one-third of the lunch and evening meals and one-third of the late and evening meals the only food shown was dessert (with coffee or wine). Similarly, M. Larson's (1991) analysis of the eating behavior of characters in three prime-time family sitcoms found little change from earlier studies. Even though children's food choices were more nutritious than those of the adult characters, the emphasis was usually on snacking.

Effects of Food-Related Imagery on Television

Studies have found that children are affected by the food advertisements they see on television. One study showed that children who were shown commercials of sugary snacks and breakfast foods were more likely to select more sugared foods than children who did not see these commercials. In addition, children who viewed public service announcements containing pro-nutritional messages were more likely to choose more healthy foods (Goldberg, Gorn & Gibson, 1978).

Heavy viewing has been shown to be related to low nutritional knowledge and incorrect perceptions about the validity of nutrition claims in food commercials, as well as greater consumption of nonnutritious foods, such as candy, salty snacks, and desserts (Atkin, 1976, 1980; Clancey-Hepburn, Hickey, & Nevill, 1974). Moreover, Atkin and Gibson (1978) discovered that frequent exposure to Saturday morning commercials contributed little to children's understanding of a "balanced breakfast." Donohue (1975) found that black children believed that to maintain good health they should take advertised medicines, eat vitamins, drink Coke, and eat fast foods. In addition, Donohue, Meyer, and Henke (1978) found that 7 out of 10 children thought that fast foods (e.g., McDonald's) were more nutritious than the food they had at home.

Signorielli and Lears (1992), in a 1991 survey of fourth and fifth grade children, found a strong positive relationship between television viewing and having bad eating habits (e.g., eating sugared cereal for breakfast, frequently eating at a fast-food restaurant, frequently eating sugared or fat-laden salty snacks, and frequently drinking soda or sweetened fruit drinks). There was also a positive relationship between viewing and giving incorrect answers to questions about the principles of good nutrition. These relationships held in a number of different demographic groups and remained statistically significant after simultaneously controlling for a number of important demographic characteristics (e.g., sex, reading level, race, parent education, and socioeconomic status). Similarly, Signorielli and Staples (1997), in a 1994 survey of fourth and fifth grade children, detected a strong relationship between television viewing and saying that they would choose unhealthy rather than healthy foods, as well as saying that the unhealthy food choice was healthier than the healthy food. Again, these relationships withstood simultaneous controls for demographic characteristics.

Finally, there is some evidence that a relationship exists between television viewing and obesity. In studies of children (Dietz, 1990), men (Tucker & Friedman, 1989), and women (Tucker & Bagwell, 1991), those who watched more television tended to be overweight. Because these studies examine the relationships between variables, these authors posit a dynamic model of mutual interaction and reinforcement—in essence a vicious circle. Viewing is often accompanied by snacking and having less time available for exercise, leading to more weight gain. This, in turn, results in more time spent in passive activities such as television viewing with its accompanying snacking.

Television thus presents very problematic and potentially harmful messages about food and nutrition. Images of food abound, but most of the food is not nutritious. All television viewers, particularly children, are bombarded with commercials for products extolling the virtues of high-fat, high-sugar foods. Characters on television seem to snack continually but not on healthy foods. Yet, at the same time, an overweight television character is a rarity.

The message may be ominous. Dieting is emerging as a regular practice of elementary school youngsters, particularly young girls (Stein & Reichert, 1990). As Dietz (1990) and others have postulated, ironically eating disorders, such as bulimia, may be the only way to eat and enjoy food but also to stay slim and stay in shape. In short, the only way a woman can eat all the food she wants and not gain weight probably is to become a bulimic or an exercise junkie.

FUTURE RESEARCH DIRECTIONS

This review has barely scratched the surface of the kinds of health-related images found on television and how these may affect viewers. It has focused in greater detail on four topics—physical health, sex and sexuality, alcohol–drugs, and food–nutrition—to show some of the depth of our knowledge. Most of the research in this area shows that many, if not most, of the images relating to health on television (and in the media in general) are in serious conflict with realistic guidelines for health, nutrition, and medicine. Research on how these images contribute to what people know about health and medicine, though somewhat scarce, consistently indicates that those who spend more time with the media, particularly television, may have beliefs about health-related issues that are in conflict with the things that should be done to remain healthy or improve the current status of their health.

Those who control the content of the media and access to it (often called *gatekeepers*) may not be overly concerned that there is a need to educate the public about health or that the images they include in entertainment programming may contribute to ill health. Institutional constraints seriously affect the type of health-related images we find in entertainment programming. Portrayals cannot be too controversial; production gatekeepers, traditionally the networks, anticipate unfavorable reactions on the part of advertisers or the audience. For example, the large food–tobacco conglomerates would probably look unfavorably on scriptwriters who include antismoking themes in programs in which they buy advertising time. In addition, some advertisers may not want to have their product associated with a deadly disease. Finally, special interest groups, such as the medical profession, may attempt to control how certain things, practices, or professions are portrayed. For example, members of the medical profession have often served as advisers for medically related dramas and may only approve the most favorable presentations of medicine and medical professionals.

The need to address these issues continues. Entertainment programming is storytelling, and any health issue that makes its way into an entertainment program must have a good storytelling component. Portrayals of health must fit with the story line and be compatible with the characterizations. Such portrayals can be incorporated in entertainment programming only if script writers and producers are aware of and take an interest in them. However, while the media can provide information, such imagery cannot, in isolation, make people change their behavior (Wallack, 1990). The media is a promising outlet for health-related information, but only through a media advocacy approach can media images be reshaped to provide more appropriate health messages to viewers.

The connections between health and the media, particularly television, are multifarious. Although the knowledge base has continued to increase, the data are still fragmentary and uneven. In some areas, notably the presentation of certain types of imagery on television, considerable progress has been made in isolating and understanding the images. In others, notably the impact of these images on society, little progress has been made, and considerable time and resources must be devoted to this effort in the future.

Glossary

accounts   Messages that convey the speaker's motives or explanations for his or her behavior.

adherence   A decision on the part of the patient to accept and follow a plan of treatment mutually agreed upon with the physician. Compare with *compliance*.

advance directives   A means for a competent patient to set out health care preferences should he or she become incompetent because of serious illness. Most advance directives are written documents (e.g., living will, durable power of attorney, and proxy appointment).

asymmetry   A characteristic of interpersonal relationships in which the two parties have differential control (i.e., a "one-up/one-down" relationship).

asynchronous electronic communication media   Communication in a noninteractive or nonsynchronized fashion. For example, sending an electronic message to another party is considered asynchronous because the other party may not be on the computer at the same time and therefore will not receive the message in real time.

autonomy   The right to be regarded as a self-determining agent and to be consulted in one's own care.

beneficence model   A paradigm for decision making that seeks actions believed to be in the best interest of the patient.

capitation   A per-member, monthly payment to a provider that covers contracted services and is paid in advance of the delivery of services. In essence, a provider agrees to provide specified services to plan members for this fixed, predetermined payment for a specified length of time (usually a year), regardless of how many times the member uses the service.

caremaps   Medical protocols or guidelines providing the caregiver with specific treatment options or steps when faced with a particular set of clinical symptoms, signs, or laboratory data in order to have an acceptable clinical outcome.

clinical information systems   A computer system dedicated to automating the functions of clinicians.

community empowerment   An approach emphasizing the sociocultural factors that influence behavior change and include the concepts of individual, organizational, and community-level control.

community health information networks (CHINs)   Networks organized to exchange data among computer systems of various health care financing and delivery organizations serving a community.

compliance   The extent to which a patient follows a treatment plan authoritatively prescribed by the health care provider.

computer-mediated communication (CMC)   Communication enabled by the use of a computer. Generally used for geographically dispersed areas.

confirmation   Communication that approves the value of the other person; communication that functions to recognize, acknowledge affiliation with, express awareness of the value of, and/or endorse the experience of the other person.

cultural diversity   The result of a more heterogeneous society, from which breakdowns in communication and interpersonal relationships can result.

culture   A symbolic meaning system (system of knowledge, beliefs, and values) shared by members of a given society; the means by which people know how to enact and interpret ''appropriate'' social behavior.

data warehouse   A collection of information gathered from many different sources allowing individuals to make database queries against the entire collection for analysis.

defensive avoidance   A situation that occurs when an individual rejects a persuasive message either because of the strength of the emotional appeal or because the message is inconsistent with other attitudes or beliefs.

demand management   Reduction of unnecessary, ineffective, or inappropriate medical services through prevention and information about health care choices.

diffusion of innovations   A theory examining the ways in which new ideas, practices, and objects are communicated through a social system.

disconfirmation   Communication that negates the value of the other person; communication that denies the existence, experience, or value of the other person.

dominance   A measure of the degree to which a person has succeeded in establishing actual control in a relationship; proportion of ''one-up'' messages to which the other's response is a ''one-down,'' or submissive, message.

domineeringness   A measure of the relative number of attempts made by an individual to establish control in a relationship; proportion of one-up messages used by an individual.

elaboration likelihood model (ELM)   An information processing model that suggests that if people are motivated and able, they will process a message centrally and carefully evaluate arguments. If people are not motivated or are unable to process a message, they will use cues to process a message peripherally.

electronic data interchange (EDI) Standardized format for data exchange electronically between sites not on the same computer network.

electronic medical records Also known as electronic patient records, computer medical records, and automated patient records. This is a computer system that stores patient information such as test results, medications, physician notes, progress notes and other aspects of patient care. All information is stored electronically.

ethnographic Studying data by ethnic groups.

extended parallel processing model A fear appeal model that proposes that when people feel threatened by a serious disease or health threat, they are motivated to act.

external communication Communication that takes place between organizations.

fear appeal A message that arouses fear in order to motivate compliance with a recommended health-related behavior.

fidelity The right to service aimed at one's own interest and the rejection of conflicting interests.

grapevine An informal communication network within an organization.

health belief model A model proposing that the likelihood an individual will take a recommended health action is based on his or her perceived susceptibility to disease, perceived severity of the threat, psychological, demographic, and structural variables, and cost-benefit analysis of perceived benefits to taking action minus perceived barriers.

health education campaigns Campaigns designed to inform the public about health issues which are conducted in a specific time frame and consist of organized, planned communication activities.

hidden curriculum The culture in which the formal curriculum is situated. The formal curriculum is likely to be successful only to the extent that messages about it are consistent with what students glean from the hidden curriculum.

inoculation An approach to promoting the resistance of unhealthy behaviors which involves exposing individuals to a threat in order for them to prepare themselves to defend against that threat.

interdisciplinary health care team (IHCT) A team composed of physicians, nurses, therapists, or other caregivers required for the care of patients.

integrated services digital network (ISDN) Essentially a digital telephone line that sends data without being converted to analog, enabling the sender to send large amounts of voice, data, and video information.

interactive media/multimedia Computer-mediated communication, usually involving some combination of text, graphics, sound, still, or full-motion video, which involves users in ways that enable them to customize the content and delivery.

interactive voice response (IVR) Technology that enables organizations to decrease time wasted on routine, inbound calls by providing answers to common questions automatically.

internal communication   The information exchange that takes place within the boundaries of an organization.

knowledge-based mail systems (KMS)   Basically intelligent electronic mail systems that have been developed to overcome the communication problems inherent in traditional systems. Control, filtering, categorization and the setting of priorities are built into the system.

living will   See *advance directives.*

local area networks (LAN)   The interconnection of computers by cables, telephone lines, or wireless communication.

local hospital system (LHS)   A system that exists if two or more hospitals in the same system are located in the same urban area or within 60 miles of the largest urban member.

lucidity   The right to full and truthful disclosure of pertinent health information.

macro-level approaches   Theories and approaches that focus on the "big picture" of health behavior change.

managed care   A system of providing health care in which administrative firms, rather than private practitioners, manage the allocation of benefits. This contrasts with conventional indemnity systems in which insurers reimburse providers for services rendered. Health Maintenance Organizations and Preferred Provider Organizations are examples of managed care organizations.

market commonality   The degree of presence that a competitor manifests in the markets it overlaps with the focal firm.

micro-level theories   Theories that focus on behavior change at the individual level.

multimedia   The use of multiple forms of media (such as voice or video) to create interesting and interactive documents.

networked technologies   Communication devices, including computers, telephones, and other wire and wireless systems, that are linked in either a closed network or to the Internet.

patient instructor (PI)   A person trained to role-play a patient and provide immediate feedback to the student. More specifically, the PI's mission is to help the student learn communication skills or physical exam skills (e.g., pelvic exam) by engaging in a realistic encounter and then providing feedback.

payers (payors)   Organizations that make payment to providers for services and goods.

PBX integration   Private branch exchange server that has evolved from merely a voice server to a more enterprisewide server that will accommodate true voice and data integration.

perceived barriers   The potential costs of performing the response recommended by a health education campaign.

perceived susceptibility   An individual's subjective estimation of the likelihood that he or she will experience a health threat.

problem-based learning (PBL)   A learner-centered technique in which students take responsibility for determining learning issues, gathering information relevant to those issues, and reporting back to their colleagues. Problems, often clinical case descriptions, are the fodder for discussion in PBL. These problems, the details of which may be revealed in stages, serve as the triggers for generating ideas regarding possible causes (e.g., the basic science pathways to the clinical manifestations), as well as collecting and integrating information. Faculty members who work with PBL groups are meant to adopt the role of facilitator rather than the role of expert.

providers   A practitioner or facility offering health care services.

quality informed consent   A process involving (a) disclosure of pertinent medical information, (b) patient comprehension of this information, (c) the voluntariness with which a decision is made, (d) competence to make the decision, and (e) and the act of consent.

RACE (Ready, Aim, Communicate, Evaluate)   A communication system developed by the New York University Medical Center to assist in the dissemination of information about the organization's position on managed care. It facilitates top-down and bottom-up communication through the use of open forums, videos and panel discussions.

reactance   A situation that occurs when individuals perceive that their freedom has been violated by a persuasive attempt and the individual subsequently resists persuasion.

relational control   Communication that establishes, maintains, or reflects who has the right to define or direct actions within an interpersonal system.

remote access   Complex structures that house reliable and easy access into the corporate network.

resource similarity   The extent to which a given competitor possesses strategic endowments comparable, in terms of both type and amount, to those of the focal firm.

Roter interaction analysis system (RIAS)   An assessment tool that can be used to measure the impact of physician skills both on the patients and on the bottom-line. The tool was developed at the Johns Hopkins University and is now widely accepted to be the most effective tool available for evaluating the communication skills of physicians.

self-efficacy   An individual's belief that he or she can exert control over his or her motivation, behavior, and social environment.

self-management/self-care   Individual initiative and responsibility for health care decisions, including the prevention and management of disease.

shared decision making   Encouragement of patient participation in medical decisions; information and educational tools that support medical decision making.

social learning theory   A theory which suggests that self-efficacy is the driving force behind human behavior and crucial for effective health campaigns.

social marketing   The application of marketing principles to social and health issues.

standardized patient (SP)   A person trained to role-play a patient and record student behavior. More specifically, the SP's mission is to provide clinical skills assessment data by engaging in a realistic encounter and then recording student behavior. As a general rule, SPs working in an assessment context do not break the patient role to provide instructional feedback to the students.

truthful disclosure   The accurate and complete revelation of a patient's diagnosis and prognosis.

videoconferencing   Interactive way of communicating across a long distance using video-audio-data digital signals usually transmitted via phone lines.

voice mail/automated attendant   Device that answers and processes incoming calls, directing callers to extension directories or live operators and attendants.

wireless   Network based on radio frequency or infrared frequencies to connect devices together.

References

Able-Boone, H., Dokecki, P., & Smith, S. M. (1989). Parent and health care provider communication and decision making in the intensive care nursery. *Children's Health Care, 18,* 133–141.

Adelman, R. D., Greene, M., & Charon, R. (1987). The physician–elderly patient–companion triad in the medical encounter: The development of a conceptual framework and research agenda. *Gerontologist, 27,* 729–734.

Adelman, R. D., Greene, M., & Charon, R. (1991). Issues in physician–elderly patient interaction. *Aging and Society, 11,* 127–148.

Adelman, R. D., Greene, M., Charon, R., & Friedmann, E. (1992). The content of physician and elderly patient interaction in the medical primary care encounter. *Communication Research, 19,* 370–380.

Addington, T., & Wegescheide-Harris, J. (1995). Ethics and communication with the terminally ill. *Health Communication, 7,* 267–281.

Agho, A. O. (1992). Problem areas faced by hospital administrators. *Hospital & Health Services Administration, 37*(1), 131–135.

Aiken, M., & Motiwalla, L. (1993). An organizational communications perspective on knowledge-based mail systems. *Information & Management, 25*(5), 265–273.

Alemi, F., & Stephens, R. C. (1996). Computer services to patients' homes through their telephones. *Medical Care, 34*(10), Supplement, October.

Alexander, J. A., Halpern, M. T., & Lee, S. D. (1996, February). The short-term effects of merger on hospital operations. *Health Services Research, 30*(6), 827–846.

Allen, M. J. (1993). Sociolinguistic dimensions of nurse practitioner practice: A question of power. (University of San Diego; 6260). *Dissertation Abstracts International, 54–03B,* 1328.

American Hospital Association & the Picker Institute. (1996). *Eye on patients: A report from the American Hospital Association and the Picker Institute.* Chicago: American Hospital Association; Boston: The Picker Institute.

American Medical Association (1982). *Future directions for medical education: A report of the Council on Medical Education*. Chicago: Author.

Anders, G. (1997, September 4). Doctors learn to bridge cultural gaps. *Wall Street Journal*, p. B-1.

Anderson, C. M., & Martin, M. M. (1995, July). Why employees speak to co-workers and bosses: Motives, gender, and organizational satisfaction. *The Journal of Business Communication, 32*(3), 249.

Anderson, L. A., & Zimmerman, M. A. (1993). Patient and physician perceptions of their relationship and patient satisfaction: A study of chronic disease management. *Patient Education and Counseling, 20*, 27–36.

Annandale, E. C. (1987). Dimensions of patient control in a free-standing birth center. *Social Science and Medicine, 25*, 1235–1248.

Anonymous. (1996, March). Communication a major factor in measuring quality of care. *Managed Health Care News* (3), 44.

Anvaripour, P. L., Jacobson, L., Schweiger, J., & Weissman, G. K. (1991). Physician–nurse collegiality in the medical school curriculum: Exploratory workshop and student questionnaire. *The Mount Sinai Journal of Medicine, 58*, 91–94.

Arntson, P. (1989). Improving citizen's health competencies. *Health Communication, 1*(1), 29–34.

Aronsson, K., & Satterlund-Larsson, U. (1987). Politeness strategies and doctor–patient communication: On the social choreography of collaborative thinking. *Journal of Language & Social Psychology, 6*, 1–27.

Association of American Medical Colleges. (1984). *Physicians for the twenty-first century: Report of the project panel on the general professional education of the physician and college preparation for medicine*. Washington, DC: Author.

Association of American Medical Colleges. (1992). *Educating medical students: Assessing change in medical education—the road to implementation*. Washington, DC: Author.

Atkin, C. K. (1976). Children's social learning from television advertising: Research evidence on observational modeling of product consumption. *Advances in Consumer Research, 3*, 513–519.

Atkin, C. K. (1980). Effects of television advertising on children. In E. L. Palmer & A. Door (eds.), *Children and the faces of television: Teaching, violence, selling* (pp. 287–306). New York: Academic Press.

Atkin, C. K., & Gibson, W. (1978). Children's nutritional learning from television advertising. Unpublished manuscript, Michigan State University, East Lansing, MI.

Atkin, C. K., & Heald, G. (1977). The content of children's toy and food commercials. *Journal of Communication, 21*(1), 107–114.

Atkin, C. K., Hocking, J., & Block, M. (1984). Teenage drinking: Does advertising make a difference? *Journal of Communication, 34*(2), 157–167.

Atkin, C. K., Neuendorf, K., & McDermott, S. (1983). The role of alcohol advertising in excessive and hazardous drinking. *Journal of Drug Education, 13(4)*, 313–325.

Atwood, J. R., Haase, J., Rees-McGee, S., Blackwell, G., Giordano, L., Earnest, D., Alberts, D., Sheehan, E., Benedict, J., Aickin, M., & Meyskens, F., Jr. (1992). Reasons related to adherence in community-based field studies. *Patient Education & Counseling, 19*, 251–259.

Backer, T. E., & Marston, G. (1993). Partnership for a drug-free America: An experiment in social marketing. In T. G. Backer & E. M. Rogers (eds.), *Organizational as-*

pects of health communication campaigns: What works? (pp. 10–24). Newbury Park, CA: Sage.

Baker, L. M., & Connor, J. J. (1994). Physician–patient communication from the perspective of library and information science. *Bulletin of the Medical Library Association, 82*, 37–42.

Bakhurst, D. (1992). On lying and deceiving. *Journal of Medical Ethics, 18*, 63–66.

Ballard-Reisch, D. S. (1990). A model of participative decision-making for physician–patient interaction. *Health Communication, 2*(2), 91–104.

Bandura, A. (1969). *Principles of behavior modification.* New York: Holt, Rinehart, & Winston.

Bandura, A. (1971). *Social learning theory.* Morristown, NJ: General Learning Press.

Bandura, A. (1977a). Self-efficacy: Toward a unifying theory of behavioral change. *Psychological Review, 84*, 191–215.

Bandura, A. (1977b). *Social learning theory.* Englewood Cliffs, NJ: Prentice-Hall.

Bandura, A. (1982). Self-efficacy mechanism in human agency. *American Psychologist, 37*, 122–147.

Bandura, A. (1989). Perceived self-efficacy in the exercise of control over AIDS infection. In V. M. Mays, G. W. Albee, & S. S. Schneider (eds.), *Primary prevention of AIDS: Psychological approaches* (pp. 128–141). Newbury Park, CA: Sage.

Bandura, A., & Walters, R. H. (1963). *Social learning and personality development.* New York: Holt, Rinehart & Winston.

Barcus, F. E. (1971). *Saturday children's television: A report on TV programming and advertising on Boston commercial television.* Newtonville, MA: Action for Children's Television.

Barcus, F. E. (1980). The nature of television advertising to children. In E. L. Palmer & A. Dorr (eds.), *Children and the faces of television: Teaching, violence, selling* (pp. 273–285). New York: Academic Press.

Barnlund, D. C. (1976). The mystification of meaning: Doctor–patient encounters. *Journal of Medical Education, 51*, 716–725.

Barrows, H. (1971). *Simulated patients (programmed patients): The development and use of a new technique in medical education.* Springfield, IL: Charles C. Thomas.

Basara, L. A. R. (1995). The impact of direct-to-customer advertising of prescription medications on new prescription volume and consumer information search behavior. (University of Mississippi; 0131). *Dissertation Abstracts International, 56-06B*, 3144.

Baxter, R. L., DeRiemer, C., Landini, A., Leslie, L., & Singletary, M. W. (1985). A content analysis of music videos. *Journal of Broadcasting & Electronic Media, 29*(3), 333–340.

Baylav, A. (1996). Overcoming culture and language barriers. *Practitioner, 250*, 403–406.

Bayles, K. A., & Kaszniak, A. (1987). *Communication and cognition: Normal aging and dementia.* Boston: Little, Brown.

Beauchamp, T. L. (1989). Informed consent. In R. M. Veatch (ed.), *Medical ethics* (pp. 173–200). Boston: Jones and Bartlett Publishers.

Becker, H. (1961). *Boys in white: Student culture in medical school.* Chicago: University of Chicago Press.

Beckman, H. B., Frankel, R. M., & Darnley, J. (1995). Soliciting the patient's complete agenda: A relationship to the distribution of concerns. *Clinical Research, 33*, 714–717.

Beckman, H. B., Markakis, K. M., Suchman, A. L., & Frankel, R. M. (1994). The doctor–patient relationship and malpractice: Lessons from plaintiff depositions. *Archives of Internal Medicine, 154*, 1365–1370.

Beckmann, C. R. B., Sharf, B. F., Baransky, B. M., & Spellacy, W. N. (1986). Student response to gynecologic teaching associates. *American Journal of Obstetrics and Gynecology, 155*, 301–306.

Beisecker, A. E. (1986). Taking charge: Attempts to control the doctor–patient interaction. Paper presented at the Second James Madison University Medical Communication Conferences, Harrisonburg, VA.

Beisecker, A. E. (1988). Aging and the desire for information and input in medical decisions: Patient consumerism in medical encounters. *Gerontologist, 28*, 330–335.

Beisecker, A. E. (1989) The influence of a companion on the doctor–elderly patient interaction. *Health Communication, 1*, 55–70.

Beisecker, A. E. (1990). Patient power in doctor–patient communication: What do we know? *Health Communication, 2*(2), 105–122.

Beisecker, A. E., & Beisecker, T. D. (1990). Patient information-seeking behaviors when communicating with doctors. *Medical Care, 28*, 19–28.

Beisecker, A. E., & Beisecker, T. D. (1993). Using metaphors to characterize doctor–patient relationship: Paternalism versus consumerism. *Health Communication, 5*, 41–58.

Beisecker, A. E., & Thompson, T. L. (1995). The elderly physician–patient interaction. In J. F. Nussbaum & J. Coupland (eds.), *Handbook of communication and aging research* (pp. 397–416). Mahwah, NJ: Lawrence Erlbaum.

Bell, C. W. (1996, July 29). Decoding health language is key. *Modern Healthcare, 26*(31), 25–26.

Benson, J. (1994). Health care executives must reengineer themselves to keep pace with industry. *Health Care Strategic Management, 12*(1), 14–15.

Benzing, J. (1991). Doctor–patient communication and the quality of care. *Social Science and Medicine, 32*, 1301–1310.

Bernstein, B., & Kane, R. (1981). Physicians' attitudes toward female patients. *Medical Care, 19*, 600–608.

Berwick, W. (1996). Ideas for medical education (preface). *Academic Medicine, 71*, 972.

Bettis, R. A., & Weeks, D. (1987). Financial returns and strategic interaction: The case of instant photograph. *Strategic Management Journal, 8*, 549–563.

Bibb, A., & Casimir, G. J. (1996). Haitian families. In M. McGoldrick, J. Giorano, & J. K. Pearce (eds.), *Ethnicity and family therapy* (2nd ed., pp. 97–111). New York: Guilford Press.

Bird, B. (1955). *Talking with Patients*. Philadelphia: J. B. Lippincott.

Blackhall, L. J., Murphy, S. T., Frank, G., Michel, V., & Azen, S. (1995). Ethnicity and attitudes toward patient autonomy. *Journal of the American Medical Association, 274*, 820–825.

Blalock, S. J., & Devellis, B. McE. (1986). Stereotyping: The link between theory and practice. *Patient Education and Counseling, 8*, 17–25.

Blanchard, C. G., Labrecque, M. S., Ruckdeschel, J. C., & Blanchard, E. B. (1988). Information and decision-making preferences of hospitalized adult cancer patients. *Social Science & Medicine, 27*, 1139–1145.

Bloom, B. L. (1988). *Health psychology*. Englewood Cliffs, NJ: Prentice-Hall.

Blum, L. H. (1972). *Reading between the lines: Doctor–patient communication*. New York: International Universities Press.

Boberg, E. W., Gustafson, D. H., Hawkins, R. P., Bricker, E., Pingree, S., McTavish, F., Wise, M., Owens, B., & Botta, R. (1997). CHESS: The Comprehensive Health Enhancement Support System. In P. F. Brennan, S. J. Schneider, & E. Tornquist (eds.), *Information networks for community health*. New York: Springer-Verlag.

Bochner, S. (1982). The social-psychology of cross-cultural relations. In S. Bochner (ed.), *Cultures in contact: Studies in cross-cultural interaction* (pp. 5–44). Oxford, England: Pergamon Press.

Bochner, S. (1983). Doctors, patients, and their cultures. In D. Pendleton & J. Hasler (eds.), *Doctor–patient communication* (pp. 127–138). London: Academic Press.

Bordage, G., & Lemieux, M. (1991). Semantic structures and diagnostic thinking of experts and novices. *Academic Medicine, 66*, S70–S72.

Borges, S., & Waitzkin, H. (1995). Women's narratives in primary care medical encounters. *Women and Health, 23*, 29–56.

Borzo, G. (1994, September). Message system sends patients lab results by phone. *American Medical News, 37*(36), 5–6.

Bowers, W. F. (1960). *Interpersonal relations in the hospital*. Springfield, IL: Charles C. Thomas.

Bowker, J. (1996). Cancer, individual process, and control: A case study in metaphor analysis. *Health Communication, 8*, 91–104.

Breed, W. J., & DeFoe, J. R. (1981). The portrayal of the drinking process on prime-time television. *Journal of Communication, 32*(2), 88–99.

Breemhaar, B., Visser, A. P., & Kleijnen, J. G. (1990). Perceptions and behavior among elderly hospital patients: Description and explanation of age differences in satisfaction, knowledge, emotions, and behaviour. *Social Science and Medicine, 31*, 1377–1385.

Brennan, P. F., & Ripich, S. (1994). Use of a home-care computer network by persons with AIDS. *International Journal of Technology Assessment in Health Care, 10*(2), 258–272.

Brennan, P. F., Schneider, S. J., & Tornquist, E. (eds.). (1997). *Information networks for community health*. New York: Springer-Verlag.

Brody, D. S. (1980). The patient's role in clinical decision-making. *Annals of Internal Medicine, 93*, 718–722.

Brody, H. (1989). The physician–patient relationship. In R. M. Veatch (ed.), *Medical ethics* (pp. 65–92). Boston: Jones and Bartlett Publishers.

Brody, H. (1992). *The healer's power*. New Haven: Yale University Press.

Brooks, K. A. (1994). The hospital CEO: Meeting the conflicting demands of the board and physicians. *Hospital & Health Services Administration, 30*(4), 471–485.

Brown, J. D., Childers, K. W., & Waszak, C. S. (1990). Television and adolescent sexuality. *Journal of Adolescent Health Care, 11*(1), 62–70.

Brown, J. D., & Newcomer, S. F. (1991). Television viewing and adolescents' sexual behavior. *Journal of Homosexuality, 21*(1–2), 77–91.

Brown, J. D., Waszak, C. S., & Childers, K. W. (1989). Family planning, abortion and AIDS: Sexuality and communication campaigns. In C. T. Salmon (ed.), *Information campaigns: Balancing social values and social change* (pp. 85–112). Newbury Park, CA: Sage.

Browne, K., & Freeling, P. (1967). *The doctor–patient relationship*. Edinburgh: E & S Livingstone.

Brownlee, S., Cook, G. G., & Hardigg, V. (1994). Genes and cancer: Tinkering with destiny. *U.S. News and World Report, 117*(8), 58–67.

Broyard, A. (1992). *Intoxicated by my illness and other writings on life and earth*. New York: Fawcett Columbine.

Brubaker, R. G., & Wickersham, D. (1990). Encouraging the practice of testicular self-examination: A field application of the theory of reasoned action. *Health Psychology, 9*, 154–163.

Buckman, R. (1992). *How to break bad news*. Baltimore, MD: Johns Hopkins University Press.

Bunker, J. P., et al. (1994). Improving health: Measuring effects of medical care. *Milbank Quarterly, 72*: 225–258.

Burg, F. D., McMichael, H., & Stemmler, E. J. (1986). Managing medical education at the University of Pennsylvania. *Journal of Medical Education, 61*, 714–720.

Burgoon, M., & Hall, J. R. (1994). Myths as health belief systems: The language of salves, sorcery, and science. *Health Communication, 6*, 97–115.

Burner, S. T., & Waldo, D. R. (1995). National Health Expenditure Projections, 1994–2005. *Health Care Financing Review, 16*(4), 221–242.

Burton, M. W., & Parker, R. W. (1994). Satisfaction of breast cancer patients with their medical and psychological care. *Journal of Psychosocial Oncology, 12*, 41–63.

Cameron, K. A., Witte, K., Lapinski, M. K., & Nzyyuko, S. (1996, November). Preventing HIV transmission along the Trans-African highway in Kenya: Using persuasive message theory to conduct a formative evaluation. Paper presented at the annual meeting of the Speech Communication Association, San Diego, CA.

Caporael, L. R. (1981). The paralanguage of caregiving: Baby talk to the institutionalized aged. *Journal of Personality and Social Psychology, 40*, 876–884.

Cappella, J. N. (1987). Interpersonal communication: Definitions and fundamental questions. In C. R. Berger & S. H. Chaffee (eds.), *Handbook of Communication Science* (pp. 184–238). Newbury Park, CA: Sage.

Carrese, J. A., & Rhodes, L. A. (1995). Western bioethics on the Navajo reservation: Benefit or harm? *Journal of the American Medical Association, 274*, 826–829.

Carter, W. B., Inui, T. S., Kukull, W. A., & Haigh, V. (1982). Outcome-based doctor-patient interaction analysis: II. Identifying effective provider and patient behavior. *Medical Care, 20*, 550–566.

Cascio, W. F. (1995). *Managing human resources* (4th ed.). New York: McGraw-Hill.

Cassata, D. (1978). Health communication theory and research: Overview of the communication specialist interface. In B. Ruben (ed.), *Communication Yearbook 2*, 495–504. New Brunswick, NJ: Transaction Press.

Cassata, D. (1980). Health communication theory and research: A definitional overview. In D. Nimmo (ed.), *Communication Yearbook 4*, 583–589. New Brunswick, NJ: Transaction Press.

Cassata, M. B., Skill, T. D., & Boadu, S. O. (1979). In sickness and in health. *Journal of Communication, 29*(4), 73–80.

Cassell, E. J. (1976). *The healer's art: New approaches to the doctor–patient relationship*. New York: J. B. Lippincott.

Cassell, E. J. (1985). *Talking with patients. Volume 1: The theory of doctor–patient communication*. Cambridge, MA: MIT Press.

Casson, R. W. (1981). Language, culture and cognition. In R. W. Casson (ed.), *Language, culture and cognition* (pp. 11–22). New York: Macmillan.

Cegala, D. J., McGee, D. S., & McNeilis, K. S. (1996). Components of patients' and doctors' perceptions of communication competence during a primary care medical interview. *Health Communication, 8*, 1–28.

Cegala, D. J., McNeilis, K. S., McGee, D. S., & Jonas, A. P. (1995). A study of doctors' and patients' perceptions of information processing and communication competence during the medical interview. *Health Communication, 7*, 179–203.

Chaffee, S. H., & Berger, C. R. (1987). What communication scientists do. In C. R. Berger & S. H. Chaffee (eds.), *Handbook of Communication Science* (pp. 99–122). Newbury Park, CA: Sage.

Chaiken, S. (1980). Heuristic versus systematic information processing and the use of source versus message cues in persuasion. *Journal of Personality and Social Psychology, 39*, 752–766.

Chamberlain, M. A. (1996). Health communication: Making the most of new media technologies—an international overview. *Journal of Health Communication, 1*(1), 43–50.

Chen, K. L. (1994). Comparing hypermedia-based user interfaces for an intelligent computerized medical record input system. (Illinois Institute of Technology; 0091). *Dissertation Abstracts International, 55–04B*, 1913.

Chen, L. (1992). Navigation in electronic space: Users' learning strategies of word processing. *Spout Masters Abstracts International, 31*, 457.

Chen, M. (1996, January). Competitor analysis and interfirm rivalry: Toward a theoretical integration. *Academy of Management Review, 21*(1), 100–135.

Cherry, K., & Smith, D. H. (1993). Sometimes I cry: The experience of loneliness for men with AIDS. *Health Communication, 5*, 181–208.

Christy, N. P. (1979). English is our second language. *New England Journal of Medicine, 300*, 979–981.

Clancey-Hepburn, K., Hickey, A. A., & Nevill, G. (1974). Children's behavior responses to TV food advertisements. *Journal of Nutrition Education, 6*, 93–96.

Clark, J. A., Potter, D. A., & McKinlay, J. B. (1990). Bringing social structure back into clinical decision making. *Social Science and Medicine, 32*, 853–866.

Clark, M. (1996, July/August). Humanizing the face of healthcare. *Healthcare Forum Journal, 39*(4), 66–71.

Clarke, D. B. (1986). Helping patients make health care decisions. *The Euthanasia Review, 1*(2), 85–96.

Clarke, D. E., Goldstein, M. K., & Raffin, T. A. (1994). Ethical dilemmas in the critically ill elderly. *Clinics in Geriatric Medicine, 10*, 91–101.

Clausen, H. (1994). Electronic mail and the information professional: A study of computer-mediated communication and its future prospects in the information field. (Aarhus Universitet, Denmark; 0814). *Dissertation Abstracts International, 55–03C*, 689.

Cleary, P. D., Edgman-Levitan, S., McMullen, W., & Delbanco, T. L. (1992). The relationship between reported problems and patient summary evaluations of hospital care. *Quality Review Bulletin, 18*, 53–59.

Cleary, P. D., Edgman-Levitan, S., Roberts, M., Maloney, T. W., McMullen, W., Walker, J. D., & Delbanco, T. L. (1991). Patients evaluate their hospital care: A national survey. *Health Affairs, 10*, 254–267.

Cline, R. J. (1983). Interpersonal communication skills for enhancing physician–patient relationships. *Maryland State Medical Journal, 32*, 272–278.

Coile, R. C. (1995, March). Managed care outlook, 1995–2000. Top 10 trends for the HMO insurance industry. *Health Trends, 7*(5), 2.

Coleman, L. (1983, July). *Social cognitions about group membership: Marking social distance in speech.* Presented at Second International Conference on Language and Social Psychology, Bristol, England.

Condry, J., Bence, P., & Scheibe, C. (1988). Nonprogram content of children's television. *Journal of Broadcasting & Electronic Media, 32*(3), 255–270.

Connors, A. F., Dawson, N. V., Desbiens, N. A. et al. (1995). A controlled trial to improve care for seriously ill hospitalized patients. *Journal of the American Medical Association, 274*, 1591–1598.

Consumer Reports. (1992). Wasted health care dollars. Vol. *7*(57), 435–449.

Cook, M. A., Coe, R. M., & Hanson, K. (1990). Physician–elderly patient communication: Processes and outcomes of medical encounters. In S. M. Stahl (ed.), *The legacy of longevity: Health and health care in later life* (pp. 291–309). Newbury Park, CA: Sage.

Costello, D. (1977). Health communication theory and research: An overview. In B. Ruben (ed.), *Communication Yearbook 1*, 555–567. New Brunswick, NJ: Transaction Press.

Costello, D., & Pettegrew, L. (1979). Health communication theory and research: An overview of health organizations. In D. Nimmo (ed.), *Communication Yearbook 3* (pp. 607–623). New Brunswick, NJ: Transaction Press.

Cotugna, N. (1988). TV ads on Saturday morning children's programming—What's new? *Journal of Nutritional Education, 20*, 125–127.

Coupland, J., & Coupland, N. (1994). "Old age doesn't come alone": Discursive representations of health-in-aging in geriatric medicine. *International Journal of Aging and Human Development, 39*, 81–95.

Cousins, N. (1979). *Anatomy of an illness as perceived by the patient.* New York: Bantam Books.

Crawford, T. J., & Boyer, R. (1985). Salient consequences, cultural values, and childbearing intentions. *Journal of Applied Social Psychology, 15*, 16–30.

Curry, R., & Makoul, G. (1996). An active-learning approach to basic clinical skills. *Academic Medicine, 71*, 41–44.

Daingerfield, M. A. Farrell. (1993). Communication patterns of critical care nurses. (Rutgers The State University of New Jersey–New Brunswick; 0190). *Dissertation Abstracts International, 54–04B*, 1888.

Dalla-Vorgia, P., Katsouyanni, K., Garanis, T. N., Touloumi, G., Grogari, P., & Koutselinis, A. (1992). Attitudes of a Mediterranean population to the truth-telling issues. *Journal of Medical Ethics, 18*, 67–74.

D'Aveni, R. (1994). *Hypercompetition: Managing the dynamics of strategic maneuvering.* New York: Free Press.

Davis, K. (1993). Nice doctors and invisible patients: The problem of power in feminist common sense. In A. D. Todd & S. Fisher (eds.), *The social organization of doctor–patient communication* (2nd ed., pp. 243–265). Norwood, NJ: Ablex.

Deber, R. B. (1994). Physicians in health care management: 7. The patient–physician partnership: changing roles and the desire for information 11. *Canadian Medical Association Journal, 1512*(2), 171–176.

Dede, C., & Fontana, L. (1995). Transforming health education via new media. In Harris L. (ed.), *Health and the new media: Technologies transforming personal and public health.* Mahwah NJ: Lawrence Erlbaum.

DeDonder, J. L. (1991). A methodological study of self-disclosure in chronically ill patients. Unpublished dissertation, University of Kansas School of Nursing.

Deering, M. J. (1997). Partnerships for networked consumer health information: summary of proceedings and follow-on activities. *Telemedicine Sourcebook 1998.* New York: Faulkner and Gray. (See also Partnerships conference web site: http://odphp.osophs.dhhs.gov/confrnce/partnr97)

Deering, M. J., & Harris, J. (1996). Consumer health information demand and delivery: Implications for libraries. *Bull MLA 84*(2), 209–216.

DeFoe, J. R., & Breed, W. (1991). Consulting with media for health education: Some new directions. Paper presented at the Annual Meeting of the American Psychological Association.

DeFoe, J. R., Breed, W., & Wallack, L. (1983). Drinking on television: A five-year study. *Journal of Drug Education, 13*(1), 25–38.

Delia, J. G. (1987). Communication research: A history. In C. R. Berger & S. H. Chaffee (eds.), *Handbook of Communication Science* (pp. 20–98). Newbury Park, CA: Sage.

Deloitte & Touche. (1992, June). U.S. Hospitals and the future of health care: A continuing opinion survey (a limited-distribution document).

Deruyte, E. (1994, June). The delivery. *The Business Journal, 12,* 16–19.

DiClemente, C. C. (1986). Self-efficacy and addictive behaviors. *Journal of Social and Clinical Psychology, 4,* 302–315.

DiClemente, C. C., & Prochaska, J. O. (1985). Processes and stages of change: Coping and competence in smoking behavior change. In S. Shiffman & T. A. Willis (eds.), *Coping and substance abuse* (pp. 319–334). San Diego, CA: Academic Press.

Did you hear it through the grapevine? (1994, October). *Training and Development, 48*(10), 20–21.

Dietz, W. H. (1990). You are what you eat: What you eat is what you are. *Journal of Adolescent Health Care, 11*(1), 76–81.

Dilenschneider, R. L. (1995, July 2). Cultivating the corporate grapevine. *New York Times,* p. F13(L).

DiMatteo, M. R. (1993). Expectations in the physician–patient relationship: Implications for patient adherence to medical treatment recommendations. In P. D. Blanck (ed.), *Interpersonal expectations* (pp. 296–315). New York: Cambridge University Press.

DiMatteo, M. R. (1994). Enhancing patient adherence to medical recommendations. *Journal of the American Medical Association, 271,* 79, 83.

DiMatteo, M. R., & DiNicola, D. D. (1982). *Achieving patient compliance: The psychology of the medical practitioner's role.* New York: Pergamon Press.

DiMatteo, M. R., Hays, R. D., & Prince, L. M. (1986). Relationships of physicians' nonverbal communication skill to patient satisfaction, appointment noncompliance, and physician workload. *Health Psychology, 5,* 581–594.

DiMatteo, M. R., Hays, R. D., Gritz, E. R., Bastani, R., Crane, L., Elashoff, R., Ganz, P., Heber, D., McCarthy, W., & Marcus, A. (1993). Patient adherence to cancer control regimens: Scale development and initial validation. *Psychological Assessment, 5*, 102–112.

DiMatteo, M. R., Linn, L. S., Chang, B. L., & Cope, D. W. (1985). Affect and neutrality in physician behavior. *Journal of Behavioral Medicine, 8*, 397–409.

DiMatteo, M. R., Reiter, R. C., & Gambone, J. C. (1994). Enhancing medication adherence through communication and informed collaborative choice. *Health Communication, 6*, 253–265.

Ditto, P. H., Moore, K. A., Hilton, J. L., & Kalish, J. R. (1995). Beliefs about physicians: Their role in health care utilization, satisfaction, and compliance. *Basic and Applied Social Psychology, 17*, 23–48.

Dolan, N. C., Reifler, D. R., McDermott, M. M., & McGaghie, W. C. (1995). Adherence to screening mammography recommendations in a university general medicine clinic. *Journal of General Internal Medicine, 10*, 294–306.

Donohue, T. (1975). Effects of commercials on black children. *Journal of Advertising Research, 15*(6), 41–46.

Donohue, T., Meyer, T., & Henke, L. (1978). Black and white children's perceptions of television commercials. *Journal of Marketing, 42*, 34–40.

Donovan, J. L., & Blake, D. R. (1992). Patient non-compliance: Deviance or reasoned decision-making? *Social Science & Medicine, 34*, 507–513.

Douglas, M. (1985). *Risk Acceptability according to the social sciences.* New York: Russell Sage Foundation.

Downie, R. S., Fyfe, C., & Tannahill, A. (1990). *Health promotion: Models and values.* Oxford: Oxford University Press.

Drucker, E. (1974). Hidden values and health care. *Medical Care, 12*, 266–273.

Duffy, M. (1996, February). Econometric studies of advertising, advertising restrictions and cigarette demand: A survey. *International Journal of Advertising, 15*(1), 1–23.

Duncan, M. M. (1994). Trespassing: Employer paternalism and health cost control. (Columbia University; 0054). *Dissertation Abstracts International, 56–03A*, 1130.

Dunning, D. B., & Lange, B. M. (1993). "Direction" in male and female dental students' interactions with patients: A confirmation of similarities. *Health Communication, 5*, 129–136.

Duryra, E. J., Ransom, M. V., & English, G. (1990). Psychological immunization: Theory, research, and current health behavior applications. *Health Education Quarterly, 17*, 169–178.

Eaker, E., Chesebro, J. H., Sacks, F. M., Wenger, N. K., Whisnant, J. P., & Winston, M. (1993). Cardiovascular disease in women. *Circulation, 88*, 1999–2009.

Eddy, D. (1990). Anatomy of a decision. *Journal of the American Medical Association, 263*, 441–443.

Egbert, L. D., Battit, G. E., Welch, C. E., & Bartlett, M. K. (1964). Reduction of postoperative pain by encouragement and instruction of patients. *New England Journal of Medicine, 270*, 825–827.

Eisen, A. (1994). Survey of neighborhood-based comprehensive community empowerment initiatives. *Health Education Quarterly, 21*, 235–252.

Eisen, M., Zellman, G. I., & McAllister, A. L. (1985). A health belief model approach to adolescents' fertility control: Some pilot program findings. *Health Education Quarterly, 12*, 185–210.

Emanuel, L. L., Barry, M. J., Stoeckle, J. D., Ettelson, L. M., & Emanuel, E. J. (1991).

Advance directives for medical care: A case for greater use. *New England Journal of Medicine, 324*, 889–895.

Ende, J., Kazis, L., Ash, A., & Moskowitz, M. A. (1989). Measuring patients' desire for autonomy: Decision making and information-seeking preferences among medical patients. *Journal of General Internal Medicine, 2*, 23–30.

Engel, G. L. (1978). The biopsychosocial model and the education of health professionals. *Annals of the New York Academy of Sciences, 310*, 169–187.

Engelhardt, J. B. (1994). Effects of interdisciplinary team care on veterans health administration health care costs. (State University of New York at Albany; 0669). *Dissertation Abstracts International, 56–05A*, 1983.

Entman, S. S., Glass, C. A., Hickson, G. B., Githens, P. B., Whetten-Goldstein, K., & Sloan, F. A. (1994). The relationship between malpractice claims history and subsequent obstetric care. *Journal of the American Medical Association, 272*, 1588–1591.

Epstein, L. H., & Cluss, P. A. (1982). A behavioral medicine perspective on adherence to long-term medical regimens. *Journal of Consulting and Clinical Psychology, 50*, 950–971.

Epstein, R. M., Campbell, T. L., Cohen-Cole, S. A., McWhinney, I. R., & Smilkstein, G. (1993). Perspectives on patient–doctor communication. *Journal of Family Practice, 37*, 377–388.

Essaw, S. E. (1996). The future of managed care in the United States health care reform. (Walden University; 0543). *Dissertation Abstracts International, 56–09B*, 4836.

Estrada, C. A., Isen, A. M., & Young, M. J. (1994). Positive affect improves creative problem solving and influences reported sources of practice satisfaction in physicians. *Motivation and Emotion, 18*, 285–299.

Evans, B. J., Stanley, R. O., & Burrows, G. D. (1992). Communication skills training and patients' satisfaction. *Health Communication, 4*, 155–170.

Faden, R., Becker, C., Lewis, C., Freeman, J., & Faden, A. (1981). Disclosure of information to patients in medical care. *Medical Care, 19*, 718–733.

Fallowfield, L. J., Baum, M., & Maguire, G. P. (1986). The effects of breast conservation on the psychological morbidity associated with the diagnosis and treatment of early breast cancer. *British Medical Journal, 293*, 1331–1334.

Fallsberg, M. (1993). Reflections on medicines and medication: A qualitative analysis among people on long-term drug regimens (compliance). (Universitet I Linkoping, Sweden; 0720). *Dissertation Abstracts International, 54–01A*, 96.

Falter, E., & Miniace, J. N. (1996, January/February). *Planning Review (a publication of the Planning Forum), 24*(1), 26–31.

Faules, D. F., & Pace, R. W. (1994). *Organizational Communication* (3rd ed.). Englewood Cliffs, NJ: Prentice-Hall.

Fedler, F., Phillips, M., Raker, P., et al. (1994). Network commercials promote legal drugs: Outnumber anti-drug PSA's 45 to 1. *Journal of Drug Education, 24*(4), 291–302.

Feighny, K. M., Monaco, M., & Arnold, L. (1995). Empathy training to improve physician–patient communication skills. *Academic Medicine, 70*, 435–436.

Feldman, J. (1966). *The dissemination of health information*. Chicago: Aldine.

Ferguson, K. J., Yesalis, C. E., Pomrehn, P. R., & Kirkpatrick, M. B. (1989). Attitudes, knowledge, and beliefs as predictors of exercise intent and behavior in schoolchildren. *Journal of School Health, 59*, 112–115.

Ferguson, T. (1995, January–February). Consumer health informatics. *Healthcare Forum Journal*, 29–32.

Festinger, L. (1957). *A theory of cognitive dissonance*. Stanford, CA: Stanford University Press.

Festinger, L. (1964). *Conflict, decision, and dissonance*. Stanford, CA: Stanford University Press.

Fidell, L. S. (1980). Sex role stereotypes and the American physician. *Psychology of Women Quarterly, 4*, 313–330.

Find/SVP, Emerging Technologies Research Group [Find/SVP] (1997). *Consumer health & medical information on the internet: Supply and demand*. New York: Emerging Technologies Research Group. Also at http://etrg.findsvp.com/health/mktginfo. html.

Fischbach, R. L., Sionelo-Bayog, A., Needle, A., & Delbanco, T. (1980). The patient and practitioner as authors of the medical record. *Patient Counseling and Health Education, 1*, 1–5.

Fischhoff, B., Slovic, P., Lichtenstein, S., Read, S., & Combs, B. (1978). How safe is safe enough? A psychometric study of attitudes towards technological risks and benefits. *Policy Sciences, 9*, 127–152.

Fishbein, M., & Ajzen, I. (1975). *Belief, attitude, intention, and behavior: An introduction to theory and research*. Reading, MA: Addison-Wesley.

Fishbein, M., & Ajzen, I. (1981). Acceptance, yielding and impact: Cognitive processes in persuasion. In R. E. Petty, T. M. Ostrom, & T. C. Brock (eds.), *Cognitive responses in persuasion* (pp. 339–359). Hillsdale, NJ: Lawrence Erlbaum.

Fishbein, M., Ajzen, I., & McArdle, J. (1980). Changing the behavior of alcoholics: Effects of persuasive communication. In I. Ajzen & M. Fishbein (eds.), *Understanding attitudes and predicting social behavior*. Englewood Cliffs, NJ: Prentice-Hall.

Fishbein, M., & Middlestadt, S. E. (1989). Using the theory of reasoned action as a framework for understanding and changing AIDS-related behaviors. In V. M. Mays, G. W. Albee, & S. S. Schneider (eds.), *Primary prevention of AIDS: Psychological approaches* (pp. 93–110). Newbury Park, CA: Sage.

Fishbein, M., Middlestadt, S. E., & Hitchcock, P. J. (1991). Using information to change sexually transmitted disease related behaviors: An analysis based on the theory of reasoned action. In J. N. Wasserheit, S. O. Aral, and K. K. Holmes (eds.), *Research issues in human behavior change and sexually transmitted diseases in the AIDS era* (pp. 243–257). Washington, DC: American Society for Microbiology.

Fisher, S. (1983). Doctor talk/patient talk: How treatment decisions are negotiated in doctor/patient communication. In S. Fisher & A. Todd (eds.), *The social organization of doctor–patient communication* (pp. 135–157). Washington, DC: Center for Applied Linguistics.

Fisher, S. (1984). Doctor–patient communication: A social and micro-political performance. *Sociology of Health and Illness, 6*, 1–29.

Fisher, S., & Groce, S. B. (1990). Accounting practices in medical interview. *Language in Society, 19*, 225–250.

Fisher, W. (1984). Narration as a human communication paradigm: The case of public moral argument. *Communication Monographs, 51*, 1–22.

Fitzgerald, F. T. (1988). Patients from other cultures: How they view you, themselves, and disease. *Consultant, 28*, 65–73.

Flay, B. R., & Burton, D. (1990). Effective mass communication strategies for health campaigns. In C. Atkin & L. Wallack (eds.), *Mass communication and public health* (pp. 129–146). Newbury Park, CA: Sage.

Fleming, R. (1997, June 9). A physician's lament. *Newsweek, 129*, 23.

Flora, J. A., Maccoby, N., & Farquhar, J. W. (1989). Communication campaigns to prevent cardiovascular disease: The Stanford community studies. In R. E. Rice & C. K. Atkin (eds.), *Public communication campaigns.* Newbury Park, CA: Sage.

Ford, C. V., & Sbordone, R. J. (1980). Attitudes of psychiatrists toward elderly patients. *American Journal of Psychiatry, 137*, 571–575.

Ford, S., Fallowfield, L., & Lewis, S. (1996). Doctor–patient interactions in oncology. *Social Science and Medicine, 42*, 1511–1519.

Fox, S. A., Siu, A. L., & Stein, J. A. (1994). The importance of physician communication on breast cancer screening of older women. *Archives of Internal Medicine, 154*, 2058–2068.

Fox, S. A., & Stein, J. A. (1991). The effect of physician–patient communication on mammography utilization by different ethnic groups. *Medical Care, 29*, 1065–1082.

Frank, A. W. (1995). *The wounded storyteller: Body, illness, and ethics.* Chicago: University of Chicago Press.

Franke, J. (1995). Boning up on bedside manner. *Texas Medicine, 91*(3), 32–36.

Franzblau, S., Sprafkin, J. N., & Rubinstein, E. (1977). Sex on TV: A content analysis. *Journal of Communication, 27*(2), 164–170.

Frederickson, L. G. (1993). Development of an integrative model for medical consultation. *Health Communication, 5*, 225–237.

Freeman, H. E. (1963). *Handbook of medical sociology.* Englewood Cliffs, NJ: Prentice-Hall.

Freire, P. (1973). *Education for critical consciousness.* New York: Continuum.

Freudenberg, N., Eng, E., Flay, B., Parcel, G., Rogers, T., & Wallerstein, N. (1995). Strengthening individual and community capacity to prevent disease and promote health: In search of relevant theories and principles. *Health Education Quarterly, 22*, 290–306.

Freudenheim, E. (1996). *HealthSpeak.* New York: Facts on File.

Fried, C. (1974). *Medical experimentation: Personal integrity and social policy.* New York: American Elsevier.

Friedman, R. B. (1996). Top ten reasons the world wide web may fail to change medical education. *Academic Medicine, 71*, 979–981.

Friedson, E. (1961). *Patients' view of medical practice.* New York: Russell Sage Foundation.

Friedson, E. (1970). *Professional dominance.* Chicago: Aldine.

Fries, J. F. (1994, March). Health care demand management. *Medical Interface*, 55–58.

Fries, J. F., Koop, C. E., Beadle, C. E., Cooper, P. P., England, M. J., Greaves, R. F., Sokolov, J. J., & Wright, D. (1993). Reducing health care costs by reducing the need and demand for medical services. *New England Journal of Medicine, 329*(5), 321–325.

Gabbard-Alley, A. S. (1995). Health communication and gender: A review and critique. *Health Communication, 7*, 35–54.

Gaines, H. (1994, July/August). The disconnect between scientists and corporations. *Business Horizons, 37*(4), 11–14.

Galpin, T. (1995, April). Pruning the grapevine. *Training and Development, 49*(4), 28–34.

Gambone, J. C., & Reiter, R. C. (1991). Quality improvement in health care. *Current Problems in Obstetrics, Gynecology, and Fertility, 14*, 169–175.

Gambone, J. C., Reiter, R. C., & DiMatteo, M. R. (1994). *The PREPARED provider: A guide for improved patient communication.* Beaverton, OR: Mosby Great Performance.

Garrity, T. F., & Lawson, E. J. (1989). Patient–physician communication as a determinant of medication misuse in older, minority women. *Journal of Drug Issues, 19*, 245–259.

Garvin, B. J., Kennedy, C. W., Baker, C. F., & Polivka, B. J. (1992). Cardiovascular responses of CCU patients when communicating with nurses, physicians, and families. *Health Communication, 4*, 291–301.

Gemson, D. H., Elinson, J., & Messeri, P. (1988). Differences in physician prevention practice patterns for white and minority patients. *Journal of Community Health, 13*, 53–64.

Gerbner, G., Gross, L., Morgan, M., & Signorielli, N. (1981a). Aging with television commercials: Images on television commercials and dramatic programming, 1977–1979. Annenberg School for Communication, University of Pennsylvania, Philadelphia.

Gerbner, G., Gross, L., Morgan, M., & Signorielli, N. (1981b). Special report: Health and medicine on television. *New England Journal of Medicine, 305*, 901–904.

Gerbner, G., Morgan, M., & Signorielli, N. (1982). Programming health portrayals: What viewers see, say and do. In D. Pearl, L. Bouthilet, & J. Lazar (eds.), *Television and social behavior: Ten years of scientific progress and implications for the eighties* (Vol. 2, pp. 291–307). Washington, DC: U.S. Government Printing Office.

German, P. S., & Burton, L. C. (1989). Clinicians, elderly and drugs. *Journal of Drug Issues, 19*, 221–243.

Gibbons, F. X. (1986). Stigma and interpersonal relationships. In S. C. Ainley, G. Becker, & L. M. Coleman (eds.), *The dilemma of difference: A multidisciplinary view of stigma* (pp. 95–122). New York: Plenum Press.

Gibbons, P., Busch, J., & Bradac, J. J. (1989, November). *Powerful versus powerless language: A peripheral cue, an "argument," or a distracter in persuasion?* Paper presented at the annual meeting of the Speech Communication Association, San Francisco.

Gibson, V. M. (1994, February). Patient–provider communication: A cost-management tool. *HR Focus, 71*(2), 14–16.

Giloth, B. E. (1990, February). Promoting patient involvement: Education, organization, and environmental strategies. *Patient Education and Counseling, 15*, 29–38.

Girgis, A., & Sanson-Fisher, R. W. (1995). Breaking bad news: Consensus guidelines for medical practitioners. *Journal of Clinical Oncology, 13*, 2449–2456.

Glajchen, M., Fitzmartin, R. D., Blum, D., & Swanton, R. (1995). Psychosocial barriers to cancer pain relief. *Cancer Practice, 3*(2), 76–82.

Glimelius, R., Birgegard, G., Hoffman, K., Kvale, G., & Sjoden, P. O. (1995). Information to and communication with cancer patients: Improvements and psychosocial correlates in a comprehensive care program for patients and their relatives. *Patient Education and Counseling, 25,* 171–182.

Goffman, E. (1963). *Stigma.* Englewood Cliffs, NJ: Prentice-Hall.

Goldberg, M. E., & Gorn, G. (1978). Some unintended consequences of TV advertising to children. *Journal of Consumer Research, 5*(2), 22–29.

Goldberg, M. E., Gorn, G., & Gibson, W. (1978). TV messages for snack and breakfast foods: Do they influence children's preferences? *Journal of Consumer Research, 5,* 73–81.

Goode, C. J. (1994). Evaluation of patient and staff outcomes with hospital-based managed care. (The University of Iowa; 0096). *Dissertation Abstracts International, 55–04B,* 1377.

Gordon, P. R., Carlson, L., Chessman, A., Kundrat, M. L., Morahan, P. S., & Hedrick, L. A. (1996). A multisite collaborative for the development of interdisciplinary education in continuous improvement for health professions students. *Academic Medicine, 71,* 973–978.

Gostin, L. O. (1995). Informed consent, cultural sensitivity, and respect for persons. *Journal of the American Medical Association, 274,* 844–845.

Gotcher, J. M. (1995). Well-adjusted and maladjusted cancer patients: An examination of communication variables. *Health Communication, 7,* 21–33.

Greenberg, B. S. (1981). Smoking, drugging, and drinking in top rated TV series. *Journal of Drug Education, 11*(3), 227–233.

Greenberg, B. S., Adelman, R., & Neuendorf, K. (1981). Sex on the soap operas: An afternoon delight. *Journal of Communication, 31*(3), 83–89.

Greene, M. G. (1987). *The physician–elderly patient relationship: An examination of the language and behavior of doctors with their elderly patients.* Final report to the AARP–Andrus Foundation.

Greene, M. G., Adelman, R. D., Charon, R., & Friedmann, E. (1989). Concordance between physicians and their older and younger patients in the primary medical encounter. *Gerontologist, 29,* 808–813.

Greene, M. G., Adelman, R. D., Charon, R., & Hoffman, S. (1986). Ageism in the medical encounter: An exploratory study of the doctor–patient relationship. *Language and Communication, 6,* 113–124.

Greene, M. G., Adelman, R. D., & Majerovitz, S. D. (1996). Physician and older patient support in the medical encounter. *Health Communication, 8,* 263–279.

Greene, M. G., Adelman, R. D., & Rizzo, C. (1996). Problems in communication between physicians and older patients. *Journal of Geriatric Society, 19,* 13–32.

Greene, M. G., Majerovitz, S. D., Adelman, R. D., & Rizzo, C. (1994). The effects of the presence of a third person on the physician–older patient medical interview. *Journal of the American Geriatrics Society, 42,* 413–419.

Greeneich, D. M. S. (1995). A model of patient satisfaction and behavioral intention in managed care (nurse practitioners). (University of San Diego; 0105). *Dissertation Abstracts International, 56–05B,* 2557.

Greenfield, S., Kaplan, S., & Ware, J. E., Jr. (1985). Expanding patient involvement in care: Effects on patient outcomes. *Annals of Internal Medicine, 102,* 520–528.

Greenlick, M. R. (1995). Educating physicians for the twenty-first century. *Academic Medicine, 70,* 179–185.

Greeson, L. E., & Williams, R. A. (1986). Social implications of music videos for youth: An analysis of the content and effects of MTV. *Youth and Society, 18*(2), 177–189.

Gregory, D. R., & Cotler, M. P. (1994) The problem of futility: III. The importance of physician–patient communication and a suggested guide through the mine field. *Cambridge Quarterly of Health Care Ethics, 3,* 257–269.

Griffin, R. J., Neuwirth, K., & Dunwoody, S. (1995). Using the theory of reasoned action to examine the health impact of risk messages. *Communication Yearbook, 18,* 201–228.

Grimley, D. M., Riley, G. E., Bellis, J. M., & Prochaska, J. O. (1993). Assessing the stages of change and decision-making for contraceptive use for the prevention of pregnancy, sexually transmitted diseases, and acquired immunodeficiency syndrome. *Health Education Quarterly, 20,* 455–470.

Grodner, M. (1991). Using the health belief model for bulimia prevention. *Journal of American College Health, 40,* 107–112.

Guttman, N. (1993). Patient–practitioner information exchange as an asymmetrical social encounter: Do patients actually know what their practitioners think they know? In J. R. Schement & B. Ruben (eds.), *Between communication and information* (pp. 293–318). New Brunswick, NJ: Transaction Books.

Haas, A., & Puretz, S. L. (1992). Encouraging partnerships between health care providers and women recommended for gynecological surgery. *Health Communication, 4,* 29–38.

Hackett, T. P., Cassem, N. H., & Raker, J. W. (1973). Patient delay in cancer. *New England Journal of Medicine, 289,* 14–20.

Hadlow, J., & Pitts, M. (1991). The understanding of common health terms by doctors, nurses, and patients. *Social Science & Medicine, 32,* 193–196.

Hall, J. A., Epstein, A. M., DeCiantis, M. L., & McNeil, B. J. (1993). Physicians' liking for their patients: More evidence for the role of affect in medical care. *Health Psychology, 12,* 140–146.

Hall, J. A., Irish, J. T., Roter, D. L., Ehrlich, C. M., & Miller, L. H. (1994). Gender in medical encounters: An analysis of physician and patient communication in a primary care setting. *Health Psychology, 13,* 384–392.

Hall, J. A., Roter, D. L., & Katz, N. R. (1988). Meta-analysis of correlates of provider behavior in medical encounters. *Medical Care, 25,* 399–412.

Hall, J. A., Roter, D. L., Milburn, M. A., & Daltroy, L. H. (1996). Patients' health as a predictor of physician and patient behavior in medical visits: A synthesis of four studies. *Medical Care, 34,* 1205–1218.

Hamel, G., & Prahalad, C. K. (1990, Spring). Strategic intent. *The McKinsey Quarterly,* 36–61.

Hamilton, M. A., Rouse, R. A., & Rouse, J. (1994). Dentist communication and patient utilization of dental services: Anxiety inhibition and competence enhancement effects. *Health Communication, 6,* 137–158.

Hammond, S. L., & Lambert, B. L. (eds.). (1994). Communicating with patients about their medications. Special Issue of *Health Communication, 6*(4).

Hampton, D. (1994). The impact of computers on nursing: A case study. *Dissertation Abstracts International, 56,* 688.

Hargie, O., Morrow, N., & Woodman, C. (1993). *Looking into community pharmacy: Identifying effective communication skills in pharmacist–patient consultations.* Jordanstown, N. Ireland: University of Ulster.

Harris. L. M. (ed.). (1995). *Health and the new media: Technologies transforming personal and public health.* Mahwah, NJ: Lawrence Erlbaum.

Harvey, L. K., & Shubat, S. C. (1989). *Public Opinion on Health Care Issues 1989.* Chicago: American Medical Association.

Haug, M. (1979). Doctor–patient relationships and the older patient. *Journal of Gerontology, 34*, 852–859.

Haug, M. R. (1996). The effects of physician/elder patient characteristics on health communication. *Health Communication, 8,* 249–262.

Haug, M. R., & Lavin, B. (1983). *Consumerism in medicine: Challenging physician authority.* Beverly Hills, CA: Sage.

Haug, M. R., & Ory, M. G. (1987). Issues in elderly patient–provider interactions. *Research on Aging, 9*, 3–44.

Hayes-Bautista, D. E. (1976). Modifying the treatment: Patient compliance, patient control and medical care. *Social Science & Medicine, 10*, 233–238.

Haynes, R. B., Taylor, D. W., & Sackett, D. L. (eds.) (1979). *Compliance in health care.* Baltimore, MD: Johns Hopkins University Press.

Health Commons Institute. (1995). *Annotated bibliography of citations on shared medical decision making.* Portland, ME: Health Commons Institute.

Health Economics Solutions in conjunction with Philadelphia's Thomas Jefferson University Hospital. *A health economics pocket glossary.* Plymouth Meeting, PA: IMS America.

Healthcare Information and Management Systems Society. (1996). *Guide to effective health care telecommunications.* Chicago: Healthcare Information and Management Systems Society.

Heavey, A. (1988). Learning to talk with patients. *British Journal of Hospital Medicine, 39*, 433–439.

Heeter, C., Perlstadt, H., & Greenberg, B. S. (1984). Health incidents, stages of illness and treatment on popular television programs. Paper presented at the annual convention of the International Communication Association.

Helling, D., Lempe, J., Semla, R., Wallace, R., Lipson, D., & Coroni-Huntley, J. (1987). Medication use characteristics in the elderly: The Iowa 65+ rural health study. *Journal of the American Geriatrics Society, 35*, 4–12.

Henderson, L. J. (1985). Physician and patient as a social system. *New England Journal of Medicine, 212*, 819–823.

Herselman, S. (1996). Some problems in health communication in a multicultural clinical setting: A South African experience. *Health Communication, 8*, 153–170.

Hickson, G. B., Clayton, E. W., Entman, S. S., Miller, C. S., Githens, P. B., Whetten-Golstein, K., & Sloan, F. A. (1994). Obstetricians' prior malpractice experience and patients' satisfaction with care. *Journal of the American Medical Association, 272*, 1583–1587.

Himmel, W., Stolpe, C., & Kochen, M. (1994). Information and communication about overweight in family practice. *Family Practice Research Journal, 14*, 339–351.

Hinckley, J. J., Craig, H. K., & Anderson, L. A. (1990). Communication characteristics of provider–patient information exchanges. In H. Giles & W. P. Robinson (eds.), *Handbook of language and social psychology* (pp. 519–536). Chichester, England: John Wiley & Sons.

Hochbaum, G. M., Sorenson, J. R., & Loring, K. (1992). Theory in health education practice. *Health Education Quarterly, 19*, 295–314.

Hodes, R. J., Ory, M. G., & Pruzan, M. R. (1995). Communicating with older patients:

A challenge for researchers and clinicians. *Journal of the American Geriatrics Society, 43*, 167–168.

Holland, J. C., Geary, N., Marchini, A., & Tross, S. (1987). An international survey of physician attitudes and practice in regard to revealing the diagnosis of cancer. *Cancer Investigation, 5*, 151–154.

Holm, S. (1993). What is wrong with compliance? *Journal of Medical Ethics, 19*, 108–110.

Holsinger, B. C. (1995). The influence of business characteristics and composition on the choice of health care benefits in Virginia businesses. (Virginia Commonwealth University; 2383). *Dissertation Abstracts International, 55–07A*, 2044.

Hooper, E. M., Comstock, L. M., Goodwin, J. M., & Goodwin, J. S. (1982). Patient characteristics that influence physician behavior. *Medical Care, 20*, 630–638.

Hornberger, J. C., Gibson, C. D., Jr., Wood, W., Dequeldre, C., Corso, I., Palla, B., & Bloch, D. A. (1996). Eliminating language barriers for non-English-speaking patients. *Medical Care, 34*, 845–856.

Hornik, R. (1991). Alternative models of behavior change. In J. N. Wasserheit, S. O. Aral, and K. K. Holmes (eds.), *Research issues in human behavior change and sexually transmitted diseases in the AIDS era* (pp. 201–218). Washington, DC: American Society for Microbiology.

Hovland, C., Janis, I., & Kelley, H. (1953). *Communication and persuasion*. New Haven: Yale University Press.

Howard, E. (1995, April). Going global: What it really means to communicators. *Communication World, 12*(4), 12–16.

Hudak, R. P., Brooke, P. P., Jr., Finstuen, K., and Riley, P. (1993, Summer). Health care administration in the year 2000: Practitioners' views of future issues and job requirements. *Hospital & Health Services Administration, 38*(2), 181–195.

Hughes, J. J. (1995). Organization and information at the bed-side: The experience of the medical division of labor by University Hospital's inpatients. (University of Chicago; 0330). *Dissertation Abstracts International, 56–03A*, 1146.

Hulka, B. S., Cassel, J., Kupper, L., & Burdette, J. (1976). Communication, compliance, and concordance between physicians and patients with prescribed medications. *American Journal of Public Health, 66*, 847–853.

Hull, W. W. (1994, August). Beating the grapevine to the punch. *Supervision, 55*(8), 17–20.

Hunter, K. M. (1991). *Doctor's stories: The narrative structure of medical knowledge.* Princeton, NJ: Princeton University Press.

Irish, J. T., & Hall, J. A. (1995). Interruptive patterns in medical visits: The effects of role, status and gender. *Social Science and Medicine, 41*, 873–881.

Israel, B. A., Checkoway, B., Schulz, A., & Zimmerman, M. (1994). Health education and community empowerment: Conceptualizing and measuring perceptions of individual, organizational, and community control. *Health Education Quarterly, 21*, 149–170.

Jackson, J. (1991). Telling the truth. *Journal of Medical Ethics, 17*, 5–9.

Jackson, J. (1993). On the morality of deception—does method matter? A reply to David Bakhurst. *Journal of Medical Ethics, 19*, 183–187.

Jackson, L. D. (1992). Information complexity and medical communication: The effects of technical language and amount of information in a medical message. *Health Communication, 4*, 197–210.

Jackson, L. D. (1994a). Ethical issues in medicine: A communication revolution. Paper presented at the Annual Convention of the Speech Communication Association, New Orleans.

Jackson, L. D. (1994b). Maximizing treatment adherence among back-pain patients: An experimental study of the effects of physician-related cues in written medical messages. *Health Communication, 6*(3), 173–191.

Jackson, L. D., & Selby, M. J. (1998). Communicating an HIV-positive diagnosis. In N. L. Roth & L. K. Fuller (eds.), *Women and AIDS: Negotiating safer practices, care and representation* (pp. 131–153). Binghamton, NY: The Harrington Park Press.

Jaco, E. G. (1972). *Patients, physicians, and illness: A sourcebook in behavioral science and health* (2nd ed.). New York: Free Press.

Janis, I. L. (1967). Effects of fear arousal on attitude change: Recent developments in theory and experimental research. In L. Berkowitz (ed.), *Advances in experimental social psychology* (Vol. 3, pp. 166–225). New York: Academic Press.

Janis, I., & Feshbach, S. (1953). Effects of fear-arousing communications. *Journal of Abnormal and Social Psychology, 48*, 78–92.

Janz, N. K., & Becker, M. H. (1984). The health belief model: A decade later. *Health Education Quarterly, 11*, 1–47.

Jeffe, D., & Jeffe, S. B. (1984, February/March). Losing patience with doctors: Physicians vs. the public on health care costs. *Public Opinion, 55*, 45–47.

Jeffries-Fox, S., & Signorielli, N. (1978). Television and children's conceptions of occupations. In H. S. Dordick (ed.), *Proceedings of the Sixth Annual Telecommunications Policy Research Conference* (pp. 21–38). Lexington, MA: D.C. Heath.

Jenkinson, C. (1994). Quality of life measurement: Does it have a place in routine clinical assessment? *Journal of Psychosomatic Research, 38*, 377–381.

Jenks, E. B. (1993). Communication in health care settings. In L. P. Arliss & D. J. Borisoff (eds.), *Women and men communicating* (pp. 122–141). Fort Worth, TX: Harcourt Brace Javanovich.

Johnson, B. T., & Eagly, A. H. (1989). Effects of involvement on persuasion. *Psychological Bulletin, 106*, 290–314.

Johnson, J. E., & Leventhal, H. (1974). Effects of accurate expectations and behavioral instructions on reactions during a noxious medical examination. *Journal of Personality & Social Psychology, 29*, 710–718.

Jones, E. E., Farina, A., Hastorf, A. H., Marhus, H., Miller, D. T., & Scott, R. A. (1984). *Social stigma: The psychology of marked relationships*. New York: W. H. Freeman.

Jones, J. A., & Phillips, G. M. (1988). *Communicating with your doctor*. Carbondale, IL: Southern Illinois University Press.

Joos, S. K. & Hickam, D. H. (1990). How health professionals influence health behavior: Patient–provider interaction and health care outcomes. In K. Glanz, F. M. Lewis, & B. Rimer (eds.), *Health behavior and health education*. San Francisco, CA: Jossey-Bass.

Joshi, N., & Milfred, D. (1995). The use and misuse of new antibiotics. A perspective. *Archives of Internal Medicine, 155*, 569–577.

Josiah H. Macy, Jr. Foundation. (1988). *Adapting Clinical Medical Education to the Needs of Today and Tomorrow*. New York: Author.

Kaiser Family Foundation & U.S. Agency for Health Care Policy and Research. (1996).

Americans as Health Care Consumers: The Role of Quality Information. Menlo Park, CA: Kaiser Family Foundation.

Kalisch, P. A., & Kalisch, B. J. (1982). Nurses on prime time television. *American Journal of Nursing, 82,* 264–270.

Kalisch, P. A., & Kalisch, B. J. (1984). Sex role stereotyping of nurses and physicians on prime time television: A dichotomy of occupational portrayals. *Sex Roles, 10*(7/8), 533–553.

Kaplan, R. M. (1991). Health-related quality of life in patient decision making. *Journal of Social Issues, 47*(4), 69–90.

Kaplan, S. H., Greenfield, S., & Ware, J. E., Jr. (1989). Assessing the effects of physician–patient interactions on the outcomes of chronic disease. *Medical Care, 27,* S110–S127.

Kasper, J. F., Mulley. A. G., Jr., & Wennberg. J. E. (1992). Developing shared decision making programs to improve the quality of care. *Quality Review Bulletin 18*(6), 183–190.

Katz, E., & Lazarsfeld, P. (1955). *Personal influence*. New York: Free Press.

Katz, J. (1984). *The silent world of doctor and patient*. New York: Free Press.

Katzman, N. (1982). Television soap operas: What's been going on anyway? *Public Opinion Quarterly, 36*(2), 200–212.

Kaufman, L. (1980). Prime time nutrition. *Journal of Communication, 30*(3), 37–46.

Keller, V. F., & Caroll, J. G. (1994). A new model for physician–patient communication. *Patient Education and Counseling, 23,* 131–140.

Kemper D. W. (1994). *Kaiser Permanente's healthwise handbook: A self-care guide for you and your family*. Boise, Idaho: Healthwise.

Kemper, S. (1994). Elderspeak: Speech accommodation to older adults. *Aging and Cognition, 1,* 246–252.

Kirkpatrick, P. R. (1994). Attracting employee patients: A study of primary care physician selection in the managed care plan of an academic medical center. (University of Alabama; 0005). *Dissertation Abstracts International, 55–12A,* 3914.

Kirscht, J. P., & Joseph, J. G. (1989). The health belief model: Some implications for behavior change with reference to homosexual males. In V. M. Mays, G. W. Albee, & S. S. Schneider (eds.), *Primary prevention of AIDS: Psychological approaches* (pp. 93–110). Newbury Park, CA: Sage.

Kishchuk, N. A. (1987). Causes and Correlates of Risk Perceptions: A Comment. *Risk Abstracts, 4,* 1–4.

Klapper, J. (1960). *The effects of mass communication*. New York: Free Press.

Kleck, R. E. (1968). Effects of stigmatizing conditions on the use of personal space. *Psychological Reports, 23,* 111–118.

Kleck, R. E. (1969). Physical stigma and task oriented interactions. *Human Relations, 22,* 53–60.

Klein, J. D., Brown, J. D., Childers, K. W., Oliveri, J., Porter, C., & Dykers, C. (1993). Adolescents' risky behavior and mass media. *Pediatrics, 92*(1), 24–31.

Klein, L. E., German, P. S., Levine, D. M., Feroli, E. R., Jr., & Ardery, J. (1984). Medication problems among outpatients: A study with emphasis on the elderly. *Archives of Internal Medicine, 144,* 1185–1188.

Kleinman, A. (1980). *Patients and healers in the context of culture*. Berkeley: University of California Press.

Kleinman, A. (1988). *The illness narratives: Suffering, healing, and the human condition.* New York: Basic Books.

Kleinman, A., Eisenberg, L., & Good, B. (1978). Culture, illness and care: Clinical lessons from anthropologic and cross-cultural research. *Annals of Internal Medicine, 88,* 251–258.

Klenow, D. J., & Young, G. A. (1987). Changes in doctor/patient communication of a terminal prognosis: A selective review and critique. *Death Studies, 11,* 263–277.

Kline, K. (1995). *Applying Witte's Extended Parallel Process Model to pamphlets urging women to engage in BSE: Where are the efficacy messages?* Paper presented at the annual meeting of the Speech Communication Association, San Antonio, Texas.

Korsch, B. M. (1989). Current issues in communication research. *Health Communication, 1*(1), 5–9.

Korsch, B. M., Gozzi, E. K., & Francis, V. (1968). Gaps in doctor–patient communication: I. Doctor–patient interaction and patient satisfaction. *Pediatrics, 42,* 855–871.

Korsch, B. M., & Negrete, V. (1972). Doctor–patient communication. *Scientific American, 227,* 66–74.

Kosa, J., Antonovsky, A., & Zola, I. K. (1969). *Poverty and health: A sociological analysis.* Cambridge, MA: Harvard University Press.

Kotler, P. (1972). A generic concept of marketing. *Journal of Marketing, 36,* 46–54.

Kotler, P. (1984). Social marketing of health behavior. In L. W. Frederikson, L. J. Solomon, & K. A. Brehony (eds.), *Marketing health behavior* (pp. 23–39). New York: Plenum Press.

Kotler, P., & Roberto, E. (1989). *Social marketing.* New York: Free Press.

Kotler, P., & Zaltman, G. (1971). Social marketing: An approach to planned social change. *Journal of Marketing, 35,* 3–12.

Kotz, K., & Story, M. (1994). Food advertisements during children's Saturday morning television programming: Are they consistent with dietary recommendations? *Journal of the American Dieticians Association, 94*(11), 1296–1300.

Kravitz, R. L., Callahan, E. J., Paterniti, D., Antonius, D., Dunham, M., & Lewis, C. E. (1996). Prevalence and sources of patients' unmet expectations for care. *Annals of Internal Medicine, 125,* 730–737.

Kreps, G. L. (1988). The pervasive role of information in health care: Implications for health communication policy. In J. Anderson (ed.), *Communication Yearbook 11* (238–276). Newbury Park, CA: Sage.

Kreps, G. L. (1989). Setting the agenda for health communication research and development: Scholarship that can make a difference. *Health Communication, 1*(1), 11–15.

Kreps, G. L. (1990a). Communication and health education. In E. B. Ray & L. Donohew (eds.), *Communication and health: Systems and applications,* 187–203. Hillsdale, NJ: Lawrence Erlbaum.

Kreps, G. L. (1990b). A systematic analysis of health communication with the aged. In H. Giles, N. Coupland, & J. M. Wiemann (eds.), *Communication, health, and the elderly* (pp. 135–154). Manchester, England: Manchester University Press.

Kreps, G. L. (1993). Refusing to be a victim: Rhetorical strategies for confronting cancer. In B. C. Thornton & G. L. Kreps (eds.), *Perspectives on health communication* (pp. 42–47). Prospect Heights, IL: Waveland Press.

Kreps, G. L. (1996a). Communicating to promote justice in the modern health care system. *Journal of Health Communication, 1*(1), 99–109.

Kreps, G. L. (1996b). Promoting a consumer orientation to health care and health promotion. *Journal of Health Psychology, 1*(1), 41–48.

Kreps, G. L. (ed.). (1996c). Special issue, messages and meanings: Health communication and health psychology. *Journal of Health Psychology, 1*(3), 259–403.

Kreps, G. L., & Atkin, C. (eds.). (1991). Special issue: Communicating to promote health. *American Behavioral Scientist, 34*(6), 645–772.

Kreps, G. L. & Kunimoto, E. N. (1994). *Effective communication in multicultural health care settings.* Thousand Oaks, CA: Sage.

Kreps, G. L., & O'Hair, H. D. (eds.). (1995). *Communication and health outcomes.* Cresskill, NJ: Hampton Press.

Kreps, G. L., & Thornton, B. C. (1984). *Health communication: Theory and practice.* New York: Longman.

Kukulska-Hulme, A. M. (1994). Effective knowledge transfer: A terminological perspective. Dismantling the jargon barrier to knowledge about computer security. (Aston University, United Kingdom; 0734). *Dissertation Abstracts International, 55–03C,* 944.

Kunkel, D., & Gantz, W. (1992). Children's television advertising in the multichannel environment. *Journal of Communication, 42*(3), 134–151.

Laine, C., & Davidoff, F. (1996). Patient-centered medicine: A professional evolution. *Journal of the American Medical Association, 275,* 152–156.

Lambert, B. L., & Gillespie, J. L. (1994). Patient perceptions of pharmacy students' hypertension compliance-gaining messages: Effects of message design logic and content themes. *Health Communication, 6,* 311–326.

Lamm, R. D. (1993). New world of medical ethics. *Vital Speeches of the Day, LIX-18,* 549–553.

Lancaster, H. (1987, April 24). Where patients are partners. *Wall Street Journal,* 5D.

Lancee, W. J., Gallop, R., McCroy, E., & Toner, B. (1995). The relationship between nurses' limit-setting styles and anger in psychiatric inpatients. *Psychiatric Services, 46,* 609–613.

Lang, F. (1990). Resident behaviors during observed pelvic examinations. *Family Medicine, 20,* 153–155.

Lapinski, M. (1997). *The impact of oral mucosal transudate testing process on counseling and testing programs in community based organizations: Analysis of results and recommendations for future data collection and analysis.* Final report submitted to Michigan Department of Community Health.

Larkin, T. J., and Larkin, S. M. (1995, March). Employee communication: Have we missed the mark? *Communication World, 12*(3), 12–16.

Larson, M. S. (1991). Health-related messages embedded in prime time television entertainment. *Health Communication, 3*(3), 175–184.

Larson, S. G. (1991). Television's mixed messages: Sexual content on *All My Children. Communication Quarterly, 39*(2), 156–163.

Lazare, A., Eisenthal, S., Frank, A., & Stoeckle, J. (1978). Studies on a negotiated approach to patienthood. In E. B. Gallagher (ed.), *The doctor–patient relationship in a changing health scene* (NIH No. 78–189, pp. 119–139). Washington, DC: U.S. Department of Health, Education, and Welfare.

Leedham, B., Meyerowitz, B. E., Muirhead, H., & Frist, W. H. (1995). Positive expectations predict health after heart transplantation. *Health Psychology, 14*, 74–79.

Lefebvre, R. C., & Flora, J. A. (1988). Social marketing and public health intervention. *Health Education Quarterly, 15*, 299–315.

Lemon, M., Yonke, A., Roe, B., & Foley, R. (1995). Communication as an essential part of program and institutional development. *Academic Medicine, 70*, 884–886.

Lepper, H. S., Martin, L. R., & DiMatteo, M. R. (1995). A model of nonverbal exchange in physician–patient expectations for patient involvement. *Journal of Nonverbal Behavior, 19*, 207–222.

Leventhal, H. (1970). Findings and theory in the study of fear communications. In L. Berkowitz (ed.), *Advances in experimental social psychology* (Vol. 5, pp. 119–186). New York: Academic Press.

Levinson, W. (1994). Physician–patient communication: A key to malpractice prevention. *Journal of the American Medical Association, 272*, 1619–1620.

Levinson, W., Stiles, W. B., Inui, T. S., & Engle, R. (1993). Physician frustration in communicating with patients. *Medical Care, 31*, 285–295.

Ley, P. (1979). Memory for medical information. *British Journal of Social & Clinical Psychology, 18*, 245–255.

Ley, P. (1982). Satisfaction, compliance and communication. *British Journal of Clinical Psychology, 21*, 241–254.

Ley, P. (1988). *Communicating with patients: Improving communication, satisfaction, and compliance.* London: Chapman and Hall.

Ley, P., & Spelman, M. S. (1967). *Communicating with patients.* London: Staples Press.

Lidz, C. W., Appelbaum, P. S., & Meisel, A. (1988). Two models of implementing informed consent. *Archives of Internal Medicine, 148*, 1385–1389.

Lin, E. H. B., Von Korff, M., Katon, W., Bush, T., Simon, G. E., Walker, E., & Robinson, P. (1995). The role of the primary care physician in patients' adherence to antidepressant therapy. *Medical Care, 33*, 67–74.

Lincoln, T. L. (1982, January 8). Medical decision-making for patients as individuals. Presented at the 148th American Association for the Advancement of Science, National Meeting, Washington, DC.

Logan, M. (1993, March). Why soaps are so sexy. *TV Guide, 20*, 8–14.

Longest, B., Darr, K., & Rakich, J. (1992). *Managing health services organizations* (3rd ed.). Baltimore: Health Professions Press.

Lorber, J. (1975). Good patients and problem patients: Conformity and deviance in a general hospital. *Journal of Health and Social Behavior, 16*, 213–225.

Lorig, K., Mazonson, P., & Holman, H. (1993). Evidence suggesting that health education for self-management in patients with chronic arthritis has sustained health benefits while reducing health care costs. *Arthritis and Rheumatism 36*(4), 439–446.

Lowry, D. T., & Towles, D. E. (1989a). Prime time TV portrayals of sex, contraception and venereal diseases. *Journalism Quarterly, 66*(2), 347–452.

Lowry, D. T., & Towles, D. E. (1989b). Soap opera portrayals of sex, contraception, and sexually transmitted diseases. *Journal of Communication 39*(2), 76–83.

Luarn, P. (1993). The relationship between computer mediated communication systems and social support (immune deficiency). (University of Wisconsin; 0262). *Dissertation Abstracts International, 54–09B*, 4862.

Luedecke, B. (1996, March). This will be our last downsizing—honest! *Canadian HR Reporter, 18.*

Luke, R. D., Ozcan, Y. A., and Olden, P. C. (1995, October). Local markets and systems: Hospital consolidation in metropolitan areas. *Health Services Research, 30*(4), 555–575.

Lunin, L. F. (1987). Where does the public get its health information? *Bulletin of the New York Academy of Medicine, 63*(10), 923–938.

Lynn, J., & DeGrazia, D. (1991). An outcomes model of medical decision making. *Theoretical Medicine, 12,* 325–343.

MacDonald, P. T. (1983). The ''dope'' on soaps. *Journal of Drug Education, 14*(4), 359–368.

MacDonald, P. T., & Macdonald, R. E. (1994). Five years of sex on prime time TV, 1989–1993. Association paper, *Society for the Study of Social Problems.*

MacMillan, I. C., McCaffery, M. L., & van Wijk, G. (1985). Competitor's responses to easily imitated new products: Exploring commercial banking product introductions. *Strategic Management Journal, 13,* 363–380.

Madden, P. A., & Grube, J. W. (1994). The frequency and nature of alcohol and tobacco advertising in televised sports, 1990 through 1992. *American Journal of Public Health, 84*(2), 297–299.

Maibach, E. W., & Cotton, D. (1995). Moving people to behavior change: A staged social cognitive approach to message design. In E. W. Maibach & R. L. Parrott (eds.), *Designing health messages: Approaches from communication theory and public health practice* (pp. 41–64). Newbury Park, CA: Sage.

Maibach, E. W., Kreps, G. L., & Bonaguro, E. W. (1993). Developing strategic communication campaigns for HIV/AIDS prevention. In S. Ratzan (ed.), *AIDS: Effective health communication for the 90's* (pp. 15–35). Washington, DC: Taylor and Francis.

Makoul, G. (1992). Perpetuating Passivity: A Study of Physician–Patient Communication and Decision Making. Unpublished doctoral dissertation, Northwestern University, Evanston, Illinois.

Makoul, G. (1995a). SEGUE: A framework for teaching and evaluating communication in medical encounters. Paper presented to Division I of the American Educational Research Association, San Francisco.

Makoul, G. (1995b). *Telemedicine Update.* Washington, DC: Annenberg Washington Program in Communications Policy Studies.

Makoul, G. (1996). Medical student and resident perspectives on delivering bad news. Poster presented at the Teaching about Communication in Medicine Conference, Oxford, England.

Makoul, G., Arntson, P., & Schofield, T. (1995). Health promotion in primary care: Physician–patient communication and decision making about prescription medicine. *Social Science and Medicine, 41,* 1241–1256.

Makoul, G., & Curry, R. H. (1998). Patient, physician & society: Northwestern University Medical School. *Academic Medicine, 73,* 14–24.

Makoul, G., & Sliwa, J. (1996). A context-based communication training program for resident physicians. Poster presented at the Teaching about Communication in Medicine Conference, Oxford, England.

Malterud, K. (1993). Strategies for empowering women's voices in the medical culture. *Health Care for Women International, 14,* 365–373.

Marshall, A. A., Smith, S. W., & McKeon, J. K. (1995). Persuading low-income women to engage in mammography screening: Source, message, and channel preferences. *Health Communication, 7*, 283–299.

Marvel, M. K. (1993). Involvement with the psychosocial concerns of patients: Observations of practicing family physicians on a university faculty. *Archives of Family Medicine, 2*, 629–633.

Marvel, M. K., & Morphew, R. K. (1993). Levels of family involvement by resident and attending physicians. *Family Medicine, 25*, 26–30.

Mason, J. L., Barkley, S. E., Kappelman, M. M., Carter, D. E., & Beachy, W. V. (1988). Evaluation of a self-instructional method for improving doctor–patient communication. *Journal of Medical Education, 63*, 629–635.

Mathys, G. (1995, February). Patient-care systems trends: The clinical data repository. *Health Management Technology, 16*(2), 12–14.

McCombs, M., & Shaw, D. (1972–1973). The agenda-setting function of mass media. *Public Opinion Quarterly, 36*, 176–187.

McGinnis, J. M., & Foege, W. H. (1993). Actual causes of death in the United States. *Journal of the American Medical Association, 270*(18), 2207–2212.

McGuire, W. J. (1964). Inducing resistance to persuasion. Some contemporary approaches. In L. Berkowitz (ed.), *Advances in experimental social psychology* (Vol. 1, pp. 191–229). New York: Academic Press.

McGuire, W. J. (1968). Personality and susceptibility to social influence. In E. F. Borgatta and W. W. Lambert (eds.), *Handbook of personality theory and research* (pp. 1130–1187). Chicago: Rand McNally.

McGuire, W. J. (1969). Attitude and attitude change. In G. Lindzey & E. Aronson (eds.), *Handbook of social psychology* (2nd ed., pp. 136–214). Reading, MA: Addison-Wesley.

McGuire, W. J. (1984). Public communication as a strategy for inducing health promoting behavioral change. *Preventive Medicine, 13*, 299–319,

McKegney, C. P. (1989). Medical education: A neglectful and abusive family system. *Family Medicine, 21*, 452–457.

McLaughlin, J. (1975). The doctor shows. *Journal of Communication, 25*(3), 182–184.

McNeil, B. J., Weichselbaum, R., & Parker, S. G. (1978). Fallacy of the five-year survival in lung cancer. *New England Journal of Medicine, 299*, 1397–1401.

Mechanic, D. (1968). *Medical sociology: A selective view.* New York: Free Press.

Mechanic, D. (1992). Health and illness behavior and patient–practitioner relationships. *Social Science & Medicine, 34*, 1345–1350.

Meeuwesen, L., Schaap, C., & van der Staak, C. (1991). Verbal analysis of doctor–patient communication. *Social Science and Medicine, 32*, 1143–1150.

Mendelsohn, H. (1973). Some reasons why information campaigns can succeed. *Public Opinion Quarterly, 37*, 50–61.

Meyer, G., & Dearing, J. W. (1996, Winter). Respecifying the social marketing model for unique populations. *Social Marketing Quarterly.*

Meyer, G., & Witte, K. (1995). Intrapersonal health communication. In J. Aitken & L. J. Shedletsky (eds.), *Intrapersonal Communication Processes* (pp. 364–375). Plymouth, MI: Midnight Oil & Speech Communication Association.

Meyers, H. (1995, May 22). Yellow pages ads still valuable despite managed care. *American Medical News, 38*(20), 19–21.

Millar, F. E., & Millar, L. E. (1976). A relational approach to interpersonal communication. In G. R. Miller (ed.), *Explorations in Interpersonal Communication* (pp. 87–103). Beverly Hills, CA: Sage.

Mishler, E. G. (1984). *The discourse of medicine: Dialectics of medical interviews*. Norwood, NJ: Ablex.

Molitor, F. (1991). How accurate is the science news we receive from the mass media? Paper presented at the Annual Meeting of the International Communication Association.

Mongeau, P., & Stiff, J. B. (1989, May). *The effects of message and source processing on attitude: Testing the elaboration likelihood model of persuasion*. Paper presented at the 56th annual meeting of the International Communication Association, San Francisco.

Morris, L. A., Grossman, R., Barkdoll, G. L., Gordon, E., & Soviero, C. (1984). A survey of patient sources of prescription drug information. *American Journal of Public Health, 74*, 1161–1162.

Morrison, R. S., Morrison, E. W., & Glickman, D. F. (1994). Physician reluctance to discuss advance directives. *Archives of Internal Medicine, 154*, 2311–2318.

Morrow, G. R., Hoagland, A. C., & Carpenter, P. J. (1983). Improving physician patient communications in cancer treatment. *Journal of Psychosocial Oncology, 1*, 93–101.

Moyer, A., Greener, S., Beauvais, J., & Salovey, P. (1995). Accuracy of health related research reported in the popular press: Breast cancer and mammography. *Health Communication, 7*(2), 147–161.

Muller, S. (1984). Physicians for the twenty first century: Report of the project panel on the general professional education of the physician and college preparation for medicine, Part II. *Journal of Medical Education, 59*.

Murphy, M. (1996, July). Cutting healthcare costs through work force reduction. *Healthcare Financial Management, 50*, 64–69.

Murphy, R. F. (1990). *The body silent*. New York: Norton.

Murray, L. S., Teasdale, G. M., Murray, G. D., Jennett, B., Miller, J. D., Pickard, J. D., Shaw, M. D., Achilles, J., Bailey, S., Jones, P., Kelly, D., Lacey, J. (1993). Does prediction of outcome alter patient management? *The Lancet, 341*, 1487–1491.

Naish, J., Brown, J., & Denton, B. (1994). Intercultural consultations: Investigation of factors that deter non-English speaking women from attending their general practitioners for cervical screening. *British Medical Journal, 309*, 1126–1128.

National Center for Health Statistics. (1986). Prevalence of selected chronic conditions, U.S., 1974–1981. *Vital and Health Statistics*, Series 10, No. 155 [DHHS Pub. No. (PHS) 86–1581]. Washington, DC: U.S. Government Printing Office.

National Information Infrastructure Task Force [NIITF], Health Information Applications Workgroup, Consumer Health Information Subgroup. (1995, September). *Consumer health information*. Draft White Paper.

Nelson, A. R. (1989). Humanism and the art of medicine. *Journal of the American Medical Association, 262*, 1228–1230.

Nelson, B. D. (1994). Decision support for utilization review using the help hospital information system. (University of Utah; 0240). *Dissertation Abstracts International, 55–11B*, 4946.

Newcomer, S. F., & Brown, J. D. (1984, August). *Influences of television and peers on adolescents' sexual behavior*. Paper presented at the American Psychological Association meeting, Toronto, Canada.

Nielsen Media Research. (1990). *Report on television*. New York: A. C. Nielsen Co.

The 1996–1997 Integrated Health Care 100 Directory. (1997). Reston, VA: St. Anthony Publishing.

Norman, N. M., & Tedeschi, J. T. (1989). Self-presentation, reasoned action, and adolescents' decisions to smoke cigarettes. *Journal of Applied Social Psychology, 19,* 543–558.

Northouse, P. G., & Northouse, L. L. (1985). *Health communication: A handbook for health professionals.* Englewood Cliffs, NJ: Prentice-Hall.

Norton, C. (1989). Absolutely not confidential. *Hippocrates, 3*(2), 52–59.

Novack, D. H., Plumer, R., Smith, R. L., Ochitill, H., Morrow, E. R., & Bennett, J. M. (1979). Changes in physicians' attitudes toward telling the cancer patient. *Journal of the American Medical Association, 241,* 897–900.

Novack, D. H., Volk, G., Drossman, D. A., & Lipkin, M. (1993). Medical interviewing and interpersonal skills teaching in US medical schools: Progress, problems, and promise. *Journal of the American Medical Association, 269,* 2101–2105.

Nussbaum, J. F. (1989). Directions for research within health communication. *Health Communication, 1*(1), 35–40.

Nussbaum, J. F., Thompson, T., & Robinson, J. D. (1989). Health, communication, and aging. In *Communication and aging* (pp. 185–197). New York: Harper & Row.

Nuttbrock, L., & Kosberg, J. I. (1980). Images of the physician and help-seeking behavior of the elderly: A multivariate assessment. *Journal of Gerontology, 35,* 241–248.

O'Connor, K. (1996). *Health care glossary of terms and definitions* (2nd ed.). San Francisco: Understanding Business Press.

Ogletree, S. M., Williams, S. W., Raffeld, P., Mason, B., & Fricke, K. (1990). Female attractiveness and eating disorders: Do children's television commercials play a role? *Sex Roles, 22*(11/12), 791–797.

O'Hair, D. (1989). Dimensions of relational communication and control during physician–patient interactions. *Health Communication, 1,* 97–115.

O'Hair, D. H., Behnke, R. R., & King, P. E. (1983). Age-related preferences for physician communication styles. *Educational Gerontology, 9,* 147–158.

Oken, D. (1961). What to tell cancer patients. *Journal of the American Medical Association, 175,* 1120–1128.

Olson, B. (1994). Sex and the soaps: A comparative content analysis of health issues. *Journalism Quarterly, 71*(4), 840–850.

Omnibus Reconciliation Act of 1990. Washington, DC: U.S. Government Printing Office, p. 152.

Ong, L. M. L., DeHaes, J. C. J. M., Hoos, A. M., & Lammes, F. B. (1995). Doctor–patient communication: A review of the literature. *Social Science and Medicine, 40,* 903–918.

Ovrebo, B., Ryan, M., Jackson, K., & Hutchinson, K. (1994). The homeless prenatal program: A model for empowering homeless pregnant women. *Health Education Quarterly, 21,* 187–198.

Paget, M. A. (1983). On the work of talk: Studies in misunderstandings. In S. Fisher & A. D. Todd (eds.), *The social organization of doctor–patient communication* (pp. 55–74). Washington, DC: Center for Applied Linguistics.

Paletta, J. H. (1995). Patients' perception of orthopaedic nursing competence. (Columbia University Teachers College; 0055). *Dissertation Abstracts International, 56–07B,* 3696.

Parrott, R. (1994). Exploring family practitioners' and patients' information exchange about prescribed medications: Implications for practitioners' interviewing and patients' understanding. *Health Communication, 6*, 267–280.

Parsons, T. (1951). *The social system*. New York: Free Press.

Peabody, F. W. (1927). The care of the patient. *Journal of the American Medical Association, 88*, 877–882.

Pellegrino, E. D. (1976). Medical ethics, education, and the physician's image. *Journal of the American Medical Association, 235*, 1043–1044.

Pendleton, D., Schofield, T., Tate, P., & Havelock, P. (1984). *The consultation: An approach to learning and teaching*. New York: Oxford University Press.

Pendleton, D. A., & Bochner, S. (1980). The communication of medical information in general practice consultations as a function of patients' social class. *Social Science and Medicine, 14A*, 669–673.

Perez-Stable, E. J., Sabogal, F., Otero-Sabogal, R., Hiatt, R. A., & McPhee, S. J. (1992). Misconceptions about cancer among Latinos and Anglos. *Journal of the American Medical Association, 268*, 3219–3223.

Perkins, H. S. (1989). Teaching medical ethics during residency. *Academic Medicine, 64*(5), 262–266.

Peterkin, B. B. (1985). Dietary guidelines, second edition. *Journal of Nutrition Education, 17*(5), 188–190.

Peterson, J. L., Moore, K. A., & Furstenberg, F. F. (1991). Television viewing and early initiation of sexual intercourse: Is there a link? *Journal of Homosexuality, 21*(1–2), 93–118.

Petroshius, S. M., Titus, P. A., & Hatch, K. J. (1995, November/December). Physician attitudes toward pharmaceutical drug advertising. *Journal of Advertising Research, 31*(6), 41–52.

Pettegrew, L. S. (1988). Theoretical plurality in health communication. In J. Anderson (ed.), *Communication Yearbook 11* (pp. 298–308). Newbury Park, CA: Sage.

Petty, R. E., & Cacioppo, J. T. (1986). The elaboration likelihood model of persuasion. *Advances in Experimental Social Psychology, 19*, 123–205.

Pfau, M., Mullen, L. J., & Garrow, K. (1995). The influence of television viewing on public perceptions of physicians. *Journal of Broadcasting & Electronic Media, 39*(4), 441–458.

Pfau, M., & Parrott, R. L. (1993). *Persuasive communication campaigns*. Needham Heights, MA: Simon & Schuster.

Pfau, M., Van Bockern, S., & Kang, J. G. (1992). Use of inoculation to promote resistance to smoking initiation among adolescents. *Communication Monographs, 59*, 213–230.

Pieters, H. M., Touw-Otten, F. W. W. M., & DeMelker, R. A. (1994). Simulated patients in assessing communication skills of trainees in general practice vocational training: A validity study. *Medical Education, 28*, 226–233.

Pingree, S., Hawkins, R. P., Gustafson, D. H., Boberg, E. W., Bricker, E., Wise, M., & Tillotson, T. (1994). Will HIV-positive people use an interactive computer system for information and support? A study of CHESS in two communities. *Proceedings of the seventeenth annual symposium on computer applications in medical care, a conference of the American medical informatics association* (pp. 22–26). New York: McGraw-Hill.

Planned Parenthood Federation of America. (1987). *American teenagers speak: Sex, myths, TV and birth control*. New York: Author.

Plough, A., & Olafson, F. (1994). Implementing the Boston healthy start initiative: A case study of community empowerment and public health. *Health Education Quarterly, 21*, 221–234.

Porac, J. F., & Thomas, H. (1994). Cognitive categorization and subjective rivalry among retailers in a small city. *Journal of Applied Psychology, 79*, 54–66.

Porter, M. E. (1980). *Competitive strategy: Techniques for analyzing industries and competitors*. New York: Free Press.

Porter, M. E. (1985). *Competitive advantages: Creating and sustaining superior performance*. New York: Free Press.

Prabhu, N. P., Duffy, L. C., & Stapleton, F. B. (1996). Content analysis of prime time television medical news; A pediatric perspective. *Archives of Pediatric and Adolescent Medicine, 150*(1), 46–49.

Prochaska, J. O., DiClemente, C. C., & Norcross, J. C. (1992). In search of how people change. *American Psychologist, 47*, 1102–1114.

Proven, K. G., & Milward, H. B. (1995, March). A preliminary theory of interorganizational network effectiveness: A comparative study of four community mental health systems. *Administrative Science Quarterly, 40*(1), 1–33.

Prutting, C. A. (1982). *Observational protocol for problematic behaviors* (Clinic manual). Developed for the University of California Speech and Hearing Clinic, Santa Barbara.

Pruyn, J. F. A., Ruckman, R. M., van Brunschot, C. J. M., & van den Borne, H. W. (1985). Cancer patients personality characteristics, physician-patient communication and adoption of the Moerman diet. *Social Science and Medicine, 20*, 841–847.

Quill, T. E., & Brody, H. (1996). Physician recommendations and patient autonomy: Finding a balance between physician power and patient choice. *Annals of Internal Medicine, 125*, 763–769.

Quine, L., & Pahl, J. (1986). First diagnosis of severe mental handicap: Characteristics of unsatisfactory encounters between doctors and parents. *Social Science & Medicine, 22*, 53–62.

Ramsey, S. (1993). New medical undergraduate curriculum. *The Lancet, 342*, 1164–1165.

Rappleye, W. C. (1932). *Medical Education: Final Report of the Commission on Medical Education*. New York: Association of American Medical Colleges.

Raudonis, B. M. (1995). Empathic nurse–patient relationships in hospice nursing. *The Hospice Journal, 10*, 59–74.

Ravitch, M. M., Brunner, E. A., & McGaghie, W. C. (1995). Effects of student group size on problem-based learning. Paper presented at the Problem Solving across the Curriculum Conference, Rochester, NY.

Ray, E. B., & Donohew, L. (1990). *Communication and health: Systems and applications*. Hillsdale, NJ: Lawrence Erlbaum.

Ray, E. B., & Miller, K. I. (1990). Communication in health care organizations. In E. B. Ray & L. Donohew (eds.), *Communication and health: Systems and applications* (pp. 92–107). Hillsdale, NJ: Lawrence Erlbaum.

Reardon, K. K. (1988). The role of persuasion in health promotion and disease prevention: Review and commentary. In J. Anderson (ed.), *Communication Yearbook 11* (pp. 276–297). Newbury Park, CA, Sage.

Regehr, G., & Norman, G. R. (1996). Issues in cognitive psychology: Implications for professional education. *Academic Medicine, 71*, 988–1001.

Reiser, S. J. (1993). The era of the patient: Using the experience of illness in shaping the missions of health care. *Journal of the American Medical Association, 269,* 1012–1017.

Reissman, C. K. (1993). *Narrative Analysis: Qualitative Research Methods Series 30.* Newbury Park, CA: Sage.

Reiter, R. C., Gambone, J. C., & Johnson, S. R. (1991). Availability of a multidisciplinary pelvic pain clinic and frequency of hysterectomy for pelvic pain. *Journal of Psychosomatic Obstetrics and Gynecology, 12,* 109–112.

Renfro, B. (1995). The influence of an educational program on professional nurses' knowledge and acceptance of a computerized information system for the documentation of nursing process. (George Mason University; 0083). *Dissertation Abstracts International, 56–05B,* 2563.

Roan, S. (1993). What to do when the news is bad. *Los Angeles Times,* October 7, A1–29.

Roberts, C. S., Cox, C. E., Reintgen, D. S., Baile, W. F., & Gibertini, M. (1994). Influence of physician communication on newly diagnosed breast patients' psychologic adjustment and decision making. *Cancer: Diagnosis, Treatment, and Research, 74,* 336–341.

Robinson, E. J., & Whitfield, M. J. (1985). Improving the efficiency of patients' comprehension monitoring: A way of increasing patients' participation in general practice consultations. *Social Science & Medicine, 21,* 915–919.

Rockefeller, R. (1994). Shared decision making and new information technologies: Transforming the health care system, an invitational conference for policy leaders, Washington, DC, May 7, 1994. Portland, ME: Health Commons Institute.

Rodin, J., & Janis, I. L. (1979). The social power of health-care practitioners as agents of change. *Journal of Social Issues, 35*(1), 60–81.

Rodin, J., & Langer, E. J. (1980). Aging labels: The decline of control and the fall of self-esteem. *Journal of Social Issues, 36,* 12–29.

Rogers, C. R. (1951). *Client-centered therapy.* Boston: Houghton-Mifflin.

Rogers, C. R. (1957). The necessary and sufficient conditions of therapeutic personality change. *Journal of Consulting Psychology, 21,* 95–103.

Rogers, C. R. (1961). *On becoming a person.* Boston: Houghton-Mifflin.

Rogers, C. R. (1962). The interpersonal relationship: The core of guidance. *Harvard Educational Review, 32,* 415–429.

Rogers, C. R. (ed.). (1967). *The therapeutic relationship and its impact.* Madison: University of Wisconsin Press.

Rogers, E. M. (1973). *Communication strategies for family planning.* New York: Free Press.

Rogers, E. M. (1995). *Diffusion of innovations* (4th ed.). New York: Free Press.

Rogers, E. M. (1996). The field of health communication today. *American Behavioral Scientist, 38,* 208–214.

Rogers, E. M., & Chaffee, S. H. (1983). Communication as an academic discipline: A dialogue. *Journal of Communication, 33,* 18–29.

Rogers, E. M., & Shoemaker, F. F. (1971). *Communication of innovations: A cross-cultural approach* (2nd ed.). New York: Free Press.

Rogers, E. M., & Storey, J. D. (1987). Communication campaigns. In C. R. Berger & S. H. Chaffee (eds.), *Handbook of communication science* (pp. 817–845). Newbury Park, CA: Sage.

Rogers, R. W. (1975). A Protection Motivation Theory of fear appeals and attitude change. *Journal of Psychology, 91*, 93–114.

Rogers, R. W. (1983). Cognitive and physiological processes in fear appeals and attitude change: A revised theory of Protection Motivation. In J. Cacioppo & R. Petty (eds.), *Social psychophysiology* (pp. 153–176). New York: Guilford Press.

Rognehaugh, R. (1996). *The managed health care dictionary.* Gaithersburg, MD: Aspen Publishers.

Rokeach, M. (1973). *The nature of human values.* New York: Free Press.

Rootman, I., & Hershfield, L. (1994). Health communication research: Broadening the scope. *Health Communication, 6*, 69–72.

Rosenberg, S. N., Gorman, S. A., Snitzer, S., Herbst, E. V., & Lynne, D. (1989). Patients' reactions and physician–patient communication in a mandatory surgical second-opinion program. *Medical Care, 27*, 466–477.

Rosenstock, I. M. (1974). Historical origins of the health belief model. *Health Education Monographs, 2*, 328–335.

Rosenstock, I. M. (1988). Enhancing patient compliance with health recommendations. *Journal of Pediatric Health Care, 2*, 67–72.

Rossi, P. H., & Freeman, H. E. (1989). *Evaluation: A systematic approach.* Newbury Park, CA: Sage.

Rost, K., Carter, W., & Inui, T. (1989). Introduction of information during the initial medical visit: Consequences for patient follow-through with physician recommendations for medication. *Social Science & Medicine, 28*, 315–321.

Roter, D. L. (1977). Patient participation in the patient–provider interaction: The effects of patient question asking on the quality of interaction, satisfaction, and compliance. *Health Education Monographs, 5*, 281–315.

Roter, D. L. (1983). Physician/patient communication: Transmission of information and patient effects. *Maryland State Medical Journal, 32*, 260–265.

Roter, D. L. (1984). Patient question asking in physician-patient interaction. *Health Psychology, 3*, 395–410.

Roter, D. L., & Hall, J. A. (1992). *Doctors talking with patients/patients talking with doctors.* Westport, CT: Auburn House.

Roter, D. L., Hall, J. A., & Katz, N. R. (1988). Patient–physician communication: A descriptive summary of the literature. *Patient Education & Counseling, 12*, 99–119.

Roter, D. L., Hall, J. A., Kern, D. E., Barker, L. R., Cole, K. A., & Roca, R. P. (1995). Improving physicians' interviewing skills and reducing patients' emotional distress: A randomized clinical trial. *Archives of Internal Medicine, 155*, 1877–1884.

Royster, L. J. (1990). Doctor–patient communication: An exploration of language use during the informed consent process. Unpublished dissertation, University of Pennsylvania.

Ruben, B. D. (1993). What patients remember: A content analysis of critical incidents in health care. *Health Communication, 5*, 99–112.

Ruesch, J. (1957). *Disturbed communication.* New York: Norton.

Ruesch, J. (1959). General theory of communication in psychiatry. In S. Arieti (ed.), *American handbook of psychiatry* (Vol. 1, pp. 895–908). New York: Basic Books.

Ruesch, J. (1961). *Therapeutic communication.* New York: Norton.

Ruesch, J. (1963). The role of communication in therapeutic transactions. *Journal of Communication, 13*, 132–139.

Ruesch, J., & Bateson, G. (1951). *Communication: The social matrix of psychiatry.* New York: Norton.

Ryan, E. B., & Butler, R. N. (1996). Communication, aging, and health: Toward understanding health provider relationships with older clients. *Health Communication, 8,* 191–197.

Ryan, E. B., & Cole, R. L. (1990). Evaluative perceptions of interpersonal communication with the elders. In N. Giles, N. Coupland, & J. M. Weimann (eds.), *Communication, health and the elderly* (pp. 173–188). London: Manchester University Press.

Ryan, E. B., Meredith, S. D., MacLean, M. J., & Orange, J. B. (1995). Changing the way we talk with elders: Promoting health using the communication enhancement model. *International Journal of Aging and Human Development, 41,* 89–107.

Said, M. B., Consoli, S., & Jean, J. (1994). A comparative study between a computer-aided education (ISIS) and habitual education techniques for hypertensive patients. *Journal of the American Medical Informatics Association,* symposium supplement.

Saint Clair, A. J. (1994). The effect of undergraduate nursing education program type on the achievement of critical thinking, field dependent-independent thinking, adaptive style flexibility and self-esteem. (University of Connecticut, 0056). *Dissertation Abstracts International, 56–04B,* 1921.

Salmon, C. T. (1989). Campaigns for social "improvement": An overview of values, rationales, and impacts. In C. T. Salmon (ed.), *Information campaigns: Balancing social values and social change* (pp. 19–53). Newbury Park, CA: Sage.

Sandman, P. M. (1976). Medicine and mass communication: An agenda for physicians. *Annals of Internal Medicine, 85,* 378–383.

Sankar, A. (1986). Out of the clinic into the home: Control and patient–physician communication. *Social Science & Medicine, 22,* 973–982.

Sanson-Fisher, R., Bowman, J., & Armstrong, S. (1992). Factors affecting nonadherence with antibiotics. *Diagnostic Microbiology and Infectious Disease, 15,* 103S–109S.

Sapolsky, B. S., & Tabarlet, J. O. (1991). Sex in primetime television: 1979 versus 1989. *Journal of Broadcasting & Electronic Media, 35*(4), 505–516.

Scheffelin, A. M. (1995). The hospital administrator: Yesterday, today and tomorrow. (Golden Gate University; 0452). *Dissertation Abstracts International, 56–04A,* 1438.

Scherer, C. W., & Juanillo, N. K. (1992). Bridging theory and praxis: Reexamining public health communication. In J. Anderson (Ed.), *Communication Yearbook 15* (pp. 312–345). Newbury Park, CA: Sage.

Scherz, J. W., Edwards, H. T., & Kallail, K. J. (1995). Communicative effectiveness of doctor–patient interactions. *Health Communication, 7,* 163–177.

Schlundt, D. G., Quesenberry, L., Pchert, J. W., Lorenz, R. A., et al. (1994). Evaluation of a training program for improving adherence promotion skills. *Patient Education & Counseling, 24,* 165–173.

Schneiderman, L. J., Kronick, R., Kaplan, R. M., Anderson, J. P., & Langer, R. D. (1992). Effects of offering advance directives on medical treatments and costs. *Annals of Internal Medicine, 117,* 559–606.

Schommer, J. C. (1994). Effects of interrole congruence on pharmacist–patient communication. *Health Communication, 6,* 297–310.

Schramm, W. (1973). *Men, messages, and media: A look at human communication.* New York: Harper and Row.

Schramm, W. (1983). The unique perspective of communication: A retrospective view. *Journal of Communication, 33,* 6–17.

Schwartz, M. P. (1994, August 8). Study finds many health reform ads misleading. *National Underwriter Life and Health-Financial Services Edition, 31,* 3–4.

Seijo, R., Gomez, H., & Freidenberg, J. (1995). Language as a communication barrier in medical care for Hispanic patients. In A. M. Padilla (ed.), *Hispanic psychology* (pp. 169–181). Thousand Oaks, CA: Sage.

Shadish, W. R., Cook, T. D., & Leviton, L. C. (1991). *Foundations of program evaluation: Theories of practice.* Newbury Park, CA: Sage.

Shapiro, A. (1960). A contribution to a history of the placebo effect. *Behavioral Science, 5,* 109–135.

Shapiro, D. E., Boggs, S. R., Melamed, B. G., & Graham-Pole, J. (1992). The effect of varied physician affect on recall, anxiety, and perceptions in women at risk for breast cancer: An analogue study. *Health Psychology, 1,* 61–66.

Shapiro, J. P., & Bowermaster, D. (1994). Death on trial: Debating the American way of dying. *U.S. News and World Report, 116*(16), 31–39.

Shapiro, J., & Saltzer. E. (1981, December). Cross-cultural aspects of physician–patient communication patterns. *Urban Health,* 10–15.

Sharf, B. F. (1984). *The physician's guide to better communication.* Glenview, IL: Scott, Foresman.

Sharf, B. F. (1990). Physician–patient communication as interpersonal rhetoric: A narrative approach. *Health Communication, 3,* 217–232.

Sharf, B. F. (1993). Reading the vital signs: Research in health care communication. *Communication Monographs, 60,* 35–41.

Shelton, N. L. (1992). Hospital competition: The impact of selective contracting of San Francisco Bay area hospitals, 1983–1989. (University of California, Berkeley). *Dissertation Abstracts International, 54–08A,* 3114.

Sherman, B. L., & Dominick, J. R. (1986). Violence and sex in music videos: TV and rock 'n' roll. *Journal of Communication, 36*(1), 79–93.

Shidler, J. A., & Lowry, D. T. (1995). Network TV sex as a counterprogramming strategy during a sweeps period: An analysis of content and ratings. *Journalism & Mass Communication Quarterly, 72*(1), 147–157.

Signorielli, N. (1987). Drinking, sex, and violence on television: The Cultural Indicators perspective. *Journal of Drug Education, 17*(3), 245–260.

Signorielli, N. (1993). *Mass media images and impact on health: A sourcebook.* Westport, CT: Greenwood Press.

Signorielli, N., & Lears, M. (1992). Television and children's conceptions of nutrition: Unhealthy Messages. *Health Communication, 4*(4), 245–260.

Signorielli, N., & Staples, J. (1997). Television and children's conceptions of nutrition. *Health Communication, 9*(4), 289–302.

Slater, M. D., & Domenech, M. M. (1995). Alcohol warnings in TV beer advertisements. *Journal of the Studies on Alcohol, 56*(3), 361–367.

Slovic, P. (1987). Perception of risk. *Science, 236,* 280–285.

Slovic, P., Fischhoff, B., & Lichtenstein, S. (1982). Why study risk perceptions? *Risk Analysis, 2,* 83–93.

Smith, C. (1991). Sex and genre on prime time. *Journal of Homosexuality, 21*(1–2), 119–138.

Smith, D. H., Cunningham, K., & Hale, W. E. (1994). Communication about medicines: Perceptions of the ambulatory elderly. *Health Communication, 6*, 281–296.

Smith, D. H., & Pettegrew, L. S. (1986). Mutual persuasion as a model for doctor–patient communication. *Theoretical Medicine, 7*, 127–146.

Smith, E. R., & Zarate, M. A. (1992). Exemplar-based models of social judgment. *Psychological Review, 99*, 3–21.

Smith, F. A., Trivax, G., Zuehlke, D. A., Lowinger, P., & Nghiem, T. L. (1972). Health information during a week of television. *The New England Journal of Medicine, 286*(10), 516–520.

Smith, R. C., & Hoppe, R. B. (1991). The patient's story: Integrating the patient- and physician-centered approaches to interviewing. *Annals of Internal Medicine, 115*, 470–473.

Smith-Dupre, A. A., & Beck, C. S. (1996). Enabling patients and physicians to pursue multiple goals in health care encounters: A case study. *Health Communication, 8*, 73–90.

Soe, L. L. (1994). Substitutability and complementarity in the diffusion of multiple electronic communication media: An evolutionary approach. (University of California, Los Angeles; 0031). *Dissertation Abstracts International, 55–08A*, 2473.

Soldo, B., & Manton, K. (1985). Changes in health status and service needs of the oldest old: Current patterns and future trends. *Milbank Memorial Fund Quarterly, 63*, 177–186.

Soley, L. C., & Reid, L. N. (1985). Baiting viewers: Violence and sex in television program advertisements. *Journalism Quarterly, 62*(1), 105–110, 131.

Sommers-Flanagan, R., Sommers-Flanagan, J., & Davis, B., (1993). What's happening on music television? A gender role content analysis. *Sex Roles, 28*(11–12), 745–753.

Spears, L. A. (1996, March). The writing of nurse managers: A neglected area of professional communication research. *Business Communication Quarterly, 59*(1), 54–66.

Speedling, E. J., & Rose, D. N. (1985). Building an effective doctor–patient relationship: From patient satisfaction to patient participation. *Social Science & Medicine, 21*, 115–120.

Spilka, R. (1995, August). Communication across organizational boundaries: A challenge for workplace professionals. *Technical Communication, 42*(3), 436–451.

Sprecher, P. L., Thomas, E. R. Huebner, L. A., Norfleet, B. E., & Jacoby, K. E. (1983). Effects of increased physician–patient communication on patient anxiety. *Professional Psychology: Research and Practice, 14*, 251–255.

Squier, R. W. (1990). A model of empathic understanding and adherence to treatment regimens in practitioner–patient relationships. *Social Science & Medicine, 30*, 325–339.

Stanton, A. L. (1987). Determinants of adherence to medical regimens by hypertensive patients. *Journal of Behavioral Medicine, 10*, 377–394.

Starfield, B., Steinwachs, D., Morris, I., Bause, G., Siebert, S., & Westin, C. (1979). Patient–doctor agreement about problems needing follow-up visit. *Journal of the American Medical Association, 242*, 344–346.

Starr, P. (1982). *The social transformation of American medicine.* New York: Basic Books.

Stein, D. M., & Reichert, P. (1990). Extreme dieting behaviors in early adolescence. *Journal of Early Adolescence, 10*(2), 108–121.

Stephenson, M. T. (1993). A subliminal manipulation of the extended parallel process model. Unpublished master's thesis, Texas A & M University.

Stevens, R. (1989). *In sickness and in wealth: American hospitals in the twentieth century.* New York: Basic Books.

Stewart, M. A. (1995). Effective physician–patient communication and health outcomes: A review. *Canadian Medical Association Journal, 152,* 1423–1433.

Stiff, J. B. (1986). Cognitive processing of persuasive message cues: A meta-analytic review of the effects of supporting information on attitudes. *Communication Monographs, 53,* 75–89.

Stiff, J. B., & Boster, F. J. (1987). Cognitive processing: Additional thoughts and a reply to Petty, Kasmer, Haugtvedt, and Cacioppo. *Communication Monographs, 54,* 250–256.

Stillman, P. L., & Swanson, D. B. (1987). Ensuring the clinical competence of medical school graduates through standardized patients. *Archives of Internal Medicine, 147,* 1049–1052.

Story, M., & Faulkner, P. (1990). The prime time diet: A content analysis of eating behavior and food messages in television program content and commercials. *American Journal of Public Health, 80*(6), 738–740.

Street, R. L. (1991). Information-giving in medical consultations: The influence of patients' communicative styles and personal characteristics. *Social Science and Medicine, 32,* 541–548.

Street, R. L., & Buller, D. B. (1988). Patients' characteristics affecting physician–patient nonverbal communication. *Human Communication Research, 15,* 60–90.

Strouse, J., & Fabes, R. A. (1985). Formal versus informal sources of sex education: Competing forces in the sexual socialization of adolescents. *Adolescence, 20,* 251–263.

Strouse, J. S., Buerkel-Rothfuss, N., & Long, E. C. (1995). Gender and family as moderators of the relationship between music video exposure and adolescent sexual permissiveness. *Adolescence, 30*(119), 505–521.

Strull, W. M., Lo, B., & Charles, G. (1984). Do patients want to participate in medical decision making? *Journal of the American Medical Association, 252*(21), 2990–2994.

Suchman, A. L., Markakis, K., Beckman, H. B., & Frankel, R. (1997). A model of empathic communication in the medical interview. *Journal of the American Medical Association, 277,* 678–682.

Surbone, A. (1992). Truth telling to the patient. *Journal of the American Medical Association, 268,* 1661–1662.

Surgeon General. (1979). *Health people: The Surgeon General's report on health promotion and disease prevention.* Washington, DC: U.S. Department of Health, Education, and Welfare, Public Health Service, U.S. Government Printing Office.

Svarstad, B. (1976). Physician–patient communication and patient conformity with medical advice. In D. Mechanic (ed.), *The growth of bureaucratic medicine* (pp. 220–238). New York: John Wiley.

Svenkerund, P. J., Singhal, A., & Papa, M. J. (1996, May). *The applicability of diffusion of innovations theory in targeting unique populations at high-risk for HIV/AIDS in Thailand*. Paper presented at the annual meeting of the International Communication Association, Chicago, IL.

Szasz, T. S., & Hollander, M. H. (1956). A contribution to the philosophy of medicine: The basic models of the doctor–patient relationship. *Archives of Internal Medicine, 97*, 585–592.

Tajfel, H. (1970). Experiments in intergroup discrimination. *Scientific American, 223*(5), 96–102.

Tannen, D. (1990). *You just don't understand*. New York: William Morrow.

Taras, H. L., & Gage, M. (1995). Advertised foods on children's television. *Archives of Pediatric and Adolescent Medicine, 149*(6), 649–652.

Tate, P. H. L., & Foulkes, J. (1996). The approach to the assessment of performance of general practitioners using observation of video-recorded surgeries in the MRCGP examination. Unpublished working paper, Royal College of General Practitioners.

Taylor, K. M., & Kelner, M. (1987). Informed consent: The physicians' perspective. *Social Science and Medicine, 24*, 135–143.

Taylor, S. E. (1979). Hospital patient behavior: Reactance, helplessness, or control? *Journal of Social Issues, 35*(1), 156–184.

Taylor, S. E. (1982). Social cognition and health. *Personality & Social Psychology Bulletin, 8*, 549–562.

Taylor, S. E., Lichtman, R. R., & Wood, J. V. (1984). Attributions, beliefs about control, and adjustment to breast cancer. *Journal of Personality & Social Psychology, 46*, 489–502.

Thompson, C. L., & Pledger, L. M. (1993). Doctor–patient communication: Is patient knowledge of medical terminology improving? *Health Communication, 5*, 89–97.

Thompson, T. L. (1984). The invisible helping hand: The role of communication in the health and social service professions. *Communication Quarterly, 32*, 148–163.

Thompson, T. L. (1986). *Communication for health professionals: A relational perspective*. New York: Harper & Row.

Thompson, T. L. (1990). Interpersonal issues in health communication. In E. B. Ray & L. Donohew (eds.). *Communication and Health: Systems and Applications* (pp. 27–50). Mahwah, NJ: Lawrence Erlbaum.

Thompson, T. L. (1994). Communication in health care. In M. L. Knapp & G. R. Miller (eds.), *Handbook of Interpersonal Communication* (pp. 696–725). Beverly Hills, CA: Sage.

Thomson, A. N. (1994). Reliability of consumer assessment of communication skills in a postgraduate family practice examination. *Medical Education, 28*, 146–150.

Thornton, B. C., & Kreps, G. L. (1993). *Perspectives on health communication*. Prospect Heights, IL: Waveland Press.

Tichenor, P. J., Donohue, T., & Olien, C. N. (1970). Mass media flow and differential growth in knowledge. *Public Opinion Quarterly, 34*, 159–170.

Todd, A. D. (1993). A diagnosis of doctor–patient discourse in the prescription of contraception. In A. D. Todd & S. Fisher (eds.), *The social organization of doctor–patient communication* (pp. 183–209). Norwood, NJ: Ablex.

Tones, K., & Tilford, S. (1994). *Health education: Effectiveness, efficiency, and equity*. London: Chapman & Hill.

Trenholm, S. (1991). *Human communication theory* (2nd ed.). Englewood Cliffs, NJ: Prentice-Hall.

Trenholm, S. (1995). *Thinking through communication*. Needham Heights, MA: Allyn & Bacon.

Tucker, L. A., & Bagwell, M. (1991). Television viewing and obesity in adult females. *American Journal of Public Health, 81*(7), 908–911.

Tucker, L. A., & Friedman, G. M. (1989). Television viewing and obesity in adult males. *American Journal of Public Health, 79*(4), 516–518.

Tucker, M. L., Powell, K. S., & Meyer, G. D. (1995, October). Qualitative research in business communication: A review and analysis. *Journal of Business Communication, 32*(4), 383–399.

Turow, J. (1989). *Playing doctor: Television, storytelling, and medical power*. New York: Oxford University Press.

Turow, J., & Coe, L. (1985). Curing television's ills: The portrayal of health care. *Journal of Communication, 35*(4), 36–51.

U.S. Congress, Senate Special Committee on Aging. (1985). *Aging America: Trends and projections*. Washington, DC: U.S. Government Printing Office.

U.S. Congress, Senate Special Committee on Aging. (1991). *Aging America: Trends and projections*. (USDHHS # (FCOA) 91–28001). Washington, DC: U.S. Government Printing Office.

U.S. Department of Health and Human Services. (1991). *Man, media and health: Opportunities of improving the nation's health*. Washington, DC: Public Health Service.

U.S. Department of Health and Human Services, Agency for Health Care Policy and Research (HHS/OPHS). (1996). *Consumer assessment of health plans (CAHPS)*. Rockville, MD: Agency for Health Care Policy and Research.

U.S. Department of Health and Human Services, Office of Public Health and Science [HHS/OPHS] (1996). *Guide to Clinical Preventive Services* (2nd ed.). Washington, DC: U.S. Government Printing Office. (GPO Publication no. 1996–415–220).

U.S. Department of Health and Human Services, Office of Public Health and Science [HHS/OPHS] (1997a). *Child Health Guide* (2nd ed.). Washington, DC: U.S. Government Printing Office.

U.S. Department of Health and Human Services, Office of Public Health and Science [HHS/OPHS] (1997b). *Personal Health Guide* (2nd ed.). Washington, DC: U.S. Government Printing Office.

U.S. Department of Health and Human Services, Public Health Service [HHS/OPHS] (1991). *Healthy People 2000: National health promotion and disease prevention objectives* (HHS Publication No. PHS 91–50213). Washington, DC: U.S. Government Printing Office.

U.S. Department of Health and Human Services, Public Health Service [HHS/PHS]. (1994). *For a healthy nation: Returns on investment in public health*. Washington, DC: U.S. Government Printing Office.

U.S. Department of Health and Human Services, Substance Abuse and Mental Health Services Administration [HHS/SAMHSA]. (April 1996). *Consumer-oriented mental health report card; Final report of the mental health statistics improvement program (MHSIP) task force on a consumer-oriented mental health report card*. Rockville, MD: Substance Abuse and Mental Health Services Administration, Center for Mental Health Services.

Van Der Merwe, J. V. (1995). Physician–patient communication using ancestral spirits to achieve holistic healing. *American Journal of Obstetrics and Gynecology, 172,* 1080–1087.

Vanderford, M., & Smith, D. H. (1996). *The Silicone Breast Implant Story.* Mahwah, NJ: Lawrence Erlbaum.

Vanderford, M. L., Smith, D. H., & Harris, W. S. (1992). Value identification in narrative discourse: Evaluation of an HIV education demonstration project. *Journal of Applied Communication Research, 20*(2), 123–160.

Vandyk, A. (1995, June). When crew cultures clash. *Air Transport World, 32*(6), 181–183.

Vanlandingham, M. J., Suprasert, S., Grandjean, N., & Sittitrai, W. (1995). Two views of risky sexual practices among northern Thai males: The health belief model and the theory of reasoned action. *Journal of Health and Social Behavior, 36,* 195–212.

Veatch, R. M. (ed.) (1989). *Medical ethics.* Boston: Jones and Bartlett Publishers.

Ventres, W. B. (1994). Hearing the patient's story: Exploring physician–patient communication using narrative case reports. *Family Practice Research Journal, 14,* 139–147.

Vera, M. I. (1996). Health care of Latina women. *Journal of the Florida Medical Association, 83,* 494–497.

Verwoerdt, A. (1966). *Communication with the fatally ill.* Springfield, IL: Charles C. Thomas.

Vickery, D. M. (1995). Demand management, self-care, and the new media. In L. M. Harris (ed.), *Health and the new media: technologies transforming personal and public health* (pp. 45–64). Mahwah, NJ: Lawrence Erlbaum.

Vickery, D. M., Golazewski, T., & Wright, E. (1988). The effect of self-care interventions on the use of medical services within a Medicare population. *Medical Care, 26,* 580–588.

Vickery, D. M., & Lynch, W. D. (1995). Demand management: Enabling patients to use medical care appropriately. *Journal of Occupational and Environmental Medicine, 37*(5), 1–7.

Virmani, J., Schneiderman, L. J., & Kaplan, R. M. (1994). Relationship of advance directives to physician–patient communication. *Archives of Internal Medicine, 154,* 909–913.

von Friederichs-Fitzwater, M. M., Callahan, E. J., Flynn, N., & Williams, J. (1991). Relational control in physician–patient encounters. *Health Communication, 3,* 17–36.

Vorhaus, M. G. (1957). *The changing doctor–patient relationship.* New York: Horizon Press.

Wagener, J. J., & Taylor, S. E. (1986). What else could I have done? Patients' responses to failed treatment decisions. *Health Psychology, 5,* 481–496.

Wagner, E. P., Barry, M. J., Barlow, W., & Fowler, F. J. (1995). The effect of a shared decision making program on rates of surgery for benign prostatic hyperplasia. *Medical Care, 33*(8), 765–770.

Waitzkin, H. (1985). Information giving in medical care. *Journal of Health and Social Behavior, 26,* 81–101.

Waitzkin, H. (1991). *The politics of medical encounters.* New Haven: Yale University Press.

Waitzkin, H., & Stoeckle, J. D. (1972). The communication of information about illness:

Clinical, sociological, and methodological considerations. *Advances in Psychosomatic Medicine, 8*, 180–215.

Waitzkin, H., & Stoeckle, J. D. (1976). Information control and the micropolitics of health care: Summary of an ongoing research project. *Social Science and Medicine, 10*, 263–276.

Waitzkin, H., Britt, T., & Williams, C. (1994). Narratives of aging and social problems in medical encounters with older persons. *Journal of Health and Social Behavior, 35*, 322–348.

Waldo, D., & Lazenby, H. (1984). Demographic characteristics and health care use and expenditures of the aged in the United States, 1977–84. *Health Care Financing Review, 6*, 1–49.

Wallack, L. (1989). Mass communication and health promotion: A critical perspective. In R. E. Rice & C. K. Atkin (eds.), *Public communication campaigns* (2nd ed., pp. 353–367). Newbury Park, CA: Sage.

Wallack, L. (1990). Improving health promotion: Media advocacy and social marketing approaches. In C. Atkin & L. Wallack (eds.), *Mass communication and public health: Complexities and conflicts* (pp. 147–163). Newbury Park, CA: Sage.

Wallack, L., Breed, W., & Cruz, J. (1987). Alcohol on prime-time television. *Journal of Studies on Alcohol, 48*(1), 33–38.

Wallack, L., Breed, W., & DeFoe, J. R. (1985). Alcohol and soap operas: Drinking in the light of day. *Journal of Drug Education, 15*(4), 365–379.

Wallack, L., & Dorfman, L. (1992). Health messages on television commercials. *American Journal of Health Promotion, 6*(3), 190–196.

Wallack, L., Grube, J. W., Madden, P. A., & Breed, W. (1990). Portrayals of alcohol on prime-time television. *Journal of Studies on Alcohol, 51*(5), 428–437.

Wallen, J., Waitzkin, H., & Stoeckle, J. D. (1979). Physician stereotypes about female health and illness: A study of patient's sex and the informative process during medical interviews. *Women and Health, 4*, 135–146.

Walsh-Childers, K. (1991). Adolescents' interpretations of the birth control behavior of a soap opera couple. Paper presented at the annual meeting of the International Communication Association.

Wang, C., & Burris, M. A. (1994). Empowerment through photo novella: Portraits of participation. *Health Education Quarterly, 21*, 171–186.

Ward, G. W. (1984). The national high blood pressure education program. In L. W. Frederikson, L. J. Solomon, & K. A. Brehony (eds.), *Marketing health behavior* (pp. 93–113). New York: Plenum Press.

Watzlawick, P., Beavin, J. H., & Jackson, D. D. (1967). *Pragmatics of human communication: A study of interactional patterns, pathologies, and paradoxes.* New York: Norton.

Weaver, C. G. (1995, June). CHINs: Making the important decisions. *Healthcare Financial Management, 49*(6), 58–65.

Weinstein, N. D. (1988). The precaution adoption process. *Health Psychology, 7*, 355–386.

Wennberg, J. (1995). Shared decision making and multimedia. In L. M. Harris (ed.), *Health and the new media* (pp. 109–126). Mahwah, NJ: Lawrence Erlbaum.

Wennberg, J. E. (1990). Outcomes research, cost containment, and the fear of health care rationing. *New England Journal of Medicine, 323*, 1202–1204.

Wertheimer, M. D., Bertman, S. L., Wheeler, H. B., & Siegal, I. (1985). Ethics and communication in the surgeon–patient relationship. *Journal of Medical Education, 60,* 804–806.

West, C. (1984a). *Routine complications: Troubles with talk between doctors and patients.* Bloomington, IN: Indiana University Press.

West, C. (1984b). When the doctor is a "lady": Power, status and gender in physician–patient encounters. *Symbolic Interaction, 7,* 87–106.

West, C. (1993). "Ask me no questions . . .": An analysis of queries and replies in physician–patient dialogue. In A. D. Todd & S. Fisher (eds.), *The social organization of doctor–patient communication* (2nd ed., pp. 127–157). Norwood, NJ: Ablex.

Whaley, B. B. (1994). "Food is to me as gas is to cars?" Using figurative language to explain illness to children. *Health Communication, 6,* 193–204.

Wheatley, M. (1992) *Leadership and the new science: Learning about organization from an orderly universe.* San Francisco: Berrett-Koehler.

White, C. M. (1995). Uses and impacts of computer mediated communication: A survey of faculty in mass communication and related disciplines. (University of Georgia; 0077). *Dissertation Abstracts International, 56–08A,* 2923.

White, J., Levinson, W., & Roter, D. (1994). "Oh, by the way . . .": The closing moments of the medical visit. *Journal of General Internal Medicine, 9,* 24–28.

WHY? (1995). Orlando Regional Healthcare System corporate communication. Orlando, FL.

Wilkerson, L., Hafler, J. P., & Liu, P. (1991). A case study of student-directed discussion in four problem-based tutorial groups. *Academic Medicine, 66,* S79–S81.

Williams, O. A. (1993). Patient knowledge of operative care. *Journal of the Royal Society of Medicine, 86,* 328–331.

Williams, T. F. (1981). The physician viewpoint. In M. R. Haug (ed.), *Elderly patients and their doctors* (pp. 42–46). New York: Springer-Verlag.

Winett, R. A., King, A. C., & Altman, D. G. (1989). *Health psychology and public health.* New York: Pergamon Press.

Winsten, J. A. (1994). Promoting designated drivers: The Harvard Alcohol Project. Special Issue: Medicine in the twenty-first century: Challenges in personal and public health promotion. Boston: Harvard School of Public Health, Center for Health Communication.

Witte, K. (1992a). Preventing AIDS through persuasive communications: A framework for constructing effective, culturally-specific, preventive health messages. *International and Intercultural Communication Annual, 16,* 67–86.

Witte, K. (1992b). Putting the fear back into fear appeals: The extended parallel process model. *Communication Monographs, 59,* 329–349.

Witte, K. (1994a). Generating effective risk messages: How scary should your risk communication be? *Communication Yearbook, 18,* 229–254.

Witte, K. (1994b). The manipulative nature of health communication: Ethical issues and guidelines. *American Behavioral Scientist, 38*(2), 288–292.

Witte, K. (1997). Preventing teen pregnancy through persuasive communications: Realities, myths, and the hard-fact truths. *Journal of Community Health, 22*(2), 137–154.

Witte, K. (1998). Fear as motivator, fear as inhibitor: Using the extended parallel process model to explain fear appeal successes and failures. In P. A. Andersen and L. K.

Guerrero (eds.), *Communication and Emotion: Theory, Research, and Applications*. New York: Academic Press.

Witte, K., Berkowitz, J., McKeon, J., Cameron, K., Lapinski, M. K., & Liu, W. Y. (1996, November). Radon awareness and reduction campaigns for African-Americans: A theoretically-based formative and summative evaluation. Paper presented at the annual meeting of the Speech Communication Association, San Diego, CA.

Witte, K., & Morrison, K. (1995). Intercultural and cross-cultural health communication: Understanding people and motivating healthy behaviors. In R. L. Wiseman (ed.), *Intercultural communication theory* (pp. 216–246). Thousand Oaks, CA: Sage.

Witte, K., Nzyuko, S., & Cameron, K. (1996). *HIV/AIDS along the Trans-Africa Highway in Kenya: Examining risk perceptions, recommended responses, and campaign materials*. Final report submitted to the All-University Research Grant, Michigan State University.

Witte, K., Peterson, T. R., Vallabhan, S., Stephenson, M. T., Plugge, C. D., Givens, V. K., Todd, J. D., Becktold, M. G., Hyde, M. K., & Jarrett, R. (1993). Preventing tractor-related injuries and deaths in rural populations: Using a Persuasive Health Message (PHM) framework in formative evaluation research. *International Quarterly of Community Health Education, 13*, 219–251.

Witte, K., Stokols, D., Ituarte, P., & Schneider, M. (1993). Testing the health belief model in a field study to promote bicycle safety helmets. *Communication Research, 20*, 564–586.

Wolf, S. M. (1988). Conflict between doctor and patient. *Law, Medicine, & Health Care, 16*, 197–203.

World Health Organization. (1947). *Constitution*. Geneva: Author.

World Health Organization. (1986). *The Ottawa charter for health promotion*. Geneva: Author.

Wunsch, J. M. (1996). Perceived threat of cancer and perceived efficacy of fruit and vegetable intake in reducing cancer risk by participants in a WIC program. Manuscript under review.

Yankelovich, Skelly, and White, Inc. (1979). *The General Mills American family report, 1978–1979: Family health in an era of stress*. Minneapolis: General Mills.

Young, M., & Klingle, R. S. (1996). Silent partners in medical care: A cross-cultural study of patient participation. *Health Communication, 8*, 29–53.

Zajec, E. J., & Bazerman, M. H. (1991). Blind spots in industry and competitor analysis: Implications of interfirm (mis)perception to strategic decisions. *Academy of Management Review, 16*, 37–46.

Zillmann, D., & Bryant, J. B. (1988). Pornography's impact on sexual satisfaction. *Journal of Applied Social Psychology, 18*, 438–453.

Zimmerman, C. (1994, February 7). Should I advertise? *American Medical News, 37*(5), 29–32.

Zinn, W. (1993). The empathic physician. *Archives of Internal Medicine, 153*, 306–312.

Zola, I. (1966). Culture and symptoms—An analysis of patients' presenting complaints. *American Sociological Review, 31*, 615–630.

Author Index

Subject Index

About the Contributors

ELLEN W. BONAGURO is Assistant Professor of Speech Communication at Ithaca College. She has written numerous grants and has served as the principal investigator for several projects under the Health Education–Risk Reduction Program funded by the Centers for Disease Control. She has published several articles and chapters on health communication, health promotion, and health education, and is active in communication organizations.

REBECCA J. CLINE is Associate Professor of Communication Studies in the Department of Communication Sciences and Disorders, University of Florida, Gainesville, where she specializes in interpersonal and health communication. Her recent research focuses on interpersonal communication and HIV/AIDS, including HIV prevention, communicating with people with HIV disease, and gender issues associated with communicating about HIV/AIDS.

MARY JO DEERING is Director, Health Communication and Telehealth Staff in the Office of Disease Prevention and Health Promotion for the U.S. Department of Health and Human Services. She is responsible for cross-cutting research, policy, and programs in health communication and for the National Health Information Center (NHIC), oversees the Science Panel on Interactive Communication and Health and the federal web site ''healthfinder,'' and serves as associate editor of the *Journal of Health Communication*.

M. ROBIN DiMATTEO is a health psychologist and Professor of Psychology at the University of California, Riverside, and a consultant in health policy to the RAND Corporation. She is a licensed psychologist in the state of California, and a Fellow of the American Psychological Association and the American

Psychological Society. She is the author of five books and over 70 research articles applying psychological principles to the practice of medicine, and is a consultant to health care organizations nationwide.

BERNARD K. DUFFY is Professor of Speech Communication at California Polytechnic State University–San Luis Obispo, where he has also served as Department Chair. Of his four books, the two most recent are *The Politics of Rhetoric: Richard Weaver and the Conservative Tradition* (1993) and *Douglas MacArthur: Warrior as Wordsmith* (1997). He is also co-adviser of the Great American Orators book series published by Greenwood Press.

SHRITI HALLBERG is a Business Systems Analyst for Orlando Regional Healthcare System in Orlando, Florida. She is currently serving as the project manager for the computerized member record. She previously worked for a hospital in Canada and has also been an independent consultant for hospitals in Canada and the United States. She is an affiliate of the American College of Healthcare Executives, the Central Florida Healthcare Executive Group, the Canadian and American Data Processing Management Association, and the National Association for Female Executives.

LORRAINE D. JACKSON is Associate Professor of Speech Communication at California Polytechnic State University San Luis Obispo. Her research interests include improving doctor–patient communication, promoting adherence to treatment, safer-sex negotiation, and women's health issues. Her research has appeared in the journal *Health Communication* as well as in scholarly books. Recent funded research involving the communication of an HIV positive diagnosis to women appears in the book *Women and AIDS: Negotiating Safer Practices, Care and Representation.*

GARY L. KREPS is Dean and Professor, School of Communication at Hofstra University. He has published extensively in the area of health communication. He has also served as editor of *Health Communication Issues* and is the founding editor of the "Health Communication" and "Communication and Social Organization" book series for Hampton Press.

MARIA KNIGHT LAPINSKI is a doctoral student in the Department of Communication at Michigan State University. Her research has focused primarily on intercultural and international issues in interpersonal communication, and most recently on social influence and health communication.

HEIDI S. LEPPER is Adjunct Assistant Professor of Psychology at the University of California, Riverside. She completed post-doctorial study at Iowa State University and the University of Iowa, and is currently writing a textbook in health psychology (with M. Robin DiMatteo). She conducts research in the care and quality of life of older adults as well as in patient involvement in medical decisions and the social-psychological principles related to medical interactions. Her work has appeared in such journals as *Health Psychology*, *Journal of Nonverbal Behavior*, *Archives of Family Medicine*, and *Birth: Issues in Perinatal Care*.

NELYA J. McKENZIE is Associate Professor in the Department of Communication at Auburn University at Montgomery, Alabama. Her research interests include gender and communication and intergenerational communication, particularly in health contexts.

GREGORY MAKOUL is Director of the Program in Communication & Medicine and Assistant Professor of Medical Education at Northwestern University Medical School. He holds secondary appointments in the Department of Medicine and the University's Department of Communication Studies. He was a senior Fellow of the Annenberg Washington Program in Communications Policy Studies from 1994 to 1996. His research focuses on the relationship between communication and control, particularly in the context of health and medicine. His work has been published in *Academic Medicine* and *Social Science & Medicine*.

RICHARD MYLES has more than 10 years of experience in management and business. He received his Baccalaureate degree Magna Cum Laude with majors in statistics/operations research and economics. He has expertise in the supervision of professional and support staff, the development of office policy and procedures, and the application of computer software programs. He is currently overseeing the construction, leasing, and operation of a 126,570 square foot medical office building and ambulatory surgery center.

ROBERT D. O'CONNOR has been a health care executive for over 32 years, including 16 years as chief executive officer of both hospitals and a managed care organization. He is the Health Services Management Mentor and Adjunct Professor at Webster University's Central Florida Campus and a Life Fellow in the American College of Healthcare Executives. His essays and articles have been published in *Trustee*, *Southern Hospitals*, *Hospitals*, *Journal of the American Hospital Association*, and the *Journal of the Healthcare Financial Management Association*.

JIM L. QUERY, JR. is Assistant Professor of Communication at Loyola University, Chicago. He was President of the Alzheimer's Association of Tulsa, Oklahoma, from 1991 to 1994. His research focuses on communicating social support during major life events such as retirement, caregiving during Alzheimer's, returning to higher education, and living with AIDS.

NANCY SIGNORIELLI is Professor of Communication at the University of Delaware, Newark. Her primary research area focuses on television content and how media images are related to people's conceptions of social reality (cultivation theory). In particular, her studies examine gender roles, media messages about health and nutrition, and television violence. She has written several books and her research has appeared in numerous journals and edited books.

TERESA L. THOMPSON is Professor of Communication at the University of Dayton. She edits the quarterly journal *Health Communication* and is the author of two books on health communication issues. She has published in *Human Communication Research*, *Journal of Nonverbal Communication*, *Cosmetic Dermatology*, *Neonatal Network*, *Communication Quarterly*, *Western Journal of Communication*, *Sex Roles*, and *Public Opinion Quarterly*. Her research focuses on issues relevant to health care provider–patient interaction.

KIM WITTE is Associate Professor in the Department of Communication at Michigan State University. Her current research centers on the responses of diverse cultures to health risk messages, the study of fear appeals, and the development of culturally appropriate public health campaigns. She is a past Chair of the Health Communication Division of the National Communication Association and is the Vice Chair of the Health Communication Division of the International Communication Association. Her work has appeared in *Social Science and Medicine*, *International Quarterly of Communication Health Education*, *Communication Yearbook*, *Communication Monographs*, *Journal of Community Health*, and elsewhere.

ISBN 0-313-29925-0

9 780313 299254

90000>

HARDCOVER BAR CODE

BUILDING
USE
ONLY

vsr99